What people are saying about Dr. David Eckman, his other books & *Becoming What God Intended*

"Isolates the issues people have and gives solutions in a way that's fresh and profoundly biblical."

—Josh McDowell, author of over 150 books

"God has given David powerful insights to help people discover who they are in Christ and show them what a huge difference this truth can make in everyday life."

—Chip Ingram, President,
Walk Thru the Bible Ministries; author of The Invisible War

"This material has a well deserved reputation for being used by God to bring positive change through the creative application of the Word of God. It has been created by a man, David Eckman, who is not only a committed student of the Word of God, but one who has lived out the principles he presents in the difficult fabric of life and demonstrated the truth of them."

-Dr. Earl Radmacher, Distinguished Professor of Theology &
President Emeritus of Western Seminary

"How many Christians really know that their heavenly Father likes them and has a passionate delight in them? That His love is not based on how well they perform? That if they are struggling with addictions, God is not there to punish them but to bless them?" "The beautiful, inspiring message woven throughout Sex, Food, and God is that God is not distant, but close—and wants to be our heavenly Father, even our 'Daddy.' "

—Bob and Geri Boyd, Issues in Education

"David Eckman is a man you can trust…His teaching resonates with God's wisdom and compassion."

—Stu Weber,
author of Tender Warrior & Four Pillars of a Man's Heart

"I enjoyed reading Becoming Who God Intended and found it both encouraging and helpful to me personally…I am a big believer in submitting our imaginations to the Holy Spirit in order to allow him to "reprogram our minds" about who our Abba-Father really is."

-Steve McVey, author of Grace Walk

"Dr. Eckman's wisdom and vision helped me come face-to-face with issues I thought I had addressed long ago. The pain I have lived with for so long is now gone, thanks to being able to give all of my family background over to God."

-Cheryl, Sacramento, California

"I can personally testify that Head to Heart is a powerful discipleship process that can bring spiritual, emotional and relational health. You will also develop some deep friendships along the journey. I recommend every leader and member of our church to participate in this spiritual growth opportunity."

-Steve Quen, Senior Pastor,
Bay Area Chinese Bible Church

Only Becoming What God Intended Ministries Certified Trainers should be teaching the material, otherwise groups should be utilizing the videos. Certified trainers should have a numbered certificate with a gold emblem. You can verify if someone is certified by emailing webmail@bwgi.org.

To become a BWGI Certified Facilitator or Trainer in Becoming What God Intended by Dr. Eckman or another BWGI Master Trainer email webmail@bwgi.org or visit WhatGodIntended.org

BECOMING WHAT GOD INTENDED

By:

David Eckman, Ph.D.

Published by Becoming What God Intended Ministries
Celebrating 25 years in ministry

Becoming What God Intended - A Study For Spiritual Transformation
Copyright © 2005, 2015, 2021, by David J. Eckman
3th edition.

Published by Becoming What God Intended Ministries
P.O. Box 5246, Pleasanton, California, 94566
Library of Congress Cataloging-in-Publication Data
Eckman, David 1947.
Becoming What God Intended / David Eckman.
p. 168 cm.

ISBN-13:978-0-9996-057-4-5

www.WhatGodIntended.org

Dedicated to
Carol Eckman

A Heart of Love and Courage
For God the Father and Her Family

Thanks to Tom and Kristen Tunnicliff and to Kristin Smith for many of the questions within the text. Thanks indeed to Janie Sheedy for her work on, "The Critical Message of Hebrews."

Tens of thousands of people around the globe have been impacted by this workbook. They have also listened and watched Dr. David Eckman speak on each chapter. The CD, DVDs and On-line videos have been used together with the workbook for an even richer group study experience.

Go even deeper with Dr. David Eckman's 5-Course Curriculum:

BC101: Becoming What God Intended: Foundations of the Spiritual Life
BC102: Theology of Romans: Mastering the 7 Skills
BC103: Head to Heart: Small Group Discipleship Experience
BC104: Theology of Emotions: How to Minister to Your Emotions
BC105: Skills For Living: An Evangelistic Tool

 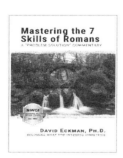   

www.WhatGodIntended.org

TABLE OF CONTENTS

CHAPTER SUMMARY: We will explore how walking by means of the Spirit addresses the moods and appetites of the flesh. We will note the negative power of this twin threat. We will find having a healthy relationship with the Trinity delivers us from the power of lusts and moods and provides us with the spiritual resources to manage our moods and appetites.

CHAPTER SUMMARY: We will explore the different ways in which the Spirit of God ministers to us. At the same time, we must recognize how radically different His ministry is versus that of the flesh. We are commanded to walk by the Spirit, to be led by the Spirit, to have the fruit of the Spirit in our lives, and to take individual steps into life by the Spirit.

CHAPTER SUMMARY: We will discover how our relationship with God the Father is expanded through prayer. Prayer is based neither on the investment of time nor the multiplication of words. Instead our prayer life is based on a set of issues we must face daily. These issues determine how we relate to God as a Father and the world about us.

CHAPTER SUMMARY: We will explore how we are to deal with the effects of sin, and the acts of sin in our lives. Sin effects us internally and it effects the Trinity. When we sin, the Father, Son, and Holy Spirit each respond differently to us. This makes confession of wrongdoing critically important in our lives. When we confess our wrongdoing, God the Father restores His hand of blessing, the Son ceases the judgment of child training or discipline, and the Spirit begins anew the process of character formation.

CHAPTER SUMMARY: God the Father could not think of a greater or nobler role for His Son than to send Him on a mission of rescue. The Son was sent to serve, to suffer, to ascend to Heaven, and to be rewarded with His reign over the universe and the church. We too are called to participate in the family business of rescue, and to consciously choose to replicate Christ's ministry in our lives. As daughters and sons of God, we have been sent. We are to choose to serve and to suffer. We will ascend in the rapture, and be rewarded by participating in Christ's reign. God could not think of a greater or nobler role for us than to participate in Christ's life pattern. This life pattern gives overall meaning to our lives.

Deepen your sense of having an Abba Father in Heaven, and develop a greater sense of affection and delight from this Father. The ***Becoming What God Intended*** Workbook is a discipleship study, a journal of your thoughts, and the foundation for the small group meetings.

Things to Be Remembered

- To obtain the greatest benefit from this work we recommend going through it slowly, and a number of times. Another way to drive home the heart changing lessons of the material is also to obtain the videos and CD's, MP3's, and Online Videos that go along with the book. As you commute, listen to them repeatedly.
- If the use of the book is with a small group, we recommend using this along with the facilitator's guide at the end of this book as well as the teaching Online Teaching Videos. The Table of Contents shows how the material can be studied for four quarters.
- The translations in the text are original & my own. They are true to the Greek text of the New Testament. The desire is to give a rich but accurate translation of what God has to say through His Word.
- The Appendix contains Small Group Material designed to make the small group a rich spiritual experience.

BECOMING WHAT GOD INTENDED

INTRODUCTION
By David Eckman

During the break in a lecture at Peninsula Bible Church in Palo Alto, California, a well-educated and thoughtful man from India, said to me, "If what you say is true, that emotions should be powerfully present in the life of the Christian, and that they indicate how well Christianity is understood - then you are talking about a complete revolution from the emotionless Christianity that most of us are used to." I assured him that was exactly what I was saying.

I began the next part of the lecture by explaining my answer. Many times people use an old-style train to describe Christianity. Fact is said to be the engine, faith is the tender with coal, and feelings are the caboose. The caboose is often misunderstood as being unimportant in the Christian life, but that is far from the truth. Certainly, the caboose is attached to the train, and must arrive at the destination sooner or later. If it does not arrive, it may mean that the engine is detached or no coal is in the tender! Emotions should and do play a major part in biblical Christianity. Feelings of confidence and hope prove the truth is accurately understood, faith is properly present, and the Spirit of God is ministering.

This book presents the premises that understanding God's ways is pivotal for the healthy emotional life of the Christian, that basic Christianity is deeply emotional, and that the presence of positive emotions strongly indicate how well we are enjoying our acceptance into the life of the Trinity.

As we proceed through the pages, the center of an emotionally vibrant Christianity will be found within the life of the Trinity. Christ has died so that the life of God can inhabit the hearts of men and women. This life revolves around a healthy understanding of the accepting relationships we have with the Father, Son, and Holy Spirit.

The acceptance existing among the members of the Trinity as applied to our lives is the change agent for a person's inner life. Understanding God's acceptance is not only an exciting pathway to solve emotional problems and change confusion to stability, but understanding the Trinity's acceptance is also the means to enter that circle of love predating time and the universe. Entering that circle begins the process of becoming the people that God intended.

In these coming pages you will learn about acceptance and God's new family, and you will learn about emotions and how to minister to your emotions. All of this learning will flow from the text of the Bible and a sound biblical theology concerning the Trinity. Yet at the same time, familiar words and concepts will be seen in a surprisingly different light. You will experience ***becoming what God Intended*** you to be. Please remember that you have in the Appendix resources for a small group.

1 | ACCEPTANCE & GRATITUDE

GROUNDING, FOUNDING & GROWING IN GOD'S FAMILY

CHAPTER SUMMARY: We will explore how growth in the Christian life is directly related to how well we respond to God, the first member of the Trinity, as a Father. Obstacles to growth often arise from one's family background. The solution is to participate in God's family so as to experience an emotionally rich sense of being loved and to have a correspondingly deep response of gratitude.

READING 1 - GOD'S FAMILY

When I was in college on the East Coast, I worked for Bethlehem Steel for a summer. I was assigned a few times to the rolling plant. Inside the Bessemer furnaces, pig iron was turned into steel by blasting air through the molten metal to burn out carbon and other impurities. The resulting red-hot steel bars glowed like orange popsicles. Rollers on either side of the furnaces applied continuous pressure on the steel to form them into precise sizes.

This rolling mill is a perfect picture of how the red-hot crucible of the family applies pressure to shape its own members. Each one bears the impression of his or her family of origin. Whether it is a healthy or unhealthy family, the pressure is ever-present, and change, healthy or unhealthy, is taking place.

Context For Growth - God's Family

A family is a very powerful force. Within the family, children are molded and shaped by pressures and expectations that will affect their entire lives. This tremendous family force applied over a long period of time conforms each member to the particular conscious and subconscious expectations of the family. As a result, each member bears the stamp of his own family throughout his life.

Describe three ways your family of origin influenced you:

1.

2.

3.

The family is the world's greatest force for molding people for good or for ill. God intended it that way. God also uses the family in His approach to positive change. He recreates family life for us, but on a healthy level, by introducing us into a new family where He is the Father, Christ is the elder brother, and the Holy Spirit is the one who conforms our character to the "genetic" make-up of the family. He uses these new family relationships to apply all the same types of family forces, positive pressures, healthy pressures, negative reinforcing pressures, even fun pressures, to conform the inner life of the child of God to the family imprint.

Simply stated, God wants to take us out of our family of origin, no matter how good it is, and bring us into a new family. The more conscious we are of that, the greater effect it will have upon us. No matter what the family, our responsibility is to consciously take the best and leave the rest. Conscious change means being personally involved in the process. We need to know what is going on and participate in an intelligent way.

The Father of the Family

The center of the new family is God the Father. Ephesians 3:14-15 tells us about God the Father and the nature of His Fatherhood.

> *On account of this I continually bow my knees to the Father out of whom every particular family in the heavens and upon the earth is named or derives its significance. -Ephesians 3:14-15[1]*

> "God wants to take us out of our family of origin, no matter how good it is, and bring us into a new family."

The Greek word for father is *pater*. The New Testament was originally written in the Greek language. It is often helpful to refer back to the Greek language to gain insights into the meaning of the words. The Greek word for family is *patria*. Our English word patriotic is derived from *patria* and is used to describe someone who is excited about the fatherland.

Paul is telling us that God the Father set the pattern for every *patria*, or family, on the earth and in the heavens. Each derives its name or significance from the existence of God the Father. In Scripture, name refers to the character, works and reputation of a person or thing. Name does not refer to what a person is called, such as "Joe," "Steve," or "John." Paul explains that every family in the heavens and on earth reflects the character, works and reputation of God the Father in some way. The implication is that the ultimate and intended father of every individual is God the Father. God created the human family as a reflection of His own. He wants to bring us into a greater emotional consciousness of our new family with Him as our Father.

How does the truth of Ephesians 3:14 begin this process of deepening our emotions toward our Heavenly Father?

Sometimes we think God accommodated Himself to us. We think that He sat up in heaven and asked Himself, "How can I communicate to mankind?" And then the light came on and He said, "I know! Since they already have families and since there are already fathers and kids, I'll call myself a father." But that is not it at all. He created families as a reflection of what already existed before the foundation of the world.

In the same way, when God formed Adam from the dust of the ground, He did not look at him and say, "Ah, I think I'll take on a shape like Adam, so when he looks at Me I won't scare him out of his wits." Just imagine this amorphous cloud forming itself into a glorified form of man. No. God formed Adam according to the image and likeness of Himself.

---

[1]   All Scripture quotations are Dr. Eckman's own translations unless otherwise stated. He is a professional translator of both Greek and Hebrew. He is a member of the National Association of Hebrew Professors and was supervised by Professor James Barr at Oxford University. James Barr is widely acknowledged as one of the leading biblical scholars of the twentieth century. Dr. Eckman is also a contributor to several books one of which is the New King James Study Bible.

Becoming What God Intended

The simple idea is this: God as a Father within the Trinity preceded any other family. He created the human family as a reflection of His own. God in His Fatherhood preceded the human family. He did not pattern Himself like the human family so that we would understand Him. Instead the human family reflects some realities of the Trinity.

> **G**od as a Father is the pivotal person for our inner change and growth, and His family is the context for that change and growth.

How does the idea that God wants to become your new father sound to you?

- ☐ Very exciting. I would love it!
- ☐ Neutral, unsure at this time.
- ☐ Very intimidating.
- ☐ Very presumptuous. I already have a father, thank you.

READING 2 - FAMILY CHARACTERISTICS

A human family is like a jigsaw puzzle and when a family member who has been away returns to his or her family, it is as if a missing puzzle piece is neatly fit into the empty spot. In a healthy family, a return to a happy place of origin is fun. In an unhealthy one, frustration results. Like stepping into a powerful undertow, the person feels the influences and expectations of the unhealthy relatives. For the healthy and unhealthy families, an aura of influence exists which deeply affects the family members.

As the deer pants for streams of water, so my soul pants for you, O God. My soul thirsts for God, for the living God. When can I go and meet with God? -Psalm 42:1-27

Like any human family, certain features or characteristics distinguish God's family. The process of knowing God as a Father and understanding the characteristics of the family will transform each new family member. Understanding and isolating these characteristics is important for a Christian for several reasons. As an example, for many people, Western Christianity has become merely a book religion in the worst sense.

Christianity was meant to be more than a religion. **True Christianity was meant to form the perspective and transform the emotions**. A religion merely of the book will emphasize acquiring information. Since in a book religion what we know is all important, what we feel and how we think will not matter. Getting to heaven is done by standing on stacks of facts reaching to the stars. Millions of facts in a mass of Biblical information in the mind of a person do not necessarily change the emotions or the heart.

A Personal Testimony

When I attended Oxford University in England, one of the students who scored among the highest on the undergraduate theology exams one year happened to be a practicing bisexual who prowled the public toilets of Oxford looking for sexual encounters. Such was common knowledge. He graduated anyway, because Christianity at the University had become merely a book religion. What a person believed or lived did not matter; only what he could recall for an exam mattered.

The characteristics of the Christian family are primarily relational, not simply informational. If we meet God merely to get more informational nuggets, we will be functioning like we are in a sick or dysfunctional home where most emotions are not allowed and selective information is just passed back and forth.

> ***Theological Jargon Box** You will have definitions of terms commonly used by Bible Teachers.

Family characteristics are powerful. I became a believer at the age of 17. One of the reasons the change took place was a result of walking out of my own house and into a friend's house. I was attending an all-male high school where I met a nice bunch of guys. One of those, a blonde-haired Italian Christian named John, invited me home for pizza one Friday night. I almost went into physical shock when I walked into his home. The first thing I noticed was that everyone was smiling. I found that strange. Secondly, everybody was in the same room. That struck me as being geographically odd. In our home, we stayed as far away from one another as possible. Thirdly, I was there for hours, and they treated each other with respect the whole time. They actually liked each other! Our home was blighted by alcoholism, and Friday night started the drinking bout that lasted all weekend; Friday night through Sunday, we avoided being home.

At that point I decided to convert. Whatever they had, I wanted it. They were simply modeling the characteristics of the true Father and His family. The characteristics of the heavenly family, the Trinity, spilled over into their personal lives. When I walked into their home, I could sense those qualities. The greatest argument for Christianity was taking place before my eyes. Not the information, but the atmosphere made the difference. The atmosphere made sense out of the information.

Similarly, God uses the characteristics of the Trinity to mold the Christian for time and eternity. These characteristics are unseen, but they can be apprehended by faith. Some of the characteristics of God's family are acceptance, worth, gentleness, trust, confidence and gratitude. We can sense the significance of God's family characteristics by examining just two of them: acceptance and gentleness.

God Is Accepting

The first thing we should notice about God's family is that each member is fully pleasing, or justified*, and completely acceptable before Him. God accepts us because He is more interested in who we are than what we have done, right or wrong.

> ***Theological Jargon Box**
> Justified: A person is all right with God forever.

> *Every variety of bitterness contaminating the spirit, and outbursts of anger, and any slow-burn, and shouting, and stupid talking, let it be taken from you along with every variety of evil malice. Be kind to each other, deeply involved emotionally, gracious forgivers of each other, even as the Father in Christ graciously forgave all of you. -Ephesians 4:31-32*

Similarly see where Ephesians 5:1 describes the family characteristics even more plainly.

> *Become then, imitators of God [we actually get the word mimic from this particular Greek word] as beloved offspring. And organize your entire conduct in relationship to love, even as Christ already loved you and gave Himself over for you as an offering, a slaughtered sacrifice* to God as a delightful aroma. -Ephesians 5:1*

These passages define God's family as one that chooses to work with people according to who they are and not what they have done. **God's family is profoundly accepting.**

> ***Theological Jargon Box**
> Slaughtered sacrifice: In the Old Testament the Israelite priest prepared cooked meat, like BBQ, to be offered to God. Meat was a more valuable commodity than it is now.

Why do shouting, bitterness, yelling, cursing, and insults inhabit homes? By choosing to keep a score card, the family members are rejecting each other's importance. An angry person typically carries a score card in his back pocket.

When somebody is in the habit of being angry for a long period of time, check the back pocket and a scorecard of about 500 pages will be in it. The more anger, the bigger the scorecard. The reason homes are more like war zones than sanctuaries is because people say, "What you have done has far more significance to me than who you are. Forget who you are! Because of what you have done, I reject your person and dislike you."

God's family does not work that way. **God is more preoccupied with the person than what the person has done.** That is the greatness of Christianity. Christianity has already solved the issue of what people have done. Jesus died for every wrong deed. He wiped them away. Only the significance of the child of God remains.

God accepts us because He is more interested in who we are than what we have done. In God's family we are highly valued and profoundly accepted. How can we actively show our understanding of God's acceptance of us?

What negative qualities or emotions diminish as His acceptance sinks in?

God Is Gentle

God is committed to the importance of persons. He treats them with gentleness. He allows them to become willing participants in His plan. God will not impose His will on anyone. As an illustration, God put the forbidden tree in the Garden of Eden because He is gentle. He placed a choice before Adam and Eve so that they could decide whether they wanted God's wonderful new world.

A perfect example of God's gentleness is given in Matthew 11:28-30.

All of you are commanded to come to me, every one of you who is working to exhaustion and who is over burdened [with religious obligation], and I shall refresh you. Right now, take my yoke upon yourselves and be continually discipled by me, because I am emotionally mild and humble in heart, and you shall find refreshment for your souls For my yoke is kindly and the weight that I put upon you is light.

Christ is speaking to people who have been deceived by a religious system that has worn them down and exhausted them. The word translated "meek" in the Authorized Version of the Bible means to be emotionally mild. When we meet Jesus in Heaven, we won't be consumed by the intensity of a divine fanaticism, but we will meet one of mild emotions. He is an easy-going God. When we talk to Him, He will set us at ease. Feelings of total acceptance will ever experience will occur. Every moment will feel like we have just come from a swim in a refreshing spring.

> *"On the first day in Heaven: Jesus didn't make one demand of me. He kept telling me to relax. I expected him to recruit me as an usher as soon as I arrived!"*

Heaven is relaxing because the God of Heaven is other-centered. He values others so much that, as a good host, He wants those in Heaven to feel special. I can imagine what might run through a person's mind after meeting Jesus face to face for the first time in Heaven. I can see the confusion in this person's eyes as he thinks to himself, "I can't believe it! Jesus didn't make one demand of me. He kept telling me to relax. I expected him to recruit me as an usher as soon as I arrived. But He didn't. He just said to relax. What a strange God. This isn't like church at all." Ironically, for many the condition of being weighed down and burdened sounds like their life in the local church.

Jesus says He is emotionally mild and humble in heart. I strain over that phrase. How can the Creator of the universe possibly be humble in heart? Yet He is because He will not impose Himself on anyone. Hell exists because God refuses to impose Heaven. The forbidden tree existed because God refused to impose the Garden of Eden on anyone.

When we don't want a garden with God or a Heaven with God, only absolute darkness and the discomfort of His absence is left. This is due to His gentleness!

In God's family, we are dealing with a gentle Father who will not impose His will on us. To some this is confusing because unfortunately, as Christians, we still sometimes live by the rules of our family of origin. We must understand that the new family does not have the same rules. People in God's family are free. They are free to make choices.

All of you are commanded to come to me, every one of you who is working to exhaustion and who is over burdened [with religious obligation], *and I shall refresh you. Right now, take my yoke upon yourselves and be continually discipled by me, because I am emotionally mild and humble in heart, and you shall find refreshment for your souls. For my yoke is kindly and the weight that I put upon you is light.*
-Matthew 11:28-30

God's gentleness in giving us free choice is also illustrated by the way He will evaluate the Christian's works in the future. At a future point called the judgment seat of Christ, Jesus will evaluate and reward the things we have done for God after we became Christians. When we get to the judgment seat of Christ, our person will be secure, but He will decide on the wage He will give us for what we have freely chosen to do for Him. He is not going to say, "I was your quarterback, you were my lineman, and now I am going to judge you by how well you read the signal I screamed at you in the middle of the game." Instead, He will say, "I am going to evaluate how you used your freedom, and how you expressed your gratitude. I'm not going to evaluate how well you read the signals from Heaven because my children aren't slaves or robots. I want to treat them as mature sons and daughters who were free to make choices."

Characteristics such as acceptance and gentleness can mark the life just as powerfully as abuse and cruelty. God uses the principle of the power of the family to form the attitudes, emotions and responses of His children. The unhealthy family is really a sick imitation of what God intended.

God's Word Emphasizes This Freedom In Christ.

Galatians 5:1 says: **"For freedom Christ did set us free."** In John 8:36, Jesus said: **"If I set someone free, they will be free indeed."** Freedom means to have a true and valid choice. The mark of God's family is the freedom to be spontaneous with the Lord. His family is not ultimately dependent upon rules and regulations, but on love and joy.

What are some unhealthy rules from your family of origin that you try to apply to God's family?

READING 3 - THE CHALLENGE TO THE FAMILY

We must overcome two challenges in order to feel the impact of God's new family in our lives. First, we have to set aside our unbelief to apprehend the ways of God's family, and second, we have to overcome any opposing influence from our own family of origin. The more unhealthy our own family background was, the more difficult it will be to imagine the way God's new family feels and relates.

Emphasis on the unhealthy family permeates book topics, talk show circuits and conversations in the United States. Family therapists, whether they realize it or not, are now agreeing with the Bible that the majority of people experience ineffective family relationships. They do not have the "happiness skills" necessary to derive benefit and enjoyment from one another. Romans 3:12 says:

They have all gone aside. Together they have become ineffective.

The word "ineffective" in our translation comes from a Greek word originally meaning a hand that was useless or atrophied. Over time it came to mean "useless" or "worthless." What Paul wrote is what family therapists have observed: people are often relationally unskilled and derive little benefit from those relationships.

The reason many individuals are unskilled, according to both the therapists and the Apostle Paul, is that they are too busy defending themselves from verbal and sometimes physical abuse. Following Romans 3:12 the apostle used graphic Old Testament language to describe what many experience.

As it is written: There is no one righteous, not even one; there is no one who continually understands, no one who seeks God. They have all gone aside, together they have become ineffective; there is no one who does good, not even one. Their throats are open graves; their tongues practice deceit. The poison of vipers is on their lips. Their mouths are full of cursing and bitterness. -Romans 3:10-14

Becoming What God Intended

He stated that their throats are an open grave or tomb. His word picture means that many people are as effective as corpses in their relational skills. He stated that the poison of asps or snakes is under their tongues and they use deceit. What they say hurts. Their feet are swift to shed blood, and violence and misery are in their paths. Verbal abuse continues on to physical abuse. Healthy families cannot exist with such characteristics.

Can you think of someone who has great relational skills and really puts you at ease when you are around them? Take a moment and write down why they stand out to you.

I recently learned a startling statistic about American women. On the average, an American woman will have more marriages than she will have children. The average American woman will be married twice and will have less than two children. This indicates that our culture has become highly ineffective in relationships. We are unhealthy. Many of us can hardly imagine what a healthy home is like. To help us out, Christian teachers and preachers need to paint vivid portraits of healthy relationships for people. In particular, these portraits should describe the relationship among the members of the Trinity and God's friendly ways. Such mental pictures will fuel the Christian's faith. Sadly, the closest many have come to experiencing a healthy family is in their imagination.

As Christians exercise faith and use their imaginations and the Word of God to involve themselves in these pictures, a life on a different dimension will challenge and change the negative effects of their past.

For the Word of God is alive and energetic, and far sharper than any double-edged sword, and is continually able to divide between soul and spirit, both joints and marrow, and is a judge of the enthusiasms and thoughts of the heart -Hebrews 4:12

What does Hebrews 4:12 tell you about the Word of God's ability to change a person's life?

READING 4 -EMBRACING THE FAMILY'S LOVE

How can God take people from their family of origin, no matter how good or bad it is, and turn them into free, grateful, loving people? Additionally, how can He help people to sense the realities of the new family and effectively respond to their new Father? The Bible has a straightforward answer.

God changes people by sharing with His new family the acceptance existing within the Trinity. He gives acceptance as a gift. He wants us to know we are more important to Him for who we are than for what we have done wrong, or what we will do right. He uses His Word to communicate this deep sense of acceptance, which then triggers (or generates) a response of gratitude within. This is the key thought for all the next eleven chapters. Acceptance is the foundation of God's family.

Our Response - Gratitude

Gratitude follows acceptance, for just as a child gets excited about a gift so an adult who understands can get excited about the gift of acceptance. A literal translation of Colossians 2:1-2 provides a picture of this process.

For I desire that you know what a great effort I am making on your behalf and those in Laodicea, and whosoever has not seen me in person, in order that your hearts might be encouraged, being knit together in love, unto all the wealth coming from __full confidence__ from understanding, resulting in a true knowledge of the mystery of God, that is, Christ Himself. -Colossians 2:1-2

"Full Confidence"

"Full confidence" comes from the Greek work *playraphoria*, which is related to euphoria. In the 20th century, euphoria means a person is practically out of his mind; but in the first century, it meant a person had good feelings in his life. Playraphoria extends that word further. *Playra* means full, and phoria means a foundation or support. We simply call it confidence, but the word picture is a solid foundation of positive emotions in the life.

The apostle was putting a great deal of personal effort into getting an emotionally positive response from the Colossians and Laodiceans. The process was labor intensive. He was striving for their encouragement and their mutual affection. Furthermore, Paul wanted the Laodiceans to have the wealth stemming from a foundation of good feelings in their lives.

His goal was not to place just a body of knowledge within the believers; his goal was to create a compellingly positive emotional environment within. This is a much different goal than the modem minister and pastor, who may feel his job is complete when the church is filled with information.

Resulting Gratitude

Paul assumed that people who understand and trust feel powerful emotions. He built his teaching method on the supposition that often an unhappy Christian did not understand and trust truth. That sounds obvious and superficial, but a revolution exists within those words.

If a person isn't thrilled with Christianity, it may be because the truth is not understood. Paul's goal, and for such a goal he labored to exhaustion, was that people would be encouraged, being knit together in love unto all the wealth stemming from a foundation of positive good feelings, based on a personal knowledge and understanding of Christ. When they had this, they would be as Colossians 3:15 says, "Grateful ones." Christians are called to experience and channel the response of gratitude, not to fake it.

Two elements, therefore, are present in a healthy Christianity: acceptance and gratitude. This creates a cycle driving the positive Christian life. A sense of acceptance and a feeling of gratitude are emotional. For many Christians, these are unknown qualities.

Can you think of two things you have done for the Lord this past year out of gratitude for His acceptance of you?

A Test At The Salad Bar

Emotions reveal much. Here is a simple test of your progress in the Christian life. Imagine you are at a restaurant filling your plate at a salad bar. Suddenly you hear an announcement: "God the Father is coming through the door in 25 seconds."

Without thinking about your response, imagine how you might react when you see the door swinging open. Choose the box that sounds closest to what your response would be:
- ☐ Do you run to the door to greet Him?
- ☐ Do you stand in place and wait for Him to come to you to let you know where you stand?
- ☐ Do you jump behind the salad bar in quaking fear, guilt and shame?
- ☐ Do you ignore Him, sit down, eat your salad and read your Bible?

Becoming What God Intended

How you react is a good indication of where you are emotionally in your spiritual life. Your reaction will tell you how much you are under girded by the emotionally rich confidence Paul spoke about. God wants us to have such confidence in His love that we will run to the door, fall at His feet and weep because we have never met anyone like Him. We should want to meet Him because we know inside ourselves no one else is like Him. No one values us more.

If you instinctively jump behind the salad bar and quiver with fear; it indicates you have not integrated the truth with your emotions. If you stand there and wait for His reaction, that indicates Christian information may be present in your life, but the life-changing emotions are not.

READING 5 - THE PROCESS OF FAMILY GROWTH

How then can God's acceptance become life-changing confidence, a solid basis for gratitude? Paul used a very definite teaching pattern in discipling people. The process was deeply involved with the individual's emotional response. **He rooted them in God's love. He laid a foundation over that love, and then he built them up.** The rooting and founding were based on God's love for the individual.

Rooting In Love - Emotional Reality

Archaeological digs have uncovered how the ancients made clay bricks and created brick pilings for their buildings. If they were going to build a two-story building, they would dig a hole and put in brick pilings 20 to 40 feet deep. Then they packed dirt and stone over the pilings until the ground was level so as to place a two- to three-foot foundation on top. Sometimes the hole they rooted out was as deep as the building was high. The builders rooted the hole, made the foundation and then built up the building. Paul used this structural design over and over again in his training of the early Christians. He rooted them deeply, he founded them squarely, and then he built them up. He did not use brick; he used the love of God.

In Ephesians 3:14-19, Paul tells us that the properly founded and rooted person can make his or her life a discovery of the dimensions of Christ's love.

> *On account of this I am bowing my knees to the Father, from whom every family in the heavens and on the earth takes its name or significance, in order that He might give to you according to the wealth of His glory, power to be strengthened through His Spirit in the inner person. With the result that Christ __makes a home__ in all your hearts through faith, having hearts __previously rooted and founded in agape love__. This will result in sufficient internal strength to lay hold of, with every one of the saints, what is the breadth, length, height and depth, and to personally know the abundant knowledge of the love from Christ, resulting in being filled unto the fullness from God. -Ephesians 3:14-19*

Paul's prayer implies a dynamic process where being rooted and founded in love is at the center of two processes. The first process is the exercise of faith by a group of Christians. This exercise of faith, if it is based on being rooted and founded in love, permits the believers to begin a lifetime exploration of the love of God. As this is done, the life is filled with the joy and fullness that God intended. Faith and the experience of being loved by God generates a powerful dynamic.

Agape Love As Our Foundation

The Greek word *agape* is used in the Bible to describe God's love. *Agape* love for many is simply an act of the will. But in the Bible, love is much more. An example of Paul's definition of love is actually found in Philippians 2:1-2.

> *If then, there is any encouragement in Christ* (and there is), *if there is any tender speaking that comes from agape love, if there is any fellowship of the Spirit, if there is any deep compassion and tender mercies, fulfill my joy and you be like-minded as I have just described. -Philippians 2:1-2*

Agape love, as described here, speaks tenderly. Encouragement is present. Deep sympathy pervades; such love is filled with tender mercies. Paul wanted believers to be rooted and grounded in *agape* love from God. God's love is not a theological abstraction. Flowing from His nature, love is filled with positive feelings for you. That is *agape* love.

Why is *agape* love so important in the rooting and founding process? In our Western culture, many people think learning about God consists of memorizing a few Bible verses. They think quoting a doctrine or the outline from one of the books of the Bible makes a person a disciple of Christ. But that is not biblical discipleship.

Feeling the Truth

Biblical discipleship occurs when we feel the truth. It is not only what you know. **Discipleship occurs when what you know grips your emotions deeply enough that it controls the subconscious part of your life and impacts your consciousness.** To simply know things was the Gnostic heresy the early Christian church challenged. Gnostic comes from the Greek word for knowledge, gnosis. The early church rejected simple knowledge as being the basis of Christianity. The relationships of faith are the basis.

A helpful theological axiom for the emotional life is:

Feelings do not authenticate truth, but they do authenticate our understanding of the truth.

It doesn't matter whether you feel that Jesus rose from the dead or not. He did. It doesn't matter whether you feel God exists or not. He does. But if you say that God is, if you say Jesus rose from the dead, then your face should reflect that reality. Paul was greatly concerned that his disciples would emotionally respond to truth.

Romans 15:13 says powerful feelings will flow out of our exercise of faith:

And may the God of the hope fill you with every variety of joy and peace in the process of believing, with the abundance of hope by the power of the Holy Spirit.

I can tell what I truly understand by what I feel about what I understand.

Describe an example in your life when you were motivated to do something positive for someone in response to their love or concern for you.

Concluding Thoughts

Feelings do not authenticate truth. Truth is truth. But feelings do authenticate our understanding of truth, and they do change our character.

In the process of discipleship, Paul rooted people deeply in God's acceptance by letting them know over and over again how God felt about them. Upon that sense of being loved, he laid a foundation for them in truth. This would keep them from being blown about by other winds of doctrine. Upon that foundation of truth, he built them up relationally.

Paul used the illustration of rooting a building, laying a foundation, and building up from the foundation to underscore a critical point. A definite, deep sense of being loved is necessary before growth can take place. A hidden depth of love in the heart (like the hidden foundation of a building) precedes visible growth.

Before life can become an exploration of God's love in Christ, the believers have to experience a sense of being loved. Practically speaking, too many Christians are being rushed through the discipleship process, which may result in a lack of inner stability.

This book is built upon two halves. The first half is an attempt to show how much we are loved. The second half is going to show what the believer can do with such a sense. This point is so important that the next four chapters are set aside to develop a sense of acceptance and a sense of being loved deep within. Chapter 6 will then show how that trust, which flows from a sense of being loved, is the basis for how we are to react to all of life. The last half of the book will be devoted to how life becomes an exploration of God's love for us.

SUMMARY OF CHAPTER 1

1. Families of origin are powerful forces in shaping our lives.
2. God wants to take us out of our family of origin and place us into His family
3. God the Father is the ultimate and intended father of every person.

TO REVIEW:

What are one or two key insights you've been challenged with this week?

Take a moment to pray and thank the Lord for what He has taught you this week.
Lord I am thankful for:

2 | ACCEPTANCE & WORTH

CHAPTER SUMMARY: We will explore how a Christian develops a healthy sense of worth. The chapter will show that a Christian is worth a Son to God. The cross illustrates that at humanity's worst season and at the time of our moral weakness, Christ died for us. This shows God values us for who we are to Him and not for what we can do for Him, either bad or good. Feeling worthwhile, feeling worth a Son to God, is an essential part of feeling loved.

READING 1 - WHAT IS WORTH?

How can the worth of a person be determined? Can it be done by the amount of money a person is worth? That may not work. J. Paul Getty, at one time the richest man in the world, died at home alone. He had already written his will and everyone knew he lived for money. So when he died, his only companion into the darkness was his wealth - a cold companion. In a very real sense, J. Paul Getty's life had no value to it. Though he was a billionaire, his life was worthless. Why? He had no true friends who would comfort him at the end. Life without relationships is no life at all.

Some college students, for example, evaluate their worth by their grades and academic achievements. The drawback is that grades go up and down like the stock market, so one's sense of worth would go up and down like the stock market. The same is true for any achievement in life. As one achieves or fails, the emotions take a terrific beating. In order to feel good about one's self, the individual would have to achieve perfectly all the time.

Sidney Lester suspected he was a worthless human being for most of his life. Nobody really loved him. After all, what had he ever done to win another person's love? Nearly everyone in his hometown had said at one time or another that he'd never amount to anything. Through a thousand repetitions, he was told by friends, relatives and even his parents that he was useless. Now, as an adult, he felt unloved and hopelessly without value. So he planned his own kidnapping. Perhaps then, he mused, he would know whether or not anyone really cared about him. Unfortunately, in response to his kidnapping, his relatives were willing to pay only $48.25.

Becoming What God Intended

Have you ever wondered what would happen if you were kidnapped? If kidnappers sent a note to your closest relatives demanding a large ransom, what would those relatives be willing to pay to get you back? How much would they sacrifice for you? The answer might be surprising, or it might be embarrassing. You might find out that you are worth a lot, a little, or nothing at all.

Most of us wouldn't risk being kidnapped just to find out how much we are worth, but it seems people from every walk of life - the rich and the poor, the highly successful and the so-called failures, the beautiful and the unlovely - all struggle with their own feelings of worthlessness.

The Self-Worth Myth

Unfortunately, we will never be able to come to a true sense of worth by looking within. Self-worth and self-esteem are misnomers in the human search for significance. Establishing one's own sense of worth is philosophically and psychologically impossible, unless, of course, one deludes oneself. Imagine a sane person saying to himself, "I am a worthwhile individual because I am rich and beautiful." When a person looks into the mirror of his conscience, his inner sense of right and wrong might reveal aberrations in his character or feelings of guilt from past failures reflecting a sense of worthlessness.

Self-worth

Self-worth is not really derived from ourselves, but is actually based upon how we perceive significant others value us.

What measure do we use to set the standard for worth or worthlessness? For each good deed or success we stack up on one side of the balance, what bad deed or failure drops in the other side to cancel it out? Self-worth, or the feeling of worth we have about ourselves, is not really derived from us but is actually based upon how we perceive how significant others value us. We need a source and a standard beyond ourselves to discover our worth, and that source must be reliable and trustworthy.

I once read a book by a counselor named Virginia Satir. The book includes a chapter on spirituality in which she tries to explain how a person can establish his own worth by going into a dark room, sitting on a chair, relaxing, and breathing deeply. Then the person is supposed to look for his innermost self and tell himself that he's wonderful, worth a lot, and unique.

While I was reading, my face blushed as I tried her method. My conscience wasn't convinced that I had a right to say anything like that to myself. We should take our conscience seriously and not attempt to brainwash ourselves into pseudo self-esteem. One of the realities of the Bible is that it takes the conscience far more seriously than the field of counseling does. God and our conscience understand, as we probably do, that our positive self-evaluations may be more wish than reality.

Read the following verses:

- Therefore I tell you, do not worry about your life, what you will eat or drink; or about your body, what you will wear. Is not life more important than food, and the body more important than clothes? Look at the birds of the air; they do not sow or reap or store away in barns, and yet your heavenly Father feeds them. Are you not much more valuable than they? -Matthew. 6:25-26

- How great is the love the Father has lavished on us, that we should be called children of God! And that is what we are! The reason the world does not know us is that it did not know him. -1 John 3:1

- But God is continually recommending His love [His own particular *agape* love] to us, because while we were yet continually sinning, Christ died on our behalf. -Romans 5:8

If our self-worth is based upon how significant others value us, what do the following verses tell you about your worth to God?

Matthew. 6:25-26:

1 John 3:1:

Romans 5:8:

If worth is not the same as self-image, or how I perceive myself instinctively, then what is it? Some years ago, I learned about the difference between worth and self-image through a heartbreaking sequence of events. I counseled a family whose son had intermittent psychotic breaks. When a family member has severe psychological problems, it is terribly tragic. In this case, the tragedy was compounded by the fact that the father had died, leaving the mother and son alone together. The son suffered from schizophrenia. He couldn't hold a job. He couldn't sustain long-term or even short-term relationships, but he was always planning how he could make his next million before he made his first one. He saw himself as one of the most brilliant young men in North America. He clung to the image of himself as sophisticated, intelligent, clever, and poetic. Clouded by delusion, he was honestly committed to an idealistic and unrealistic self-image.

Perhaps all these traits seem rather harmless, but there was another darker side to this man's disorder. Every once in a while, he would become abusive or threaten harm to his mother. I was concerned that two casualties would eventually result, so I approached the mother about institutionalizing her son or moving him to a halfway house. She found my suggestion unthinkable even though she knew her son was demented and could be dangerous. Her reason for not sending him away was simply stated, "I am his mother, and he is my son. He is worth everything to me." The young man had a hopelessly flawed view of himself, and yet he was worth everything to his mother. His self-image was how he instinctively viewed himself. His worth was what his mother was willing to give for him - her life.

An experience I had with my own son as he struggled through first grade is another good example of the difference between worth and self-image. My son is very bright, but at that time he didn't see any value in keeping two connected thoughts close together. Why bother with a train-like logic when you can have fireworks logic? Because of that propensity, his first grade year was abysmal.

After a particularly rough day, he would come home saying things like, "I'm stupid, I'm no good, I'm dumb." As parents, we wanted to communicate something else to him. No matter what his grades were, we wanted him to know he was worth everything to us. Every once in a while when he wasn't doing so well, we would throw a little party to celebrate "him" and assure him of his worth to us.

Self-image or self-perception may depend upon a lot of factors: external, internal, achievement, you name it, but worth is something that can only be established by another.

Take a moment now to thank God for loving you and valuing you so highly!

Who have you depended upon for your feelings of worth? Your parents' view, your spouse's view?

What are some problems that arise from depending on these sources?

READING 2 - WORTH, TIME & PROBLEMS

The Bible is a guide to discovering how God establishes our worth. In chapter five of the book of Romans, the Apostle Paul paints a vivid picture of what each human being is worth to God. This passage is critically important to an understanding of Christianity, and psychologically it is crucial for self-growth.

Romans is Paul's longest exposition on the basic values of Christianity. The first four chapters provide a backdrop for what follows in chapter five. The first chapter gives an account of the wickedness of the whole world culture and expresses God's anger about it. His description of the world during the 1st Century AD

Becoming What God Intended

is alarmingly similar to that of the 20th century. Chapters two and three show how the individual man, no matter how religious or moral, is guilty and without excuse before God. Romans 3:10 says we are all in the same boat:

There is no one righteousness, no not one. There is no one who understands. There is no one who seeks after God.

The marvel of the gospel is that God's righteousness becomes our righteousness* when we accept Christ as God's gift. Romans 3:24-25 introduces the value of Christ's propitiation,* or payment for us. By His death on the cross, Christ took our place. Our sin triggered the sentence of death. Someone had to pay the penalty, and only Jesus Christ was capable of completely satisfying the just demands of a holy God in relation to all humanity's sin. Sin damages people. Sin damages the sinner as well as others around him, and that's why God hates it.

> ***Theological Jargon Box**
> <u>Righteousness:</u> Both the Old and New Testaments describe how God freely gives a person access to a relationship with Himself. This is righteousness. In this relationship, the goal is to conform our character to Christ through the Father/son, Father/daughter relationship.
> <u>Propitiation:</u> Refers to the effect Christ's sacrifice has on God the Father. He is appeased concerning our sin and is infinitely satisfied concerning our person.

Chapter four cites examples from Old Testament history to exhibit the personal importance of trust or faith. Abraham exercised it, David exercised it, and we need to exercise it. The same faith that worked for them will work for us.

In one sense, chapter five could be directly linked to chapter three, which introduces what salvation means to the Christian. The forgiveness described in chapter three is further developed by the worth God gives us in chapter five. Chapter five tells us that we are worth more to God than time, and our problems are no hindrance to God's love. The reason why is spelled out graphically in this chapter.

God's quality of love radically affects us, including our relationship to time. Time does not control God's love; God's love controls time.

We Are Worth More To God Than Time

We are worth more to God than time. God's quality of love radically affects us, including our relationship to time. Time does not control God's love; God's love controls time.

Romans 5:1-2 shows how God's love affects our relationship to time. Notice that the love we are involved in has implications for the past, the present and the future.

Having then been justified directly out of faith, we have peace with God through our Lord Jesus Christ, through whom we also permanently have access into this grace in which we permanently stand. We are continually boasting in the hope of the glory from God. -Romans 5:1-2

- **Past:** justified by faith

- **Present:** peace, grace, and access to God through Christ

- **Future:** glory from God

From Romans 5:1-2, what has already taken place in the Past? What is true in the Present, and what is certain about the future?

Past:

Present:

Future:

As far as the past is concerned, God has said we are right with Him. *In the present*, we have peace with God, we are permanently standing under His grace or favor, and we have access to Him. *In the future*, we will participate in the glory of God. Real love - God's love - is not defined by time, but by the depth of relationship. God's love is insulted when we ask if it is possible to lose our salvation in the future because His love is not restrained by the dimension of time.

Romans 2:17 and 22 tells how the Jew boasted in the Law of Moses.* But the Christian can boast in the certain hope of sharing the glory and splendor of God. The thought of this kind of boasting creates an image in my mind of a football quarterback carrying the ball across the goal line and then jumping into the air, smashing the football into the ground, and dancing around because he has scored

> ***Theological Jargon Box** Law of Moses: The Old Testament moral and religious guidelines that God gave to Moses.

some points. We can experience that same feeling, but we have infinitely more to rejoice and boast over than scoring a few points in a football game. We can boast in the fact that someday we will be in His presence.

God's Love Is Greater Than Our Problems

Christians sometimes fear that time's passage may separate us from God's love. To that underlying suspicion the Christian will sometimes add doubts caused by the presence of problems and difficulties in life. Paul transitions from talking about how God's love is greater than time to how the problems of life should never be used to define the depth of God's love.

Romans 5:3 shows how God's love also radically affects our relationship to problems:

And not only, but also we are boasting in our particular troubles or tribulations. -Romans 5:3

Not only can we boast about our future, but we can boast about our problems. The Law of Moses* may be the great glory of the Jew, but the greater glory of the Christian is the problem he faces right now. Isn't that ironic? Isn't that good news? Inflation, recession, losing a job, marital strain, rejection by friends, our own inadequacies or failures, any problem we are facing as a Christian is something we can boast about. We can boast in the fact that God will use 100 percent of our problems to conform us to the character of Jesus Christ. We are not under the Law of Moses, but under God's great parenting principle that promises to use every event in our lives to make us like Christ. Knowing this, we can approach our problems in a totally different way.

A Christian who doesn't understand this principle will most likely respond inappropriately to trials. The first question that usually comes into a Christian's mind when she has a big problem (when a child dies or she learns she has cancer) will probably be, "What have I done wrong?" Yet the Bible says something else should come to mind. Knowing what God is going to do with our problems should cause us to exclaim, "This is an opportunity to participate in being made like Christ!"

Whether a great difficulty or a small irritation, God's goal is the same. Even if the difficulty is death and we end up with God in heaven, we will learn how God sustains people who trust Him in death. Through serious illness or loss of a loved one, God understands and carries us. If friends misunderstand or disappoint us, causing strain or heartache, God promises to work through it for our well-being. If we struggle financially, we can learn that God is able to meet every real need. Each trial provides a divine opportunity for us to grow.

> "We can boast in the fact that God will use 100 percent of our problems to conform us to the character of Jesus Christ."

This principle is confirmed many times in scripture. Romans 8:28 states:

And we know that all things work together beneficially for those that love God, who are the called according to His purpose.

James 1:2-3 further encourages us to count it all joy when we fall into various trials, knowing that the testing of our faith produces patience.

Becoming What God Intended

How's Your Batting Average?

Some Christians use a "batting average approach" with respect to problems. They wake up in the morning and walk out the door to find their car has a flat tire. If they think they are batting 500 spiritually (which is a pretty exceptional average), they'll look at the flat tire and say to themselves, "Since I'm batting 500, God will use this incident for my spiritual well-being. God is looking out for me in some way I can't understand, so I'll just trust in His goodness."

If, on the other hand, they think they're only batting 106 (they haven't had devotions*, haven't been tithing* at church lately, or haven't shared the Gospel with someone recently), they might walk out the door, see the flat tire, and automatically assume God is punishing them - sending them a shape-up warning, or just trying to get their attention. Either of these batting average extremes are wrong, because they focus on self and not on God.

> ***Theological Jargon Box**
> <u>Devotions:</u> A personal time set aside to pray, read the Bible, and meditate on Bible verses. <u>Tithing:</u> Some Christians believe they should give 10% of their income or tithe to the church.

Can you think of a time when you bought into "Batting Average Christianity"? How did you feel about yourself and why?

As Christians, we must realize that God works through our tribulations for our well-being - not just some of the time, but every single time. If He gave us His Son, will He not spare us the small change? Or as Paul puts it in Romans 8:32:

If He gave us the Son, will He not also freely give us all things?

> **I**f we can learn to see all our problems through God's principle of growth, our whole perspective will change. God's great goal in the believer's life is to make the believer like the Son. That is the greatest thing He can do for any of us.

Each time we face a problem, we need to remember we are not under the Law of Moses or the Law of Batting Averages; we are under the parenting principle of growth in Christ Jesus. Even if we don't remember, God will still stand by His word. It won't make a difference if we go to the grave refusing to believe it; the fact remains that God always brings good from our tribulations. Notice how Romans 5:3-5 defines problems as a growth process:

And not only do we boast in our future hope of the glory of God, but we boast in our present problems. We boast in tribulations, knowing that tribulation works out patience (the ability to sustain pressure) *and patience works out tested character. And the tested character gives hope. And that hope doesn't put us to shame because we have God's kind of love to sustain us. -Romans 5:3-5*

Bursting the Bubble

My wife and I have had several experiences in our life that we call "bursting the bubble." Early in our Christian life, we set boundaries God was not allowed to trespass. We assumed that God would never let our savings go below $1,000, or allow us to own two houses at once so we'd have to pay two mortgages, or keep us from having enough money to feed our children.

But one day it happened. While I was going to Oxford University, and during the time of the 1982 recession, the Eckman family was practically financially crushed. I turned to God and tried to remind Him of His duty by saying, "God you're forgetting to keep the rules of the Eckman bubble. You can't push us outside the bubble of our expectations."

He not only pushed us outside the bubble, He blew the bubble up! I looked at the responsibility of two mortgages to pay, a family to feed, bills to pay and my academic program, and I thought, "I do not have a category in my Christian life to cover this. God has cheated me."

That chilling experience turned out to be one of the best things that ever happened to my wife and me. We discovered, however painfully, that God's faithfulness was better than money in the bank. That is a lesson every Christian should start learning, but the only way we began to learn it was by having our little world blow up. Only then could we see that He is able to work all kinds of circumstances for our good.

Hope In Times of Desperate Need

In serious problems, we need to know whether we can trust the motives of our God. If God gave us His Son, aren't His motives clear? Can we not be assured He will be loyal to us in the little difficulties as well as the serious problems of life? Of course the answer is a hearty 'yes.' We can boast in the fact that He will be personally faithful, no matter how far we are pushed out of our own private bubbles.

Deferred hope makes the heart sick, but if we know we are loved by a good Father, we'll be sustained. Since we know we are loved with a love that is not concerned with whether we are going to do right, or how many things we've done wrong, or how weak or godless we are, or what we will become, we have reason to rejoice. The kind of love we receive from God is based on what we mean to Him (and we mean a Son to Him) - since that's the kind of love we receive from God - we have reason to rejoice.

Significance In Spite of Sin

With this background in mind, Romans 5 shows our significance to God in spite of our sinful actions. We can understand this evaluation by looking very closely at several verses. Translated from the Greek text, Romans 5:5 begins:

And the hope (we have in the future) *is not putting us to shame.*

The hope we have doesn't embarrass us or shame us. Originally, shame was born out of mankind's first experience with disobedience. Do you recall what happened in Genesis 3 to Adam and Eve when they ate from the tree in the Garden after God had forbidden it? First of all, their perspectives were profoundly changed. They were used to living in a world where God walked and talked freely with them, and suddenly He was not there. Secondly, they experienced shame for the first time in their existence, and their immediate impulse was to hide themselves from God. Shame is the refusal to reveal who we are. This sense of instinctive self-rejection is the awful emotional product of sin. When hopes fail, it can be deeply hurtful or shaming. If a person hopes for success and fails, he or she can be eaten up alive by shame.

READING 3 - GOD'S KIND OF LOVE

Unforgettable Love

Romans 5:5 continues to explain why the hope we have doesn't give us any reason to hide, to be ashamed, or to be embarrassed about who we are:

*Because that love from God (**agape** love) has been poured out into our hearts and it has left a present effect through the Holy Spirit, the one He has given to us as a comforter. -Romans 5:5*

Agape love is the subjective feeling God has for us; this feeling is not an abstract concept with God. Pulsing with vibrant emotion, love is a kindly, intended enjoyment. He enjoys the object of His love. The use of the Greek perfect verb tense means that the action of God's love being poured out on us happened in the past and left a present effect. This present effect is a deeply felt memory.

A beautiful revelation of how God's love leaves an indelible mark in a person's heart occurred during a testimony meeting at a church where I once was pastor. People from the congregation stood one at a time to share about the time they first recognized God loved them. It was fascinating! I noticed that people were extremely specific in their descriptions. They talked about where they were, how they were dressed, and what was going on at the exact instant when they were filled with a deep sense of being loved by God. They said over and over again, "It was unforgettable."

One of the church deacons said, "I was driving down Highway 1 on the Peninsula going down to Pacifica on the grade, and at that precise moment it hit me. God loves me!" He described the ocean. He described the time of day, where he was, and the way the road slanted. He said, "It hit me how God loved me. I can't forget it!" Considering the mass of detail that he used in his description, it was obvious, he could not forget it. God's love had gushed into his heart in the past, leaving a permanent effect.

Can you remember the first time you realized God loved you? What was it like? If no particular time stands out for you, what do you think it should be like?

Paul says that this sense of being loved by God keeps believers from being ashamed of who they are and of the hope they have. After talking about this highly subjective love, Paul defines God's love very objectively in verse 6:

For yet while we were being weak, yet in the right season (a strategic or right time) *Christ died on behalf of the ungodly. -Romans 5:6*

The word "for" is translated from the Greek word *gar*, and it has several different uses in the Greek New Testament. It is used here to introduce an illustration. Paul is going to describe God's subjective love in very concrete and objective terms through the most significant event of all time - Christ's death on the cross. Whenever we want to know the dimensions of God's love for us, we can look to this historical reference. And from that reference, we can understand why this love has such a powerful effect on us that we cannot forget the sense of being loved by God.

Love Strategically Timed

According to verse 6, God's timing in demonstrating His love for us was "strategic." The Greek language uses two different words for time. One is *kairos* and the other is *chronos*. A watch uses *chronos* time. The word here is *kairos*, which is invariably used of a season or a strategic time.

For example, the invasion of Normandy occurred in 1944 as far as *chronos* time goes, but it turned out to be a *kairos* time (very strategic time) for the allies to invade. When Lord Wellington faced Napoleon at Waterloo and saw that Napoleon had committed his reserve troops, Wellington realized that it was the critical time, *kairos*, to commit everything. The result was a stirring victory that determined the future of Europe.

God chose to reveal our worth to Him at this same type of strategic time. This time was when we were weak and ungodly, as described in Romans 5:7-10.

For hardly on the behalf of a righteous man (a religious person) *someone will die, possibly on behalf of a beneficial man* (a good person) *someone also might dare to die. But God is continually commending His love* (his own particular *agape* love) *to us, because while we were yet continually sinning, Christ died on our behalf. How much more then, being justified now by His blood, we shall be saved through Him from the wrath. For while we were haters* (*Echthros*: the strongest word for enemy in the New Testament, meaning vindictively hateful)*, we were reconciled through the death of His Son . . . -Romans 5:7-10*

When you read *"While we were yet continually sinning, Christ died on our behalf"* in Romans 5:8, how does that make you feel towards God?

God isolated this strategic season to prove His love poured out upon us at the very moment we were continually sinning, while we were continually weak, while we were continually ungodly, and while we were haters of God.

Using the four seasons as an illustration for thought, God could have chosen any season for His Son to die on the cross, but He chose winter, the least promising season, so that we would know he was interested in our person and not in the promise we showed.

Theologically speaking, God was free to place the cross anywhere in time, since its benefits would be applied everywhere in time. The cross wasn't placed in the Garden of Eden before the onset of our sin, nor in the future Kingdom when our sin would be obliterated, but in the middle of our sin. When we had the least to offer, He offered the Son.

Unconditional Love

God is driving home a very important truth here.

God does not love us for what we will become or what He is going to turn us into.

This is the whole point of the passage. God picked a strategic time to allow His only Son Jesus Christ to die for _us_ thereby establishing our worth to Him so we could recognize the incredible fact that His interest in us is based _only on who we are to Him._

I can't emphasize this enough. **God's love is not based on right or wrong, and it is not based on what we will become. It is based on what we mean to Him.**

Mothers usually have this non-discriminating type of love for their children. I heard a story about a famous swimmer and diver who overcame any apprehension he felt when he stepped up to dive off the edge of a 100-foot high precipice by telling himself, "It doesn't matter if I fail or not. Mom will still love me." Because he was assured of his mother's love, it did not matter to him whether he became a world champion diver or not. If he failed or succeeded at a particular dive, it did not matter. His mother's love was what gave him his sense of value. Her affection sustained him.

> "God's love is not based on right or wrong, and it is not based on what we will become. It is based on what we mean to Him."

Romantic love provides another powerful mental image of God's kind of love. I'm not talking about lust or friendship, but the mysterious thing called romantic love, in which one person becomes completely absorbed in the being of another person. This kind of love may be characterized by a sudden, unexplainable fascination. True love relationships, however rare, do exist - and God is the epitome of true love.

The word _agape_ is also used sometimes in the Greek Old Testament. For example, _agape_ is used in Genesis 29:18 of Jacob's love for Rachel. This love delights in another person, and it is the most exciting kind of love. In the story Jacob worked for fourteen years to marry Rachel. Sacrifice in such a love affair, even fourteen years of labor to earn the right to marry her, is unimportant. This is the magnificent kind of love that God extends to us. The sacrifice is not uppermost in the giver's mind, the beloved is!

READING 4 - WORTH & SIN

God's Ultimate Expression of Love

God's ultimate expression of love for us came when we were in the pit of sin and ungodliness. God's love raised a cross over that dark pit and Jesus' outstretched arms displayed the dimensions of His love. The quality of that love is not based upon what we did right, because we were not doing anything right. The word "ungodly" is translated from the Greek _asabeia_, meaning a person who doesn't know how to act around, respect, or respond to God.

Amazingly, according to the latter part of Romans chapter 5, Jesus died for those who are destined to become believers as well as those who won't become believers. His death was not a stock market investment based on financial wheeling and dealing for His own gain. His death was based on what He felt all of us were worth to Him.

Imagine A Walk With God

To illustrate this, take a moment to imagine the time in your life when you committed your most embarrassing sin or set of sins. Imagine that time. Dredge it up. Pull it up to your consciousness, no matter how red-faced you get. The sin might have been only a trifle, or it might have been something absolutely terrible.

Once you have it in your mind, imagine that in the midst of committing that sin, you hear a knocking at the door. The knocking is steady. The knocking is persistent. You know you must answer it. In great embarrassment and discomfort you go to the door. Your mind races. You wonder who it might be - the neighbors, the police, your spouse. Whoever it is, you know you have been caught at your most shameful, guilty moment.

You open the door with great fear, but to your surprise, you are met with the most understanding and compassionate facial expression you have ever seen in your life. The individual at the door looks into your eyes and says, "I am God the Father. I have picked out this moment because I need to talk with you. Let's go for a walk."

With great hesitation, you step alongside Him. He looks at you again with that same striking facial expression - total understanding marked by real compassion. Then He says, "I know you are weak. I know what you were doing. I know, whether you recognize it or not, that you intensely dislike me. And I know that deep at the core you have no great interest in a relationship with me. You're ungodly. **But I need to share with you that I am the only one who knows who you are.** You don't even know who you are. You are chained by guilt, you are bound by shame, and you are running on deep resentment."

"But I can see beyond your problems and I can see someone you have never seen - I can see you. Because I know who you are, I've intervened at this moment to show you what you are worth to my Son and Me."

At that point, His hand directs your eyes to a hillside where you see a cross bearing a young man whose face radiates with that same astonishing expression - total understanding marked by real compassion. You suddenly realize that the man on the cross is God's Son. The Father says softly, "We picked this strategic moment. We didn't pick the moment when you will be wonderful and successful in the future. We chose this moment to show you how serious we are and how significant you are to us. My Son is dying for you because you are worth a Son to Me. You are worth more than your guilt to Us. We are the only ones who know who you are!"

In the "walk with God," God's expression is one of "total understanding marked by real compassion." How is this image of God different or similar to the previous picture of God in your mind?

Describe the emotions you think you would feel on your "walk with God."

Counterfeit Love

Immersed in sin and unbelief, we are still worth a Son from the perspective of this generous-hearted God. Many of us, however, are used to a totally different kind of love. Fair-weather friendships can be heartbreaking experiences. Perhaps all of us have experienced relationships where someone has told us they love us, but we find out they love us only for what we can do, what we've got, or who we know. This is not love, but a sour counterfeit that leaves an emptiness that is hard to overcome.

Have you ever been involved in a situation where you thought you had an everlasting friendship with someone but later found out they had ulterior motives? All of us want to be loved for who we are. Yet we are unwilling to risk exposure of our true selves because we are scared to death that if somebody finds out who we are, they'll run from us.

> *"Someone has told us they love us, but we find out they love us only for what we can do, what we've got, or who we know... Our hearts droop!"*

Take a moment to write a note to the Lord. Express to Him how you feel about Him.

We don't have to run from God's love for His love hunts us down. The great word for God's love in the New Testament is *agape*. In the Old Testament Hebrew, one of the great words for God's love is *Kesed*. *Kesed* not only underscores God's affection for His own; it also has the element of loyalty in it. Meaning "loyal affection", it occurs in Psalm 23:6 where King David said, *"Only goodness and 'loyal affection' has hunted me all the days of my life"* The Israelites, the Philistines, the Edomites, the Ammonites and nearly everyone else in the ancient world tried to catch and kill King David. But when his life was nearing its end, his observation was that only God's affection and loyalty caught him. Often our world only offers short-term loyalty and "stock market" like affection. God not only offers long-term loyalty with infinite affection, but He places it upon His own.

READING 5 - WORTH A SON

The Best Kind of Love

> ***Theological Jargon Box** Omniscient:*
> *An attribute of God that means He is all-knowing.*

In a wonderfully strange way, God knows us absolutely and loves us anyway. He is omniscient*, He knows absolutely everything about us, and He is all-wise. With His infinite knowledge and wisdom, He loves us exactly as we are with a love that will not shame us. God does not love us for what He can get from us. He loves us for who we are.

The best kind of love is when somebody says, "I enjoy you - not what you do for me - but you! There is just something about you that jazzes me." God doesn't want us for what we can do for Him - anything He wants He can make. He wants our companionship because He enjoys us.

God enjoys you for you who are, not what you do.

Do you see how powerful that kind of love is? That kind of love results in a dance, and not in a production line. When somebody walks up and says, I need you on my tomato canning line because we're short of workers. Come to work for us." That's not Christianity. But when someone walks up to you and says, "I know you and I enjoy you. Let's dance." You've got Christianity.

C.S. Lewis described Christianity as the great dance. People go to a dance to appreciate and be appreciated, and to enjoy the companionship of someone else. Dancing conveys beauty, companionship, grace and a steady thrill. If you watch dancers, they are sweating as much as people lifting weights, but they don't notice it, because they are immersed in the dance. They are enjoying each other too much to be self-aware. C.S. Lewis' imagery of the Christian life is beautifully accurate because God's love invites His own to dance with their Beloved forever.

> ***Theological Jargon Box** Trinity: The God of the Bible is continually three persons existing within one nature.*

Where Does This Love Come From?

We are privileged to share God's acceptance, friendship and trust through our faith in Jesus. God shares with us the exact same quality of relationship that exists among the members of the Trinity* (one God in three persons: the Father, Son and

Becoming What God Intended

Holy Spirit). This love existed before the foundation of the world. Christ says that we should participate in this Trinitarian love in John 15:9:

Even as the Father has loved me (agape), I have loved you. Remain in my kind of agape love.

2 Corinthians 5:21 explains that we can share the righteousness of the Trinity also:

And the one who did not personally know sin, on the behalf of us He was made sin in order that we might have the righteousness of God in Him.

Concluding Thoughts

At the introduction, we made the distinction between self-worth and the worth that is established by another. A mother's love for an errant son depicts how a son may be worth everything to the mother regardless of what he has done. All acceptance with God is based on the fact we are worth a Son to Him. Worth must be defined apart from self-image, because God says we are worth a Son regardless of how we look at ourselves.

God defined His love for us at our weakest point, and He paid a precious price so that we would understand He only wants us. Even though God paid this extravagant price for us, we are strangers to our own selves. The person that Christ died for is unknown even to ourselves because we're blinded by guilt, shame, and weakness. **From God's perspective, we are worth a Son to Him just as we are.**

The subjective love from God is unforgettable. The book of Romans objectively illustrates it (Romans 5:6-8), so we can always look at the cross to remind ourselves of the kind of love we are invited to enjoy. By imagining God catching us at our most sinful moment, we get a glimpse of the profound consequences of God's love.

God's love may not be what we are used to, but our obligation is simply to start dancing and jumping up and down like little kids who are melted by the fact that they have met a relative who likes them. That's the response we are supposed to have. Christians need to make a habit of reminding themselves of this every day of their lives.

"Worth must be defined apart from self-image, because God says we are worth a Son regardless of how we look at ourselves."

God's love has implications for the past, the present and the future. When we face circumstances that cause us to doubt our worth, we should ask ourselves the rhetorical question, "What am I worth?" And then let our hearts answer, "I'm worth a Son."

You can face any problem with assurance. Next time your boss calls you into his office to berate you, remind yourself what you are really worth. You can celebrate whether you succeed or fail because you know what you're worth.

You are worth a Son to God.

These are not just empty words, but a profound lyrical outburst of song that will transform your life. You can endure the moment of failing because at the moment of your failure you are still worth a Son to God. If you want to know the dimensions of God's love, don't look to the world around you, look at the cross. You have been invited into the circle of love shared by God the Father, the Son and the Holy Spirit, which existed before the earth was formed and cannot be altered by time. Your responsibility is to enjoy His embrace. You are worth a Son.

Has your perception of who you are changed since becoming a Christian? How?

How does knowing you are worth a Son to God affect your relationships with others?

SUMMARY OF CHAPTER 2
1. True self-worth comes from knowing how much God loves you.
2. The cross of Christ is the ultimate example of God's love.
3. Feeling "worth a Son to God" is an essential part of feeling loved.

TO REVIEW:

What are one or two key insights you've been challenged with this week?

Take a moment to pray and thank the Lord for what He has taught you this week. Lord I am thankful for:

3 | ACCEPTANCE & GOD THE FATHER

CHAPTER SUMMARY: We will explore how our acceptance is uniquely linked to each member of the Trinity. The first member of the Trinity is our ultimate and intended Father. He has a deeply emotional attachment to us called "agape love," and we are to respond to such love with gratitude.

READING 1 - OUR HEAVENLY FATHER

Significance Of Our Earthly Fathers

The Minirth-Meier Clinic in Dallas, Texas, one of the largest nationally known psychiatric clinics in the world, was founded by two uniquely qualified graduates from Dallas Theological Seminary. Both men have doctoral degrees and extensive backgrounds in the field of psychiatry. They have written more than thirty books. Drawing upon their own counseling experience and upon various clinical studies, Frank Minirth and Paul Meier cite five elements which form the basis of a good self-concept during childhood. Both parents are involved in helping the child develop each element, and even more specifically, the father has a singularly important role.

Minirth & Meier's Five Elements of a Good Self-Concept

1. Unconditional Love

First of all, a person needs to experience unconditional love as he or she is growing up. Every child deeply needs unconditional love that is based not upon performance or upon how much they please others, but upon what they mean to their parents. This unconditional, non-performance love shows a parent's loyalty to a child in a healthy way.

2. Discipline

Second, a person needs to experience correct forms of discipline. Parents who show love to their children by carefully setting limits and boundaries give them a healthy sense of security. Insecurity, on the other hand, leads to a poor self-concept.

3. Consistency

Third, a person needs to experience a consistently nurturing environment. A child should be able to predict what his parents are going to do. Children who have a consistent pattern to follow not only feel good about themselves, but learn predictability and trust in life. Inconsistency and surprise cause confusion and mistrust.

4. Good Examples

Fourth, a person needs a good example to follow. Good examples provide vivid pictures of correct behavior to draw upon and imitate in order to reinforce a good self-image.

5. A Strong Father

Fifth, a person needs his or her father to be present as the head of the home as he or she is growing up. One of the most common complaints Minirth and Meier hear from people who seek their counsel is that their father is or was not affectionate enough or did not provide strong leadership in the home. According to their statistics, 80 percent of children needing psychiatric help grew up in a home with a dominating mother and a weak, passive or absent father.

The same problems also seem to influence criminal tendencies in a person. Two common factors were found to exist between 714 prisoners interviewed in a Texas prison. Each had a multiplicity of caregivers through childhood, and each lacked a stable father figure in the home.

Minirth and Meier also believe that lack of a father in early years (age six and under) contributes to a high incidence of homosexuality in boys and sexual promiscuity in girls. They contend that these problems stem from an incorrect response to a male, because a lack of a healthy father figure causes maleness to be ill-defined in their lives. Without a clearly defined father figure, a child will have to sort out problems while growing up that may lead to significant issues in later life as well. I'm convinced that homosexuality is not a result of anything genetic, but from pent up bitterness and hatred that has developed from childhood because of an incorrectly defined father figure.

Reflecting on your own earthly father, select the box that would best describe him.

☐ My father was basically warm and loving

☐ My father was emotionally distant

☐ My father was a good dad but didn't know how to express himself

☐ My father was never around

☐ Other, describe your father:

Christianity not only presents the Father God as having these five characteristics but many more. These other qualities are presented all through the New Testament, but they are particularly found in the Gospel of John. The word 'Father' used for God occurs approximately two hundred and sixty times in the New Testament. Nearly one third or one hundred and seventeen times the word Father is found in the Gospel of John. That is the most instances of any New Testament book.

The ways of the Father and the Son are developed in the Gospel of John. The Father's will is to share with us the same quality of relationship that He has with the Son. This means that the five qualities Minirth and Meier mentioned are far surpassed by the relationship God the Father shares with us. For example, God shares more than a relationship with us. He shares eternal life with us. For John 3:36 says:

The one continually believing upon the Son has eternal life, but the one continually disbelieving the Son shall not begin to see life, but the wrath of God continually remains upon him.

We participate in more than principles of relationship but also a quality of life, eternal life. Eternal life encompasses not only time, but a quality and way of life.

Becoming What God Intended

Give examples of how God has provided these five elements in your upbringing as His child.

READING 2 - THE FATHER & PRAYER

One God in Three Persons

In discussing God the Father, let me make a few comments on the doctrine of the Trinity. Scripture teaches that there are three Persons and one God. That's very easy to believe if you don't try to be simplistic. Logical arguments based upon how we are constituted when applied to the Trinity collapse under their own weight every time. But it's very easy to understand three persons who are one God as long as you don't try to make God analogous to human beings who are only one person and one nature. Scripture is pretty straightforward in presenting three persons as divine in both the Old and New Testaments. The Old Testament presents a Father God, a messenger or Angel of the Lord, and a Spirit of God.

Each is presented as divine. The New Testament presents a Father God, a Son Jesus Christ, and a Holy Spirit. Consistently throughout the Old and New Testaments, one God is manifest in three persons. In fact, the New Testament declares even more than the Old Testament that only one God exists.

Practically speaking, a person cannot learn Trinitarianism* by taking a course in theology or philosophy. One learns Trinitarianism by having a well defined picture of God the Father, a well-defined picture of God the Son and a well-defined picture of God the Holy Spirit. We also learn Trinitarianism by reacting and acting in a healthy way with each of the Persons of the Triune God. The early church practiced Trinitarianism long before they figured it out. They responded to God the Father, God the Son, and God the Holy Spirit as individuals doing separate things. They worshipped three Persons as one Deity.

> ***Theological Jargon Box**
> Trinitarianism: Comes from the term 'Trinity' or 'Tri-unity' and is used for how the three Divine persons all participate equally in the divine nature.

This practical Trinitarianism is based upon the Person of God the Father as shown in Scripture. Ephesians 3:14-15 emphasizes this important point:

> *On account of this I am bowing my knees to the Father, from whom every family in the heavens and upon the earth takes its significance, or its name.*

Every family that exists derives its form from God as a Father within the Trinity. God did not say within Himself, "Since the earthly family already exists, and in order to communicate with humanity, we are going to pretend that I am a Father, Jesus is a Son, and the Holy Spirit is the conformer of our character." It was not that way at all. God was not going to *pretend* that, He was *that*. Instead, He said, "When We create the universe, it will be based on a family pattern, like Us, where there is a Father, a Son and a Holy Spirit."

The question naturally arises: Where does the female gender fit in? Genesis chapters 1 and 2 give the answer. These chapters teach that God the Trinity has both feminine and masculine characteristics. The feminine aspects were created into the woman, while the masculine aspects were created into the man. Both man and woman are absolutely equal in worth, value, intelligence, and will. One is feminine and one is masculine, but both reflect the nature of God. God had no problem saying, "I am like a nursing mother to Israel." Moreover, to have a true picture of what God is like in the Trinity, we need to have persons of equal worth and significance in relationship, like a husband and wife. The church has had no difficulty assuming that God has feminine and masculine characteristics. In fact, believers should have no problem with the following statement: God is far more compassionate and nurturing than the most compassionate and nurturing of women, and God is far more courageous and purposeful than the most courageous and purposeful of men. Christ's compassionate courage has won the loyalty of our hearts, and the Father's nurturing discipline has won our allegiance.

Think of the most compassionate and nurturing woman you know and the most courageous and purposeful man you know. Now envision these as you try to grasp God's feminine and masculine characteristics.

How have you personally experienced these qualities of God at work in your life?

Discovering God the Father Through Prayer

The first thing of significance about God as a Father is that He is supposed to be sanctified* in our thinking and in our relationship to Him. The Father should not be confused with the Son or the Holy Spirit. Christians are Trinitarian, not Unitarian. Trinitarianism is theologically a very significant belief because it is based upon the reality of the relationship among the three members of the Trinity.

> ***Theological Jargon Box** Sanctified: This means to be separated unto God and distanced from that which would keep us from God.

In Matthew 6:8, Christ introduces to the disciples how to set God the Father apart in prayer. The passage has been called the Lord's prayer. Christ begins in verse 5 by telling his disciples where to pray. In verse 7 he tells them not to use pointless repetitions as the heathen do:

Don't then, be like them [heathen who use a lot of words]. *For God the Father knows the needs that you have before you ask Him. Therefore then, you are commanded to be continually praying this way.*
-Matthew 6:7

An Interesting Side Note About Prayer:

In the New Testament, communication to God is never built around time. In fact, no Scriptural teachings exist regarding the amount of time a person is supposed to spend praying. God is not a timekeeper in this regard. He is far too sophisticated and much more concerned about what a person understands and believes and trusts than the amount of time he prays. A person could pray eight hours a day and still be in trouble with God if he didn't believe Him once in all of those eight hours. Or a person could pray for only two seconds, trusting God, and God would be delighted and bless that person. **God's pleasure in a person's prayer doesn't correspond to the amount of time spent praying, but rather to the quality of faith invested.**

Jesus' prayer is not designed for verbal word-by-word repetition. Instead, prayer is designed as a set of issues which should be faced every time a person prays. **New Testament prayer is issues-oriented and not time-oriented.**

Our Father, the one in the heavens, let your character, works, and reputation be set apart by me.

Jesus is saying that the way to approach God the Father in prayer is by asking him to help us separate out (because that is what the word sometimes translated as "hallowed" means) His name, character, works, and reputation. Christ was teaching His disciples to define a picture of God the Father. He wanted his disciples to make an issue out of the Father's character, works, and reputation, and to let them be sanctified. Sanctification simply means to be separated unto something. He wanted them to separate the Father in their minds, to have a clear picture of Him.

Often as I pray I make it a practice to address the issue of God as Father. I'll talk it over with Him and work at it until I have a clear picture. Prayer does not revolve around time, but a sincere grappling with issues, such as the significance of God as our Father.

Take a few moments right now to pray and address God as "Heavenly Father." Ask Him to help you see Him more clearly as your "Father in Heaven" and yourself as His deeply loved son or daughter.

READING 3 - THE INTENDED FATHER

Our Ultimate And Intended Father

The second point regarding God as a Father is that He is the ultimate and intended Father for everyone, as written in Ephesians 3:14-15. This is the first thing we need to know about God the Father. **Every earthly dad, whoever he is, is merely a caretaker.** His responsibility is to turn his children over to the ultimate and intended Father. Some dads do a wonderful job. Some dads fail. But every dad is merely a caretaker, a pale imitation of the ultimate and intended Father. After all, fatherhood does not come from mankind, but from God.

Christianity simply brings people back to the originator of the family - God the Father. Every family in heaven and on earth takes its significance from God the Father.

God: The Only One We Should Call Father

Another point concerning God as our Father can be illustrated by Matthew 23:8-9. Christ was telling His disciples the difference between Pharisaism* and Christianity. Christ attacked Pharisaism as a religion because it did not make a significant issue about what was going on inside a person. Outward appearances were what mattered. **Christianity, on the other hand, is preoccupied with what is going on inside a person.** Without speaking in hyperbole or metaphor, Christ gave a very simple, straightforward command:

> ***Theological Jargon Box** Pharisaism: A Jewish religious sect that emphasized external rules versus internal change.

And don't you call anyone "Rabbi," for there is one teacher for you, and all of you are brethren. And don't you call any person upon the earth "father." For there is one Father for you, the heavenly one. And don't you call anyone way-showers [guides], because your way-shower is one, the Christ. -Matthew 23:8-9

The followers of the Pharisees were originally dependent on their earthly fathers for spiritual instruction. Then, they switched their allegiance to the Rabbis and called them "Father." Christ forbade this. If a person takes this command seriously, he or she will have a crisis. Why? Because he will have to sort out earthly relationships. How good or ineffective an earthly father or earthly teacher is does not make any difference. The crisis comes from trying to understand how to obey a command that says don't call anyone father. What does a person do with that? How can he respond to it? What does Christ really mean?

Part of the characteristic teaching method of Jesus Christ was to create a crisis within people. The purpose of this tension was to force a person to work through the implications of having a relationship with God and with Jesus. He creates the tension here by simply saying, "Don't call anyone Father." A person is stuck, because the next time he meets with his Dad or thinks about his Dad, he has to say to himself, "Jesus has commanded me not to call you Father, so I've got to do something with you." A godly father would understand that.

> *"A godly father can tell his child, "The greatest thrill in my life is to introduce you to God as a Father, because He will succeed where I have failed."*

Remember when Jesus was inside teaching and all of His relatives showed up outside of the house? Someone in the crowd came up to Him and said, "Your mother, your brothers, and your sisters are outside." Jesus' candid answer was, "You are my mother and brothers and sisters. For anyone who does the will of God is my mother and brother and sister, for we have become common brothers and sisters underneath the Fatherhood of God and prior relationships of the family of origin are negated because we have met the ultimate and intended Father."

Why do you feel Jesus put such a high value on the role of the father?

How does understanding His intention help us put our earthly father into a healthy perspective?

A godly father can tell his child, "The greatest thrill in my life is to introduce you to God as a Father, because He will succeed where I have failed. He will be kind where I have been mean. He will be compassionate where I have been hard hearted. He will discipline you in a healthy way where I have been simply dictatorial. He will have the wisdom that I lack. My goal in life is to introduce you to the ultimate and intended Father, and it is fine if you just call me a friend the rest of your life, if it means you understand that your real, ultimate, and intended father is God."

The Reparenting Exercise

In order to catch this concept, I would suggest an imaginative exercise for people who come from the minority of humanity who had good parents. Imagine your good dad taking you to God the Father and saying, "Let Him define what a true family is. Let Him define father/son, father/daughter. Let Him be the Father you need."

For the vast majority of people who did not have a good dad, I suggest doing a "Bradshaw exercise." John Bradshaw is a lecturer on the family. He's not a theologian, but just the same, he's brilliant. He once told a group of people in a seminar, who were each holding teddy bears, to imagine they were quite young (four to six years old). He told them to further imagine they were at home with their parents (and it was understood their homes were unhealthy, dysfunctional homes). They were then to return home as an adult and rescue themselves: to go up to the door, knock, introduce themselves as an adult to their parents, and say, "I am coming here to take away me as a child because this child needs to be raised by someone else. This child has been frozen as a child and has not been allowed to grow. I'm the adult that child became. I'm coming back to rescue him now so that he can grow and flourish."

Bradshaw told the people to imagine going into the living room, sitting down with their parents (as an adult) and saying, "You've lived in pain, you'll die in pain, you started in pain and I have nothing to do with your pain. I have an obligation to myself to unfreeze and become an adult. I'm going to walk this child out of here."

Then Bradshaw explains how the parents try to manipulate the adult child. He tells the person to reply, "No, you were unhappy before I came, you will be unhappy after I leave. I have to take this child out of here." As the adult walks "himself" out, the parents call to the child because they want the child to absorb their pain. They want the child to stay with them to keep their minds off their own problems and bad marital relationship. But the adult stoically walks himself out. He keeps walking, out the door and down the street, with the parents calling out to him.

Bradshaw's next instruction is horribly tragic. He tells the people to turn the child over to themselves (as adults) and to God as they understand Him. Turning ourselves over to another adult is questionable but it is even more disconcerting to turn ourselves over to God *as I understand Him.*

> "Bradshaw's next instruction is horribly tragic. He tells the people to turn the child over to themselves (as adults) and to God as they understand Him."

Bradshaw makes an important point. His answer is not adequate, though, because the child is left with the help of an amorphous or poorly defined God and a goofed up adult. People need a clearly defined Father to trust.

If a person comes from a good family background, it's not too hard to imagine a good dad giving his child into the kind hands of God the Father. If a person comes from a stressed out or unhealthy family background, he can imagine turning the child of his youth over to God the Father to be raised correctly. Either way, the reality is that Jesus tells us through His Word that He intends for God the Father to become more real than our father of our family of origin.

Ｗe should have a greater emotional investment in this ultimate and intended Father than our father from our family of origin. No matter how good that earthly father was or how evil he was, we are intended to positively pursue God as a Father.

What kinds of things can we do that will enable us to begin seeing and feeling God as the "more real Father?"

READING 4 - THE FATHER'S ACCEPTANCE

God The Father Defines Our Acceptance

God the Father has defined the nature of our acceptance with Him by having Jesus Christ die in our place on the cross. Notice carefully Romans 5:8:

And God recommends His own love unto us, because while we were yet sinners Christ died on our behalf.

God the Father (not Jesus Christ, because He is already referred to in the passage as the one on the cross) recommends or presents His own *agape* love to us. God defines the nature of His relationship to us, which is not based on what we do, what we have done, or what we will become. His acceptance is based upon His love for us, His enjoyment of us, His life in us.

How God The Father Demonstrates His Love

I am reminded of God's own demonstration on the cross where He put His Son on display in front of the entire universe so He could say to men and angels, "This is what you are worth to me as you are." **We cannot allow our problems to define God's love for us.** Only the cross can define God's love for us. Any time you want to know the quality of love God has for you, any time you question His love because of the problems in your life, you can go directly to the cross and say to yourself, "That is God's demonstration of love for me. His Son died for me when I was weak, ungodly, continually sinning, and hating Him. He did that based not on what I would become, but on who I am to Him now." The cross is based on something more powerful than right or wrong - love. God's kind of love does not disappoint and never puts us to shame.

The Successful Father

The greatest challenge of parenting comes at the moment of a child's significant failure. Anyone can raise a perfect child. It takes a real Dad to raise an imperfect one. Raising children who are imperfect is God the Father's art form.

The Quality Of Our Father's Love - God Loves And Accepts Us

This is the quality of love that any good father should have. The worst thing in the world we can do to children is to make them feel that our love is dependent upon how well they do. Isn't that a great curse in life? That curse has affected many lives, and it causes children to lose the value of who they are. God says, "Before you ever enter into Christianity, let's settle something. You are worth a Son to Me as you are. You don't have to become anything to be loved by Me." That kind of blessing sets us free!

This Father is well worth knowing because His quality of love does not depend upon performance or potential, but upon our person. We are a grand mystery, fearfully and wonderfully made, and God is in love with us. He paid an awesome price for each one of us. He defines our acceptance by the dimensions of the cross. More so, Romans 8:31-32 says He is quite willing to continually accept us and pronounce us "not guilty" and "right" before Him:

What then shall we be saying to these things? Since God is on our behalf, who can be against us? [The obvious answer to this rhetorical question is no one.] And He indeed who did not spare His own unique Son, but on the behalf of us all He handed Him over. How shall He not also with Him graciously give everything to us? -Romans 8:31-32

A*fter you give a man or a woman your son, everything else is incidental.*

God Justifies Us

Romans 8:33 tells us that it is God the Father who continually justifies us:

Who shall bring a legal or legitimate charge against the chosen ones of God? It is the God [the Father] *who is continually making us right* [or pronouncing us right]. *-Romans 8:33*

As we fall short of His perfection everyday, He justifies us everyday. Why does He do it? Because we are involved in the Trinitarian kind of acceptance that is not based on what we do but on who we are to Him. God continually pronounces us "not guilty" and "right." He is the one who is keeping us saved.

What does this mean? God is our ultimate and intended Father and He has created a relationship with us that is pure acceptance. He is convinced that exposing a person to pure acceptance and getting him off the performance mode and onto the acceptance mode will be revolutionary.

God uses acceptance to raise His children. He also uses consistency and discipline, but He's totally on our side because He is interested in the growth principle and not the trap of being preoccupied with performance.

What aspects of God's name, character, works, and reputation help you define a picture of Him? In picturing Him, what first comes to mind?

The Father & Our Sins: Jesus Our Propitiation

1 John 4:10 says Christ is our propitiation.

In this is agape love, not that we ourselves have loved God, but that He Himself has loved us and sent His Son as a propitiation concerning our sins. -1 John 4:10

> "Trusting in the person of Christ is what gets a person to heaven."

Propitiation simply means satisfaction or a price paid. If we were to give God the Father a stream of consciousness test, and if we said the word "sin" to Him, do you know what He would say? "Satisfaction." If we said the word "guilt," He would say "Payment by the blood of Christ." He has a sufficient rationale to be satisfied concerning the issue of sin. He has no problem with sin in the universe because the Son has satisfied Him. The issue for Him is no longer sin, but the Son. Sin is an issue before we know Christ, but not after. When we proclaim the gospel, this is what we tell the world. Look at 1 John 2:1-2.

My little children, these things I am writing to you in order that you should not sin. And if anyone should sin, we have a Helper personally present with the Father, Jesus Christ the righteous One. And He Himself is the propitiation concerning our sins. And not concerning ours only, but also concerning the entire world. -1 John 2:1-2

Becoming What God Intended

What does that mean? God has decided that His Son is sufficient to satisfy Him concerning sin. Then God the Father, who is very realistic, turns to the world and says, "If you want to get to heaven, you have to accept the Son." The issue to get to heaven is not sin but the Son. You have to believe that Jesus Christ has already died for your sins and that if you trust Him, He will protect you forever and will someday take you home to heaven to meet your Father. The issue is trusting the Son, not sin. That is very straightforward in the New Testament. We proclaim forgiveness of sins in the name of Jesus Christ. Trusting in the person of Christ is what gets a person to heaven. That is Christianity. Ours is the only religion in the world that is not preoccupied with guilt. We are preoccupied with the Son.

From 1 John 2:1-2 and 4:10, how would you explain what propitiation means to a child in 4th grade?

God Is Delighted With Jesus' Sacrifice

I remember when it first dawned on me that God took pleasure in His Son's death. I got excited about it and began to share that fact with a non-Christian relative. He looked at me in disbelief and said, "God took pleasure in His own Son's death? How sick!" Suddenly I thought, "Hmm... perhaps you're right. Maybe it is sick." But over time, I concluded a father could take pleasure in his son's death in the following sense.

As the story goes, some teenagers were studying the Vietnam War in their American history class. The instructor told them that the Vietnam War was stupid, dumb, un-American and that the America's soldiers were drug addicts and worse. According to the teacher, the war could be boiled down to one sentence: "It was just a bunch of black guys recruited by rich white guys to kill little yellow guys."

These naive teenagers accepted what they were hearing, and happened to discuss the issue that afternoon on their way home on a city bus. They were a bit overzealous in repeating their instructor's description of the war until a black man in the back of the bus couldn't take it any longer. Finally, this tall, muscular man with a slightly scarred face stood up and shouted, "Shut up!" Everyone in the bus froze. Tension mounted until the agitated man got his composure. "Turn around and look at me," he told them.

"He gave his life willingly so that others would be spared from death and separation from God."

"I heard what you said. But you're wrong. My son fought in Vietnam. He was not a drug addict, he was not a bum, and he wasn't dumb. He was a good son and I am very proud of him." Tears filled his eyes and his face tightened as he continued. "My son wrote me a letter the day he was killed. It said, 'Dear Dad, We're in a terrible situation. I'm not sure I'm going to get out of here alive. And if I do, I will probably be seriously wounded. But Dad, I want you to remember something no matter what happens. I believe in what I am fighting for. If I should be wounded or worse, you must not dwell on my pain.

You must dwell on the fact that you have a son who was willing to suffer for something worthwhile.

That's why God the Father finds pleasure in His Son's death. Not because He enjoyed seeing His Son suffer, but because His Son died for a noble cause. He gave his life willingly so that others would be spared from death and separation from God. A father can take pleasure and satisfaction in a son who has made him proud. Out of the pleasure and satisfaction God the Father feels over His Son's noble death, He has decided not to make sin the issue, but to make the issue His Son. He has set His Son as the mediator between God and mankind. God views sin as something to be seriously dealt with, but He allowed His Son to make the payment - so that we might have a Father/son, Father/daughter relationship with Him. The goal of all is relationship.

John Calvin, one of the founders of Protestantism, in his Commentaries and Institutes said that the primary reality of Christianity is the filial relationship between a son and his Father God. It is a Father/son relationship. Martin Luther, another founder, said the primary relationship in Christianity is the relationship of trust between the child of God and God as his Father. This is classic Christianity - where we enjoy profound acceptance based upon a sufficient atonement*.

> ***Theological Jargon Box** <u>Atonement:</u> Refers to the price Christ paid for us, the friendship He provides, and the family status the Father gives to us.

READING 5 - THE FATHER'S LOVE

The Father's Emotional Involvement With Christians

Many Bible teaching churches seem emotionless. I think one reason for this is that they are built on abstract bits of information that cannot reach us emotionally. If God is presented as a Platonic* God and not the emotionally rich God of the Bible, the church will function as a college classroom instead of a living fellowship. God gave us emotions to use. Our emotions are analogous to God's emotions. His

> ***Theological Jargon Box** <u>Platonic God:</u> Refers to Plato's idea that God is unreachable and not interested in a personal relationship.

were first. **We are made in His image. We have emotions because He does.** God is emotionally involved with us, but many Christians have instinctively concluded that the God of the Bible is not emotionally involved with them.

They're not even sure if He likes them. They just suppose He is neutral about everything. But nothing could be further from the truth. The God of the Bible is passionately in love with each of us! He likes us! If you are a lady, He'd take you for a walk and a talk. If you are a man, He'd go fishing with you. He is a lover of men and women. Psalm 103:13 reinforces this:

> *Just as a father has deep emotional involvement with his children, so Yahweh* has compassion, or deep emotional involvement, on those who have a respect for Him. For He Himself personally knows our frame. He remembers that we are but dust.*
> *-Psalm 103:13*

> ***Theological Jargon Box** <u>Yahweh:</u> The personal Hebrew name for God. It means, "He who is."

David uses the model of a human father for how God works. "Just as a father" implies a good father, assuming families in David's time were not as dysfunctional as they are in our time. David says that the Lord has compassion like a father. The Hebrew word translated compassion is *reghemim*. As a noun in the singular it refers to a woman's womb and to the intestines of a man. The Hebrew word is used of that which is felt deeply. As a noun in the plural it refers to emotional involvement or deep compassion. Commonly the Hebrew language uses bodily organs to represent psychological states.

These verses are sometimes translated to say that the Lord has compassion on those who fear Him. The Bible never endorses cringing fear. The phrase for fearing Him always refers to a deep respect for who He is and what He says.

The Christian's Emotional Involvement With God

In Deuteronomy 6:4-5 God commands us to have *agape* love for Him:

> *Hear O Israel, Yahweh is our God. Yahweh is one* [an absolute unity]. *Since that is so, you shall love Yahweh your God with all your heart and with all your soul and with all your might.*

Agape love brings the entirety of who a person is into a harmony where the heart, soul and complete being of a person is properly related to someone else. *Agape* love is that which brings a person's emotions, thinking, and will into a harmonious healthy relationship with another.

Love is not knowledge - you can know everything and still not have love. Love is not faith - you can move mountains and still not have love. And love is not sacrifice - you can give your body to be burned and still not love. *Agape* love is where a person is properly emotionally involved, mentally involved, and volitionally involved with another. You can never have *agape* love by yourself. When we properly love someone else, we will be emotionally involved.

Becoming What God Intended

Agape love is more than just doing things. It is a whole-soul response to somebody else. We only have *agape* love when we feel it. Such is not a mental abstraction or a choice of the will.

God's Soul Is Involved In Loving Christians

God's love is holistic. His soul is involved. The following are just a few of the many verses which express this truth:

- Leviticus 26:11 says: "God's soul abhors… "

- Isaiah 42:1 says: "God's soul loves… "

- Luke 1:78 says: "God's bowels of compassion are open to us. "

- Philippians 2:1 says: "If there is any tenderness, any compassion from love, be like-minded to one another."

The whole point is, God is emotionally involved with you. He is not distant. He is interacting emotionally with you. He has far more compassion for you than you have ever had pity for yourself as we find in 2 Corinthians 1:3.

Blessed be the God even the Father of our Lord Jesus Christ. The Father of tender mercies and God of every variety of encouragement.

There are three different words for mercy in the Greek New Testament. One means "I'll have mercy on you." Another means "I'm going to graciously forgive you."

But the word here means "to be tenderly merciful." It means He not only forgives, but He puts His arms around you and says, "It is all right. I tenderly forgive you. Don't feel guilty anymore. My Son died for you. Don't despair, and don't be afraid. Let me comfort you. You're worth more to me than what you've done wrong. I want you more than I want you to be perfect." That's how God works. Think of every time you have been encouraged in life. That's what God does. He's the God of tender mercies and the God of encouragement.

> Y**ou're worth more to me than what you've done wrong.
> I want you more than I want you to be perfect.**

Christians Are To Share God's Encouragement With Others

2 Corinthians 1:4 tells us what results we can expect from experiencing God's tender mercies.

The one who is continually encouraging us concerning every particular tribulation, with the result that we'll be able to encourage the ones who are in every variety of tribulation, through the encouragement with which we ourselves have been encouraged by God.

If I really know that I have a Father of tender mercies, then I can trust Him as a tender, merciful and encouraging God. If I trust Him to be who the Bible says He is, then I'll be able to get through that problem with the result of being able to help someone else on the other side. When I see somebody in a problem I'll be able to say, "I need to talk to you about Dad. You've got a good Dad who is going to be with you in this problem. You can trust Him. You can know Him. He is tender. He is not responding to you based on your guilt. He's responding to you based on His love for you."

I became a believer at 17. I became a pastor at 25. All through my time as a pastor, there was a question that I always avoided asking myself because I didn't know enough about the Bible to have an answer. When I was growing up, my dad was an alcoholic. On a weekend, one of us would get cornered and we would be browbeaten for hours. The end result was that my internal emotional life was suppressed until it disappeared. Years later, I went into ministry with my emotions still repressed.

> *"When I was too scared to cry, confronted with an alcoholic dad who could do anything to me, the God of the Bible was weeping for me."*

For a long period of time, a question nagged at me. It bothered me to think about it. Every time it would creep up into the back of my mind, I would push it back. I didn't have an answer for it. The question made me extremely uncomfortable. The question was this, "Where was God when I was cornered by my father?"

One day I was reading in Ephesians where it says that God is rich in compassion. That phrase triggered a train of thought that finally released me from the pain of that question. I finally had an answer. When I was too scared to cry, confronted with an alcoholic dad who could do anything to me, the God of the Bible was weeping for me. He was emotionally involved! He was there!

Perhaps you think that I'm over-dramatizing, but what that thought did for me was wonderful. I could finally face those fearful memories and realize God hadn't forsaken me. As I was frightened, He was weeping. At that point I granted God His emotions. When I did that, for some reason I had far more respect for Him. The other platonic, distant, uninvolved God was too much like my earthly dad.

The God of the Bible is richly emotional. He is the Father of all mercies; He is the source of every variety of encouragement. On top of that He even likes you! If we set apart God as a Father in our hearts intelligently, imaginatively, and faithfully, it will change us.

SUMMARY OF CHAPTER 3

1. God the Father should not be confused with the Son and the Holy Spirit.

2. New Testament prayer is issues oriented, not time oriented.

3. God the Father has a deeply emotional love for us.

TO REVIEW:

What are one or two key insights you've been challenged with this week?

Take a moment to pray and thank the Lord for what He has taught you this week.
Lord I am thankful for:

4 | ACCEPTANCE & THE SON

CHAPTER SUMMARY: We will explore the truth that salvation is a Person and not a religious system. That person, Jesus, is dedicated to delivering us from our past failures and sin, giving us peace in the present, and securing our future with Him. To appreciate Him adequately we must make certain we do not have an "evil conscience," an instinctive belief that to feel accepted with God we must add religious works to the work of Christ.

READING 1 - SALVATION IS A PERSON

In the New Testament, each member of the Trinity is involved in our acceptance. The acceptance of the circle of love existing among the Father, Son, and Holy Spirit becomes the acceptance that is shared with us through believing the Gospel. Acceptance is the bond holding God's circle of love together. God's circle of love is the Trinity, and that circle of love predates time. We become transformed people when we boldly enter into that circle.

In Chapter 3, we defined our relationship with God the Father. This chapter will define our relationship with Jesus Christ. Chapter 5 will define our relationship with the Holy Spirit.

Acceptance is a central person, Jesus Christ, and not a religious system. The Father loves us, the Son redeems us, and the Holy Spirit keeps us safe and empowers us. Each of these is a person, and what they have done, are doing, and will do, creates the truths of Christianity. The central figure within the Trinity we must respond to is Christ, for through Him we enter the family of God.

The Meaning of Redemption

In both the Old and New Testaments, redemption* is personal and familial. In the Old Testament Law, family members were obligated to rescue a family member in trouble or avenge a family member who was killed. A person could only be rescued or redeemed by his closest family member (Lev. 25:48-49). If he became financially destitute, the family member paid off the bills and delivered him from poverty. If he was enslaved, the family member bought him out of slavery (Lev. 27:13-31). If he or she were killed,

> ***Theological Jargon Box** <u>Redemption:</u>
> Refers to the care, concern, and deliverance that family members provide for one another in the Old Testament, and also refers to the same help that God provides for His own children.

the family member avenged the death. The whole system of family relationships acting to rescue a relative was called redemption. The theological name for this system is called the kinsman redeemer model. The kinsman redeemer was the closest relative who was under the obligation to rescue. God uses that model of redemption to explain our salvation (Job 19:25; Isa. 41:14; 43:14). Money is not the motive, nor debit or credit. The heart of it all is family. Because we are his family members, God rescues us and is willing to satisfy His sense of justice concerning our sins.

Imagine for a moment that you have been out of work for a long time. You have charged up your credit cards to their limits and taken out a number of loans. Although you've just been hired on at a new job at the same salary, there is no realistic way you can ever pay off your debts.

How does this make you feel about yourself and your future?

Now imagine your uncle Ken, a multi-millionaire, comes out of the blue and pays off all your debts and puts an additional fifty thousand dollars in your savings account. How has your perspective of yourself and your future changed?

Some schools of Christian thought are caught up with trying to figure out how the payment of Christ's death is applied and how it benefits different classes of people, namely Christians and non-Christians. In the dust of the dispute, however, a fundamental reality is overlooked: Salvation is a person. Salvation is not a divisible transaction, because a person cannot be divided. Notice I Corinthians 1:30.

Directly from Him, you yourselves are in Christ Jesus, who has become for us wisdom from God, both righteousness and sanctification and family redemption.

Christ is made our wisdom, our understanding of life, our righteousness, sanctification, and **family** redemption. God is saying that He is your closest relative, the only one who has the legitimate right to rescue you. God the Father has saved us not on the basis of a principle or a transaction, but based on a person who is placed centrally between the Father and ourselves.

Since Christ is in a central position between God and humanity, 1 Timothy 2:4 tells us we should pray for everybody.

Who is desiring that every kind of person be saved, and to come unto a full personal knowledge of the truth. -1 Timothy 2:4

Then notice in verse 4, Paul gives us the reason by describing God's desire for every person.

For there is one God, and one go-between standing in the midst of God and men, a man, Christ Jesus. The one having given himself as a ransom on the behalf of every kind of person; the witness to be shown in its own particular season. Unto which I myself have been placed as a proclaimer, an apostle (I tell you the truth, I'm not lying), a teacher of Gentiles in faith and truth. -1 Timothy 2:5-7

According to Greek grammar, the context is talking about every type of individual: men, women, princes, kings and slaves. Notice how verses 5-7 go on to describe Jesus as the go between. If you have a translation that reads "the man" Christ Jesus, it should read "a man" instead, because the text is emphasizing the humanity of Jesus Christ. Jesus Christ, a go-between who is a man, stands between God and every kind of person.

Becoming What God Intended

God wants every kind of person to be saved, and the desire is sincere. Does God have desires that His plan does not fulfill? The biblical answer is, "Of course, just as we do." We are made in His image. God has a genuine desire for every kind of person to be saved, but He places Jesus Christ in the midst. Then He says, "What are you going to do with Him?" He doesn't say, "What are you going to do with your sins?" He has already paid the family ransom. Christ, your kinsman redeemer has already secured the family redemption.

If Jesus is our kinsman redeemer, our redemption pleases God the Father (Ephesians 1:5) and He gets enjoyment out of it, why don't many of us seem to be enjoying the process of our salvation?

Personal Relationship Versus Religious System

Christian Bible teachers and theologians often teach a system to explain how salvation works. In doing so they give a false impression. The false impression is that the goal is to understand the system. That is not the goal. The goal is to recognize that Christianity is a Person and not a system. Religious systems among many Christian theologians miss the point of God's plan of salvation if they don't focus on God as a person. I can fall in love with a person, but can I fall in love with a system? If I like to play abstract games, I can. But a system can't like me. A system can't make me feel worthwhile. A system can't say what Jesus says in Matthew 11:28-29.

All you who are weary and heavy laden, come unto me and I will give you rest. Take my yoke upon you and be discipled by me, for I am gentle and humble in heart; and you will find rest for your souls.

When Arminians* and Calvinists* argue about whether believers can lose their salvation, the arguments may take interesting twists and turns. A nice abstract argument is going on until we go a little bit deeper. If we forget the systems and think about the person, the argument is really about whether God is going to drop the ball. If we push aside the systems and make it personal, the way the New Testament does, then the ultimate issue is the loyalty and faithfulness of God Himself. When salvation is a person, then it takes on a whole different light.

> ***Theological Jargon Box**
> <u>Arminian:</u> refers to one who is committed to the teachings of Jacob Arminius (1560-1609). His system emphasized man's choice for God and our weakness.
> <u>Calvinist:</u> refers to one who is committed to the teachings of John Calvin (1509- 1564). His system emphasized God's choice of us and His awesome power.

READING 2 - THIS PERSON DEALS WITH OUR PAST, PRESENT, & FUTURE

Delivered: Past, Present and Future

Our salvation is designed for personal interaction with God and protection. Our acceptance with God - our salvation - is caught up with a person whose responsibility is to deliver us from our past failures and sin, and protect us in the present and in the future. This deliverance is based upon the character, faithfulness, and integrity of that person. The system is not simply Calvinistic or Arminian, but is best illustrated by the Old Testament high priest. In the Old Testament, the high priest was continually involved in protecting the people from the penalties due for their sins. He went into the presence of God in the temple once a year to plead for the nation Israel, and to make satisfaction for the nation's sins.

We have two lines of Old Testament truth coming together to emphasize how personal our New Testament salvation is. One line of truth is the kinsman redeemer concept that emphasizes deliverance must come through our closest relative. The second is the high priest concept that underscores the reality that redemption is based upon the faithfulness and character of a person. Both of these lines of truth highlight what the New Testament so beautifully teaches - salvation is a person, Jesus Christ.

Past Deliverance

Romans 3:23-26 tells how Jesus delivers us from our past.

For everyone of us has sinned and we are continually falling short of the glorious presence of God. Now we are continually justified freely as a gift by His grace through the family redemption which is in Christ Jesus, whom God set forth as a propitiation through faith in His blood for a display of His righteousness, through the passing over of the previously done sins. -Romans 3:23-26

We are free from every trace of guilt over past wrongs because of Jesus, and He is the only one who can accomplish this for us. When the darkness of our past tries to haunt us through the terrible reminders of other people, the accusations of Satan, or our own guilty thoughts and memories, we can smile and say, "God doesn't remember that anymore. I may have guilt feelings, but I have no guilt before God because Jesus has delivered me."

Present Deliverance

1 John 2:1-2 tells how Jesus delivers us from our present sins.

My little children, these things I am writing to you in order that you should not sin. And if anyone should sin, we continually have a helper, an advocate, in the personal presence of the Father, Jesus Christ the righteous one. He Himself is the satisfaction concerning our sins and not concerning ours only, but also concerning all the world. -1 John 2:1-2

God has paid the bills for the sins of the world. God has satisfied Himself concerning our sins and He has made the way of salvation a person. Jesus Christ the righteous is the answer for our present sins. The biblical picture here is interesting. The Bible assumes we are capable of losing our salvation every day and Christ has to protect our salvation every day. Because He is consistent and righteous, we are protected every day. Our assurance and insurance is a person, not a system. If He should cease helping, we would be in trouble.

God knows we are spiritually unintelligent individuals who are continually getting ourselves lost and going astray. That is the nature of sheep, and that is why Christians are compared to sheep. If you do not continually get lost and go astray, you cannot qualify for being protected by a shepherd. You may think that you are too smart to have a shepherd. The task of convincing Christians they really do things that are wrong and that they really do need a shepherd is very difficult. In fact, finding non-Christians who will admit they are not exactly angels is just as difficult. But Christ is our Shepherd, and He is looking for those who will admit they are in need and are continually getting into trouble so that He can continually protect them.

Future Deliverance

Hebrews 7:25 shows us Jesus delivers us from our future sins.

Whence He is able to save unto the complete end the ones who are coming to God through Him because He always lives to intercede for them.

The word "end" is ***panteles***, a Greek word made from two other Greek words: ***Pas*** meaning all, and ***telos*** meaning until the very end. Sometimes the word is translated "forever," but it is not really relating to time; it is relating to a process - the process of being saved. If you run up to Jesus and say, "I trust you," Jesus will turn to you and say, "Now I am your high priest. I have also been the sacrifice for all of mankind, but now I am your high priest. You have put your hand on the sacrifice and identified yourself with it."

What I am referring to is the Old Testament process of purification. Some sacrifices were made in order to satisfy God for all of Israel. But the protection and purification was for those who came to the priest and placed their hand firmly upon the head of the animal sacrifice and said by doing that, "I will identify with the sacrifice." Jesus Christ stands between God and man. He is the sacrifice for all of mankind. He is the bronze altar of sacrifice for all of mankind, but He is the high priest only for those who come forward and identify with the sacrifice. At that point, those who come are justified by faith in the person of Jesus Christ who will protect them forever. Salvation is a Person.

Salvation is not a system. Salvation is a Person, Jesus Christ.

When you go to sleep tonight, you are protected by a person. You are not protected by a legal clause or a system. You are protected by a person who loves you and who agrees with God the Father that you are worth His suffering. Jesus is the person who delivers us from the past, who sustains us in the present and who will complete the process in the future. He is the one who, as the Hebrew *go'al* - the family kinsman redeemer - paid our debts from the past, delivers us from slavery to sinful habits in the present, and will rescue us from the threat of the worldwide tribulation period and the Antichrist* in the future.

Salvation is a person who is related to us as our closest family member. **If anybody asks you who your relatives are, you have a legitimate right to say, "Jesus Christ is my closest relative."** If you find that strange to say, the truth has not been adequately integrated into your heart. Work that through in your mind. Compare each of your family members with Jesus Christ. According to God's perspective, Jesus is a closer family member to you than your father, your mother, or your brothers or sisters. The kinsman redeemer accepted the obligation of the closest family member. God is claiming family rights as a Father and as the kinsman redeemer. You are in an entirely new family!

> ***Theological Jargon Box**
> Antichrist: Eventually Satan plans to produce a fake Christ who ends up with worldwide political support. This future world ruler is a Satanic counterfeit and miracle worker. He will be condemned along with Satan.

Picture in your mind the Lord Jesus Himself stopping on the way to the cross. He turns and looks right at you, bends down and says, "Place your hand upon My head. I will become the sacrifice for your sins, once for all eternity. You will be completely forgiven of all your sins." He then continues on to the cross and is crucified by Roman soldiers.

How would you feel about placing your hand upon His head?

What would it feel like to be totally forgiven of every past sin and failure?

What difference does it make to you to know all your future sins are forgiven?

READING 3 - THE REALITY OF THE CONSCIENCE

Salvation Pleases God

Salvation is also something that pleases God the Father. He is a delighted deity who is enjoying the whole process of our salvation. See how Ephesians 1:5 portrays this.

> *Having set out the limits around our lives, He predestined us unto adoption as adult daughters and sons through Jesus Christ unto Himself, according to the good thought of His settled desire.*

Notice the emphasis on desire and pleasure. The same word for good pleasure is used when God the Father refers to Christ in Matthew 12:18:

This is my beloved Son, in whom I am well-pleased.

The terminology is exactly the same. He feels good about His Son and He feels good about what His Son is doing to produce many sons and daughters. God is delighted with His noble Son, and He wants more sons and daughters. The term for settled desire is the basic Greek word for wanting something. Why does God do what He does? The reason is the same for God as it is for the child who is sucking a lollipop; they both are enjoying themselves. There is no great deep reason to explain the existence of Christianity, other than the fact that God is enjoying Himself. Using His Son on our behalf brings good pleasure to Him that satisfies His desires.

Isaiah 53:10 is an interesting prophetic verse referring to the future sufferings of Christ on the cross. It says: *It delighted God to crush Him.* The work of the cross brought great pleasure to God the Father. He decided sovereignly to enjoy the nobility of what Jesus did, while consciously choosing to overlook the pain His Son went through for our benefit. Love always overlooks pain to benefit someone else.

Notice how Ephesians 1:9 reiterates that God was delighted in the rescue of His children.

Having made known to us the mystery of His settled desire, according to His good pleasure which He purposed in relationship to Him.

Classic Calvinism says the purpose of mankind is that we might enjoy God and glorify Him forever. That views it from our perspective. If you take a step back and ask what God gets out of the work of salvation, the biblical answer is delight and enjoyment. At the center of everything is a God who is enjoying what He is doing. He is very much enjoying having His Son protect those who have trusted in Him. He is very much enjoying conforming our character to the character of Jesus Christ.

Salvation Should Please The Christian

If God is having such a good time, then His children should have a good time too. Then why aren't we? I personally believe, based upon many years of talking to Christians, a very simple reason exists as to why so many Christians are emotionally neutral about their Christianity.

We can find the reason in what the Bible teaches about the conscience. The subject of the conscience is hardly dealt with either in psychological literature or in preaching and teaching. Yet it is the very root of our ability or inability to enjoy life. A Christian who has a poorly trained conscience can be beaten up by that conscience, scandalized by that conscience, and even emotionally destroyed. There are at least five kinds of consciences in the New Testament: a healthy conscience, a burned out conscience, a weak conscience, a strong conscience, and an evil conscience. As a significant example, see how I Corinthians 8:7-13 describes the weak conscience.

But not in everyone is the knowledge [that there is only one God and that idols are nothing], *but some until now have a conscience trained to the idol. They are eating as if the food were offered to idols. And their conscience being weak is polluting them. Now food does not bring us to God, nor if we should eat food offered to idols are we the less. Nor if we should eat, will we abound. Watch lest the freedom or authority of yours does not become a stumbling place to the weak. For if a certain one should see you, the one having personal knowledge reclining to eat in a place of idolatry, would not his conscience being weak be built up to go unto the place of idolatry to eat? For* [inevitably] *the one being weak will be destroyed by your knowledge, this brother on account of whom Christ died. And thus sinning against the brothers and wounding their conscience, you sin against Christ. Wherefore if food scandalizes* [causes my brother to trip and be damaged,] *I will never eat meat until the end of the age in order that my brother should not be scandalized.*

Many who converted to Christianity two thousand years ago were raised in families and cultures where idolatry was everywhere. From the earliest years, the young person experienced idolatry as the center of family life. When they were converted, this family background was still a part of their subconscious belief system.

Becoming What God Intended

Very sympathetically, Paul taught that converts from idolatry should not be put in a position where that background may trip up the former idolater. He told the Christian who was not worried about idolatry not to eat in the temple of the idol, even if it has the best food in town, because the former idolater may be encouraged to eat food offered to idols and his subconscious instincts from his past will rise up and devastate him. This passage is saying that if we went to a place of idolatry where they served great food, and as a result, a brother stumbled emotionally, we should be concerned. If the brother sincerely believes that idols should be taken seriously, he has a weak conscience.

The person who, in his Christian liberty*, eats a hamburger that was sacrificed to an idol is unloving toward the weaker brother who might imitate him. If the weaker brother eats a hamburger because he saw a more mature Christian eat one and feels terrible inside, it is because he violated his own conscience.

> ***Theological Jargon Box** Christian liberty: This normally refers to the many issues of life where God has given us free choices. Many times Christians differ over what is the correct choice, but almost always the issues do not involve moral questions.

Strangely the person who has the incorrect information is damaged by the individual who has the correct information. The correctness of our doctrine is not the only thing that matters; the love we feel for the other is the proof of our Christianity.

None of us knows perfectly, but he who loves is known of God. -1 Corinthians 8:2-3

Being weak scripturally is to have an incorrect knowledge. Paul is saying that if a person's conduct is out of harmony with his subconscious belief, he's just living a weak Christian life. Three things will happen: his spiritual effectiveness will be ruined, his conscience will be wounded, and he will be scandalized. A powerful emotional response will devastate this individual because his weak Christianity has contradicted his subconscious beliefs. Those instinctive subconscious beliefs that came from being raised in a culture of idolatry will devastate a person whose Christianity is only imitated outwardly and not integrated inwardly. We can be sailing along, imitating Christianity, but when we go against what we believe deep down inside, it hurts us.

The conscience, then, is the doorway to our subconscious beliefs. These beliefs are more powerful, strong, and fearsome than most of us imagine. When a person's subconscious beliefs conflict with the beliefs of Christianity, inner turmoil will affect that person's ability to enjoy his salvation.

Some Christians have difficulties believing an subconscious part of our lives exists. The difficulty with proving an subconscious part of our life exists is simply that we are not used to asking the right questions or thinking in biblical categories. Sigmund Freud revolutionized man's view of himself by showing there really was an subconscious. Unfortunately he proceeded to misuse his insight by creating "Freudianism." His basic insight was valid; his application was wrong.

The Bible's Proof of the Subconscious

The Bible has a very well documented doctrine of the subconscious. The book of Proverbs says one can take a foolish person, grind him with a mortar and pestle, and the folly will still never come out of him. In other words, foolish beliefs are part of a person. They become subconscious realities. A part of us is instinctive and subconscious.

What are some areas in which we can overlook pain or inconvenience to ourselves in order to benefit someone else because of our love for them?

Think for a moment of a young adult who was raised in a church with the constant message, "Don't break the rules. Stick to the rules and you'll be O.K." This person then begins attending a church that does not emphasize "the rules," but emphasizes the love of God and loving relationships.

How do you suppose his conscience will affect his participation and enjoyment of the new church?

READING 4 - THE EVIL CONSCIENCE

The Conscience: Guardian of Subconscious Beliefs

The conscience is the guardian of our subconscious beliefs. With the quickness of a computer, it instantly tells us when we have violated our subconscious beliefs. Comparing what we do with what we sincerely believe, the conscience will allow us to feel good if they match. If no match exists, we feel deep emotional, powerful, destructive, scandalizing, wounding pain.

Notice how Hebrews 10:19-30 describes how a Christian is supposed to protect himself from an evil conscience.

We should enter in with a true heart and a fullness of positive feelings from faith. Having permanently sprinkled our hearts from an evil conscience, and washed our bodies in pure water. -Hebrews 10:22

As believers, we can walk directly into the presence of God and say, "Hi Father. Here are my problems. Here is my weakness. Here is my sin. Here is my guilt. Here I am." We can be free and at ease speaking in the absolute presence of God, because we have access through a great high priest who, by His sacrificial death on the cross, has opened the way to God that we may enter in. **And, we are to come with a true heart overflowing with confidence from faith. We are supposed to come into the presence of God with a full assurance or a solid foundation of positive emotions that come from faith. If we are exercising faith correctly, we feel it. If we don't feel anything, we may be profoundly misunderstanding.**

The Attack of the Evil Conscience

> "If you have such an evil conscience, you don't need Satan, because you are carrying a substitute for him around inside of yourself."

What is an evil conscience? The word for evil in Hebrews 10 is *poneros*. The word *poneros* is used in the Lord's prayer to describe Satan. When I was growing up, we lived next to a junkyard. Junkyard dogs were fun as long as you had a wire mesh fence between you and the dogs because they were trained to attack. A *poneros* conscience is malignantly evil and trained to attack. This conscience is not defunct, nor immobilized, nor weak. This evil conscience is trained to attack. If you have such an evil conscience, you don't need Satan, because you are carrying a substitute for him around inside of yourself, and the substitute will point out your defects and attack you.

The evil conscience is called malignantly evil because is not only attacks and hurts you, but it also attacks the work of Christ. In the Old Testament, before a priest was put into service, a hyssop branch was dipped into the blood of a sacrifice and the blood was sprinkled on him and his body was considered washed. Then he put on clean garments and he served. This was done only once to bring him into the priesthood. In a sense, we must do this as well. We have to find our conscience, dip some hyssop into the blood, and sprinkle the blood on our conscience to clean it up.

The "Christ Plus" Conscience

But why is the conscience evil? In Hebrews, the conscience was evil because it was a "Christ Plus" conscience. Look at Hebrews 10:1.

For the law, since it has only a shadow of the good things to come and not the very form of things, can never by the same sacrifices which they offer year by year, continually make perfect those who draw near.

Becoming What God Intended

This letter was written to Hebrew Christians living in the city of Jerusalem. On the Sabbath, these Christians would go to the temple and watch the blood of bulls and goats being applied to the bronze altar as a sacrifice. Years before, they had trusted in Jesus Christ as their Messiah, but every week they would go to the temple and see the blood of bulls and goats being sprinkled on the altar. Because of this custom, they assumed it was Christ plus the blood of bulls and goats that made them acceptable to God. Hebrews 6:1 also refers to slain animal sacrifices. Nothing is deader than a goat with a slit throat.

The believers in Jerusalem were being told to shun dead works and rely solely on the blood of Christ. Going back to Chapter 10:3, we see why the Hebrew Christians were told to do this:

> *For in those sacrifices there is reminder of sins year by year. For it is impossible for the blood of bulls and goats to take away sins.*

The people were going to the temple week after week, month after month, year after year. They believed in Christ, but they were still going to the temple.

- Verse 10 says: *By this* [the will of Christ and His sacrifice] *we have been sanctified through the offering of the body of Jesus Christ once for all.*

- Verse 14 says: *For by one offering he has perfected for all time those that are sanctified.*

- Verse 19 says: *Now where there is forgiveness of these things there is no longer any offering for sin* [as in the animal sacrifice].

If you have cleansing justification through the blood of Christ, you don't need any more offerings. That being the case, notice the last application the writer makes to the Hebrew Christians in chapter 13:10. The message to the Hebrew Christians is never to go back to the temple again. Don't demean the blood of the God-Man by going back to the temple again! Jesus died outside the city. They didn't kill him on the altar in the temple. We are to go outside the city and bear His reproach. What was His reproach? He was a criminal on a cross, like a criminal in an electric chair. He had no glorious temple, no golden altar, no altar of incense, no candlesticks - He had a cross.

What does this have to do with our conscience? Old Testament law required the sacrifice of bulls and goats and pigeons while the world waited for the completed sacrifice of Christ. There was a legitimacy to those sacrifices. They were biblical and legal until the Messiah appeared.

Believers today might have had their conscience trained the way the early Hebrew believers were trained by the sacrifice of bulls or goats. Our consciences may have been trained by a long list of religious works and good deeds. For us it might be

- Christ plus our witnessing equals positive feelings of acceptance.

- Christ plus our tithing equals acceptance. Christ plus our good works equals acceptance. Christ plus our perfect lives equals acceptance.

- Christ plus reading our Bible this morning equals acceptance. Christ plus obeying our elders equals acceptance.

- Christ plus any figment of our imagination that makes us feel good about ourselves equals acceptance.

In effect we are saying to God the Father, "It is perfectly all right that Your Son died and shed His blood for me to be accepted by You, but if you don't mind I'd like to make <u>sure</u> I'm saved by reading my Bible this morning and I'll trust in the blood of Christ plus my Bible reading to feel comfortable with You."

Do you ever feel that you need to do certain "Christian things" to feel acceptable to God? If so, check the following boxes that apply:

- ☐ I read my Bible on a regular basis
- ☐ I have daily prayer time
- ☐ I share my faith with others
- ☐ I tithe at church
- ☐ I (fill in the blank)

How can you combat the "Christ Plus" mentality when your evil conscience is attacking you?

Take a moment now and write a note to God and ask Him to help you fully appreciate what Jesus has already done for you.

D̲o you ever feel you have to read your Bible to feel acceptable to God?
If so, the Bible says you have an evil conscience.
No amount of Bible reading is equal to the Son of God.

Believers do a horrendous thing to a Father who has given a Son for our sins. If you add your Bible reading to Him as a way of buying off your conscience, you are in sin and should feel guilty about it. If you add things to the work of Jesus Christ, it is rebellion and sin! If you want to feel good and guilty, feel guilty about saying this to yourself: "Christ plus having a pure mind equals acceptance with God." Let me tell you, the purity or impurity of your mind is not the basis of your acceptance to God. If you are a lesbian or homosexual, let alone a religious person, God will accept you and work with you as you are because His Son has already died for you. If you trust in Him as you are, He won't be offended, because the blood of His Son protects you. You need not add anything to that. If you do add your religious activity to what Christ has done, feel guilty, for that is true guilt. Feel guilty enough to abandon yourself to what Christ has already done for you!

READING 5 - CLEANSING THE HEART FROM AN EVIL CONSCIENCE

The Hebrew Christians added 1500 years of perfectly legal traditions to the blood of Christ. Notice what 10:26 says to them.

For if we go on sinning willfully after receiving the knowledge of the truth, there no longer remains a sacrifice for sins [because there is only one] *but a certain terrifying expectation of judgment and the fury of a fire which will consume the adversaries. -Hebrews 10:26*

This is the strongest language in the New Testament, but what is the sin to which this passage refers? In the context of this verse, if I sin continually and willfully by adding any of my good deeds or religious works to the work of Jesus Christ, even though I have become aware of how crucial and central Christ is, I get myself into trouble.

If I walked up to a man who had just given his son to die for me and I said, "You know that is a nice gesture you did for me - giving your son. I'm going to add my small change to it." What would the father of that son say? In rage and indignation he would say, "Forget your small change. I had one son. I have given him for you. If you add anything to him, all you can expect is my anger!"

That should scare you into joy. If God is so convinced that His Son satisfies Him, I better believe and be afraid to add anything to His satisfaction. When you get up in the morning don't say to yourself, "I will say I am accepted by God after I read my Bible, after I pray, etc." You should be able to say, "Since I am accepted before God the Father by the work of Jesus Christ, I can lay here forever. I can say nothing and do nothing and I'm still accepted. Because I am related to this crazy and wonderful God who doesn't keep any of the religious rules, I think I'll read His Bible because He's got to be a curious and interesting God. And, I'll tell others about Him, too. I'll say, "I met a strange God. He's not religious. He's not preoccupied with your church attendance. The issue is not whether you're homosexual. He only cares about what you do with His Son."

Do you see the power of that? Christ's work strips away all the Republican issues, all the Democratic issues, all the religious issues. What are you going to do with His Son? That's the only issue that matters. Notice how serious God is about this in verses 28-30.

> *Anyone who has set aside the law of Moses died without mercy on the testimony of two or three witnesses. How much greater punishment do you think you will deserve who has trampled underfoot the Son of God, and has regarded as unclean the blood of the covenant by which he was sanctified and has insult ed the Spirit of grace? For we know who has said, Vengeance is mine I will repay. And again, the Lord will judge His people. -Hebrews 10:28-30*

This may sound overly harsh, but if ever the evangelical church gets judged, it will be for having a cheap view of the blood of Jesus Christ.

Why should God be upset? Imagine the scene. Here is the blood of Jesus Christ in God's presence in heaven and I walk up to that blood with the goat's blood of my good works and I pour the goat's blood into the blood of Jesus Christ and then say, "At last my conscience is satisfied." If you were God the Father, what would you do? Would you sit there and say, "Oh that's all right. He's just my Son." If the Spirit of God told you that you had a Father and a Son taking care of your salvation, would you respond by saying, "No, all I have is guilt and I have to work harder"?

One of the greatest spiritual problems that exists among evangelical believers is a "Christ Plus" religion. Being deeply ingrained into our conscience, "Christ Plus" religion takes away the joy we should be feeling. "Christ Plus" religion is Christ plus my knowledge of the Bible, Christ plus my perfect marriage, Christ plus my perfect kids, Christ plus my daily Bible reading, Christ plus my witnessing, Christ plus no sexual sins, Christ plus voting Republican, Christ plus whatever.

When we allow the "Christ Plus" religion to overtake our belief system, all joy disappears. If we sincerely believe that Christianity is "Christ Plus" our works, our conscience will pain us whenever we don't do those things that we think we have to add to the work of Christ.

Because of the work of Christ, Christians should not live a performance based life. How we perform after we trust Christ adds nothing to God's acceptance of us. The truth is that Christ and Christ alone is our acceptance before God, and the second we allow that truth to flow deeply into our inner lives, we can experience the intense freedom and pleasure God intended for us.

How Do You Change An Evil Conscience?

It is very simple. I strongly recommend taking an imaginary walk inside your heart. Find that evil conscience, take the blood of Christ and throw it at the evil conscience. Say out loud, "Take that! Jesus' blood is the perfect sacrifice. I choose to trust in Him alone." Keep sprinkling Christ's blood upon the evil conscience until it shrinks the way the evil witch did in the Wizard of Oz. The writer to the Hebrew Christians uses the imagery of the priest cleansing himself as a means of communicating the truth that Christ has provided everything we need to come into the Father's presence. In the same way, we can picture the blood of Christ sprinkling our heart free from an evil conscience.

Three Challenges

Christians find themselves often facing three challenges: <u>first</u> is the challenge of confusing one's family of origin with God's new family and the Trinity; the <u>second</u> is the "Christ Plus" mentality, wherein we add our religious works to the death of Christ in order to feel emotionally accepted before God; and finally, the <u>third</u> challenge is to fully adopt our new identity in Christ. In this chapter, the challenge we faced is that of recognizing how great is the deliverance we have through Christ.

Christ is not a religious system; He is a Person. Christ is a person who will deliver us from our past, grant us peace in the present, and secure our future. Our danger is to minimize the immense significance of His death to God. We can do this by adding our religious works to the work of Christ. When this becomes a habit, our conscience can actually become convinced that this is desirable and normal. We must aggressively deal with that mistake and cleanse our hearts from an evil conscience. These works are worthwhile responses to what Christ has done for us, but they should not be added to what Christ has done for us. Christ and Christ alone must be allowed to save us.

We experience freedom and pleasure when we realize that Christ alone is our acceptance. Conversely, what emotions are prevalent in our lives when we operate off of a performance-based mentality?

SUMMARY OF CHAPTER 4

1. Christ is not a religious system; He is a person.

2. When we add our "religious works" on top of Christ's sacrificial death, it feeds an evil conscience.

3. Christ and Christ alone must be allowed to save us and cleanse the evil conscience.

How will you do the following this week?
1. Cleanse my heart from an evil conscience?

2. Rest in what Christ alone has done to make me acceptable to God?

Take a moment to pray and thank the Lord for what He has taught you this week.
Lord I am thankful for:

The Critical Message Of The Book Of Hebrews

How the Book of Hebrews is arranged gives us insight into how important it is to have a deep appreciation for what Christ's death means to God the Father. The Book of Hebrews shows a comparison between Old Testament religious realities and obligations as opposed to the greater obligation that we have to Christ. The way Hebrews is arranged shows Christ to be superior to seven different people and things from the Old Testament. The chart in the middle of this page shows in order from the greater to the lesser the importance of these seven. Note, the most important in this arrangement is the prophets (Hebrews, Chapter 1); the least in importance are the animals that were sacrificed (Hebrews, Chapters 9-10).

For fifteen hundred years prior to Christ, the Jews had been sacrificing animals as part of their religion. When numbers of Jews became Christians shortly after Christ's resurrection, they still continued on in a robotic like fashion offering animal sacrifices as they had been obligated to do in past religious observance. They had not worked out the reality that Christ was a complete end to these sacrifices. But, what was even more troubling was that those sacrifices were inferior to most other things in the Old Testament. Unconsciously, the Christian Jews were adding the least important things to Christ's death. The animal sacrifices that are the last in the list and of least importance were the things that the Jewish Christians were adding to the work of Christ. The point being that Christ's work is infinitely valuable to God the Father, so nothing need be added to it. To add anything to Christ's work is to imply that His death is not adequate. The following chart illustrates the above:

CHRIST IS SUPERIOR TO:

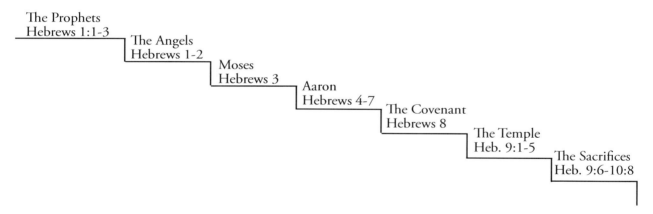

The spiritual and psychological problem was that the heart of the Jewish believers had been trained to add animal sacrifices to the blood of Christ, resulting in the conscience approving of these degrading additions to Christ's work (9:9,14; 10:2,22). That conscience has to be changed by faith by believing that Christ's blood is totally effective in making them right with God the Father. The purpose of the Book of Hebrews was to change the beliefs of these Jewish Christians so they would abandon the sacrificial system and solely cling to Christ's death.

How does this apply to us today? Once and only once, God the Father happily humiliated Jesus for the children's benefit. We must recognize that God angrily refuses to allow His children to humiliate Christ again by adding anything to Christ's work. This adding shows a lack of confidence in His Son's blood (10:30). He will tear away anything we add to Christ's blood (10:26-29). He rejects as malignantly evil any conscience that tries to improve on the blood of His Son (10:22). His most severe warnings and strongest child training (12:5-13; 10:26-39) will fall upon the Christians who devalue His Son's death. Grace is a free gift, but such grace was gained by the Son's suffering. We have no right to add anything to that suffering.

5 | ACCEPTANCE & THE HOLY SPIRIT

CHAPTER SUMMARY: Two payments have been made that should cause the believer to feel accepted. The Son was a payment for sin to the Father, and the Holy Spirit is a permanent down-payment to us signifying God's intention to finish our salvation. The Holy Spirit also has a primary ministry of reminding us that God is our Heavenly Dad. This Father wants us to have a mature and affectionate relationship with Him.

READING 1
THE HOLY SPIRIT AS A DOWN-PAYMENT

The goal of discipleship is to learn and emotionally integrate God's acceptance of us, and then to cultivate a normal response of gratitude. The first five chapters of this workbook are an attempt to show the means by which the Trinity has chosen to win our confidence. The means of building confidence are found in the New Testament as the processes of rooting, grounding, and building up.

The first chapter of this workbook illustrated the two different families into which the human race is divided: the family of Adam and the family of God. The second chapter dealt with acceptance and worth. As we step through the door of Christianity, we need to have a very clear picture of what we are worth to God. At the strategic moment, in the face of our weakness, our ungodliness, our hate of Him, our continual sinning, in the face of our deeply flawed character and regardless of what we would become, God gave His Son for us. Through this public demonstration on the cross, the question of our worth is settled. Secondly, we must realize that we are involved in a love that would never allow us to dwell in shame. If He loved us this much while we were awash in the gutter, how much more does He love us now that we've trusted in Him? When we were in the gutter, He loved us enough to publicly display on the cross the dimensions of His love for us. If salvation is not based on us, but based on Him as the cross has demonstrated, it leaves us free to be loved. **We are worth a Son to God, regardless of what we will become.** That was the thrust of the second chapter.

Becoming What God Intended

Chapters three, four, and five deal with how the Trinity wants us to be people of confidence and assurance. The last chapter dealt with God the Son and our acceptance. We saw that He is our great high priest, and His blood cleanses us from a maliciously evil conscience. Such a wretched conscience tries to convince us to add our religious works to the work of Christ to feel approved and accepted by God. We'll be looking at acceptance and God the Holy Spirit.

Acceptance & The Holy Spirit

God knows that we are fearful, suspicious people. We are far more fearful than we ever would want to admit. We are far more suspicious than we will ever really acknowledge. Knowing our frame, God has been absolutely extravagant in the demonstration of His love for us. First of all, He gave a Son publicly on the cross on our behalf. Secondly, Ephesians 1:13 and 14 state that a third member of the Trinity is involved in God's demonstration of His love for us. This is true of believers, and it is not true of non-Christians. Verse 13 says:

> *In whom also you yourselves having previously heard the word of the truth, the good news of your deliverance, in whom also having believed, you were sealed with the Holy Spirit of the promise* (referring to the promise of the Gospel of John 14:16-17 where Jesus said He would send another comforter) *who is an 'arrabon' of our inheritance unto a full deliverance as a permanent possession unto the praise of His glory.*

The Word *Arrabon*

If we went to Greece today and met an engaged lady and asked to see her *arrabon*, she would put out her hand with an engagement ring on it. In modern Greek that is what the word means. A hundred years ago, if a woman received an engagement ring, it meant the fellow promised he would follow through on that marriage. If he did not, the lady kept the ring. The piece of jewelry was a down payment reflecting his intentions. If the woman was attractive and calculating, she could make a necklace out of the rings of the victims she ensnared. The rule was, the lady kept the ring. *Arrabon* is a word derived from ancient Greek. In ancient Greece, an *arrabon* had to do with property. An *arrabon* was a non-returnable down payment on a piece of property that was going to be completely purchased later. A contract was made, and because it involved property, the purchaser gave a non-returnable down payment called an *arrabon*. The buyer gave it to the owner of the property. If the buyer did not follow through with the full purchase price, the owner kept the *arrabon*.

Think this through: the third member of the Trinity is our *arrabon*. There is no reason in the world for God to give us the third person of the Trinity as a down payment. He knows that He's going to follow through, but the question is: do we really believe that He will follow through on His intentions? We are often suspicious and fearful. God, the Trinity, contains three members: one is a Father, one is a Son, and the other is the Holy Spirit. God the Trinity gave one of its members on the cross to pay for our wrongdoing. God the Trinity gave the third member of the Trinity, God the Holy Spirit, as a down payment to us. In a real sense, two members of the Trinity are involved in our assurance. The giving of the third member of the Trinity is as significant as the gift of the second member of the Trinity.

The torment of the second member of the Trinity lasted hours. As for the third member of the Trinity, His torment may last our lifetime. He is in us, listening to us, spending time with us. When we sin, His pain or grief exists because He dwells in us. Being mindful of this, the letter to the Ephesians says not to pain or grieve the Holy Spirit of God in whom we are sealed until the day of redemption (Ephesians 4:30).

That third member of the Trinity is given to us because God wants us to know that He will follow through with His intentions. Why is He doing this? Because He's going to forget? Because He's dishonest? Because He has to force Himself into a comer? None of those reasons. He publicly displayed His Son on the cross so that we would know what we are worth to Him. He has personally placed the Holy Spirit in our lives so that we would have confidence that He will follow through. Theoretically if He doesn't follow through, we keep the third member of the Trinity. Theoretically if we went to Hell, He would be there with us. I don't know what we would do with Him in Hell, but He is our *arrabon*.

> "The torment of the second member of the Trinity lasted hours. As for the third member of the Trinity, His torment may last our lifetime."

Have you ever had someone promise you something and fail to follow through? A broken engagement? A business deal with a friend? A promised vacation with a loved one? How did you feel at the time and what effect did it have on your relationship with that person?

What are some reasons that we might need the Holy Spirit as a down payment in order to build our confidence in God?

How did you respond when you read Ephesians 1:13-14, that says God has given you the person of the Holy Spirit as an irrevocable down payment guaranteeing you are His child for all eternity?

- ☐ Skeptical
- ☐ Thankful
- ☐ Blown away
- ☐ Indifferent
- ☐ Overwhelmed with gratitude

READING 2 - THE HOLY SPIRIT AS A SEAL

Two-thirds of the Trinity has been given to win our assurance. God has not given money for us. God has not given things for us. He has given two persons for us. One cannot give more than oneself. God has given His Son as the once-and for-all sacrifice. He has given His Spirit as the once-and-for-all down payment. Something else is said in Ephesians 1:13:

In whom also you yourselves, having believed the word of the truth, the good news of our deliverance, in whom also having believed, you were sealed.

In the Roman world, a seal did two things. It declared ownership and it declared the owner's intention to protect his property and to go after the person who attempted to break the seal. The Romans shipped grain from Egypt by sea to Italy in order to keep themselves alive. They had given up farming, and now they relied on the Egyptian breadbasket to keep them going. When the Egyptians shipped the millions of bushels to Italy, the grain was put into burlap bags, which were then sealed with a dried clay seal. The Roman seal said two things: this belongs to Rome and Rome will protect it. If pirates stole it, the Roman fleet found them and destroyed them. They protected it. Paul used the symbol of the seal the same way. God is not going to break the seal because the Holy Spirit is His *arrabon*. If anyone else attempts to break the seal, the presence of the Spirit of God proclaims two things: this person is owned by God, and this person will be protected by God. The Holy Spirit is the *arrabon*. After we believed, we were sealed by the Holy Spirit of the promise, who is an *arrabon*, a non-redeemable down payment of our inheritance.

Notice the term inheritance. Inheritance is the completion of everything we're supposed to receive. God gives us the Holy Spirit as proof that we're going to receive everything He intends. He has promised: heaven, glorification, ruling, rewards, the New Jerusalem, the presence of Jesus Christ throughout eternity, joys forever more at His right hand, the position of exalted sonship above angels, and the recognition of our authority throughout the universe because we've been joined to Christ. All of those things are our inheritance. The proof of that future inheritance is the person of the Spirit of God. God has given two-thirds of the Trinity to us. To win our allegiance One person was given on the cross, the other is the person of the Spirit of God. Then after doing that, in effect He says, "Make sense out of it, make sense of how important you are. Make sense of how loved you are. Look at those gifts and think it through, because this is God who is giving these gifts." The cross defines our worth. The person of the Spirit of God defines our security. Two-thirds of the Trinity has been given to win our allegiance.

Another way of looking at this is in the book of Hebrews. Go to Hebrews 6:16 for a human principle:

For, as an illustration, men swear by someone greater, and every oath for them is an end for legal confirmation.

That is a long way of saying, ". . . among men an oath certifies legal confirmation." Among twentieth century people, an oath simply means we have just begun to lie. In the ancient world, an oath said more. Verse 16 says that among men, an oath confirms matters. Verse 17 says something about God:

By which God, being abundantly determined to display to the heirs of the promise, the unchangeableness of His determination, gave as a mediatorial reality, an oath.

In the Sermon on the Mount, Jesus Christ said not to swear or take an oath. In the book of James it says, not to swear. In the book of Hebrews, however, God takes an oath. Why? Well first of all, God is not bound by His own rules, He is bound by His own character. Just because He gives a rule, that does not mean He cannot break it. If a larger reason exists for Him to break it, He will break it.

Christian theology always recognized that God works according to a hierarchy and people are more important than rules. So God established a rule: Don't swear. But He says, "People are more important than that rule, so I'm going to give an oath." Notice the oath He gave in Hebrews 6:18-20.

... in order that through two unchangeable things, by which it is impossible for God to lie, we might have powerful encouragement. Those having fled to take strong hold of the hope set before us which we have as an anchor of the soul of our emotional life, secure and legally confirmed, and entering unto the midst of the veil. Where one, Jesus, having gone before on the behalf of us, has become according to the order of Melchizedek a high priest unto the ages. -Hebrews 6:18-20

What is this saying? God wants us to be confident people. The Greek word for powerful encouragement is *kratatos*. It is the strongest adjective in Greek for powerful. God, wanting us to be people of courage, swore an oath, so that we would have two unchangeable things to encourage us: His oath and His character.

Why does He go through all of this trouble? Because you and I are far more fearful than we'll ever admit. We're like little kids out in the dark next to a graveyard, and we're desperately afraid of admitting how much fear we have. God the Father has come to us and said, "I know you are afraid." Before we even start, before we even enter the door of this thing called Christianity, He displayed His Son openly on a cross for us, at our worst moment, so we would know what we are worth to Him. Secondly, He gave the Spirit of God to us after we trusted in the gospel so that we can have strong assurance that He won't betray us. God wants us to have powerful encouragement, so He, who says "don't swear an oath", swears an oath to us, because we're more important to Him than His rules. We are far more important to God than His rules, because we are persons. A person is infinitely worth more than rules. There is nothing wrong with rules, but persons are infinitely more valuable than rules because persons are made in the image of God; rules are just approximations of behavior.

Have you ever had someone in authority bend the rules for your benefit? How did you feel about that?

One Sabbath, Jesus was going through the grain fields, and as his disciples walked along, they began to pick some heads of grain The Pharisees said to him, "Look, why are they doing what is unlawful on the Sabbath?" He answered, "Have you never read what David did when he and his companions were hungry and in need? In the days of Abiathar the high priest, he entered the house of God and ate the consecrated bread, which is lawful only for priests to eat. And he also gave some to his companions. Then he said to them, "The Sabbath was made for man, not man for the Sabbath. So the Son of Man is Lord even of the Sabbath."
-Mark 2:23-28

From Mark 2:23-28, how did Jesus bend the rules for His disciples? How do you think they felt about it?

Looking at this again, the Holy Spirit is God's down payment to us. The Holy Spirit is a seal. A seal does two things: it shows ownership and it gives protection. This protection is alluded to in 1 John 4:4:

Greater is He that is in you than he that is in the world.

This shows we have unlimited protection from Satan. Secondly, this seal, who is a person, is an ***arrabon***, a non-redeemable down payment guaranteeing we will get our full inheritance. Two persons are involved in our redemption, the Son on the cross and the Spirit of God who is given for us.

Two-thirds of the Trinity has been given for us. What more can God give?
God gives Himself as a Father; His Son gave Himself as a sacrifice;
the Spirit gave Himself as a down payment to us.

What's left for us to give? We cannot give our character or our good works; the only thing we can give is our trust. He doesn't ask for our character. He doesn't ask for our good works. He asks for the only thing that we can sovereignly give, our trust. Christianity is absolutely brilliant because it focuses on the one thing that can radically change people: trust.

Have you ever committed to a long-term relationship with someone you did not trust? Chances are you have not. What have you seen in this section that would encourage you to put your complete trust in God?

How does it make you feel to know that you have unlimited protection from Satan?

READING 3 - THE FATHERHOOD OF GOD

The Spirit's Message About the Fatherhood of God

The Holy Spirit has another important ministry. The Holy Spirit wants to impress upon us that we have a Father in heaven. The Father issue is extremely important. The Spirit of God has come into our lives, shouting that we have a Dad in Heaven. Looking at Romans 8:12-16, this message is developed in the passage:

Therefore then, brethren, we are debtors, not to the flesh, according to the flesh to live, for if according to the flesh you are living, you are about to die.

This is a really interesting Greek phrase, ". . .you're about to die." If we live according to the moods of the flesh*, such as animosity, hatred, envy, pain, or callousness, we're about to die. Romans 8:13 continues:

> ***Theological Jargon Box**
> <u>The Flesh:</u> God intended that our imagination, relationships, and perspectives should control our emotions, moods, and appetites. Because of sin, the order is now reversed. The human body is often now controlled by appetites, negative moods, and uncontrolled emotions. When we are driven by these things, the scripture calls that "the flesh."

For if according to the flesh you are living, you are about to die; but if the practices of the body you are continually putting to death, you shall live. For whosoever, by the Spirit of God, is being drawn along (translated "led," but it has the idea of being drawn along), *these are the mature sons of God.*

Notice the phrase, "mature sons of God." It is important to pick up on this phrase. The mature daughter or son of God is simply the person who is drawn along, or led by the Spirit of God. The picture we should have in our mind is that of the Spirit of God walking up and lightly touching the hand of the mature child of God and leading her or him. Each is drawn along, not dragged along. The mature daughter or son is not lectured along, but is drawn along by the fruit of the Spirit. A delightful verse in Psalm 32:8 illustrates this:

"I will guide you by my eye."

When my children were younger, and in a stranger's home, they were led by glances from my eyes. When my wife and I are out visiting, with a glance from her eyes I learn everything I need to know. She doesn't have to say a word. In just the same way, when communicating to her, I don't need to say a word. We can glance at each other, and all we need to know to make a decision, we know. A mature relationship between two people who know each other very well can be an eyeball relationship, "I'll lead you by my eye." A glance will tell everything needed to be known because of the close harmony.

A mature son of God is simply a believer who is drawn along, pulled along by the Spirit of God. The Spirit of God prompts him or her to be generous, and the person says within, "I think I'm going to be generous, I feel like I'm going to be generous." The Spirit of God prompts sorrow, and one sorrows. The person does it naturally. As the Spirit of God places the fruit of the Spirit in the life, the person is just led along. Not pulled like a goat or a donkey or a horse, but the person is softly prompted. Psalm 32:8b, 9a reads:

"I will counsel you with My eye upon you. Do not be as the horse or as the mule which have no understanding."

This is a definition of Christian maturity. The person who is responsive to the emotionally rich prompting and insights from the Spirit of God is the mature Christian. Another factor is added to the definition of maturity in Romans 8:15. Not only is the mature Christian led; the mature Christian has a rising swell of joy pouring from the heart. We have received the Spirit of adult son placement, and because we have received that Spirit, we are continually shouting, "Daddy-Father." <u>***Abba***</u> is Aramaic, not Jewish. Aramaic is a sister language to Hebrew. <u>***Ab***</u> means Father, <u>***Abba***</u> means "the Dad." It's an affectionate term for Daddy. Father is Father, and in combination with <u>***Abba***</u>, the meaning of the phrase is Daddy-Father. The mature believer is being influenced along by the fruit of the Spirit, and responds to the Spirit of adult son placement by continually shouting, "Daddy Father." The Greek text implies this is something one does continually throughout the day. The maturity of a believer is measured by how well he knows the heavenly Dad, and frankly, how well he has recognized the difference between his family of origin and his new Father. Among the Rabbis it was agreed that the term "daddy" should not be used of God. They felt the term was too familiar and not reverent enough. Two rabbis, Jesus and Paul, were the great exceptions to that rule.

Recognizing the difference between the family of God and one's family of origin has profound implications not only for the spiritual life, but also for Christian psychology. One of the problems with psychological counselors, to put it jokingly, is that they often stir the pot and then they let the beans burn. They stir the pot and they never make a meal. It takes no genius to tell a client that the family of origin had significant problems. The real challenge is learning how to rise above such a family and pursue health.

The Bible's genius is to say in a sense, "Put 30 percent of your effort into sorting out issues from your family of origin, but spend 70 percent of your effort in getting to know this new Father and family." The negative experience has to be pushed aside by a positive passion. That positive passion is getting to know God the Father, who has a love for us that will never shame us, because it's not based on what we do or what we will become. It is based on who we are to Him.

Galatians Chapter Four

In Romans eight, we're shouting, "Daddy-Father." In Galatians four, Paul tells us that the Spirit of God is shouting at us. *Kradzone*, the Greek word for shouting is the strongest Greek verb for raising your voice. *Kradzone* means to shout, to herald, to proclaim. It could be translated any of those ways. In Galatians four, Paul describes to the Galatians a unique ministry of the Spirit of God. The ministry is stated in Galatians 4:6:

> *And because you are mature sons, God has sent out the Spirit of His Son into our hearts continually shouting, "Abba, Father."*

The one message the Spirit of God has for every Christian is this: you have a Daddy-Father. You have a Daddy-Father that will fulfill every daydream you've ever had for a healthy and happy family. You have a Daddy-Father who, with great joy, anticipates meeting you in person in heaven. You have a Daddy-Father who enjoys your company, who knows you better than you know yourself, and He finds great beauty and delight in who you are. He knows you, He knows your frame, He remembers that you are but dust, and as a father has pity on his children, so God has pity on us (Psalm 103:13). He is emotionally involved in who we are. God in heaven is our Father, the ultimate and intended father for all of us. Galatians 4:7 continues this idea:

> *So that no longer you are a slave, but a mature son;* [it's important in Greek to pick up that he's talking about a mature son] *and if a son, also an heir through God.*

Let me describe the best illustration I know concerning what the New Testament is getting at. I attended a wedding several years ago that left an indelible impression on me. A fine Christian man was getting remarried. He had adult sons and daughters. One son looked like a truck driver: strong, powerful, tall; the other son looked like a tenor, thin and slight. At the wedding reception for their father, the two sons sang a gospel song to the dad and his new wife. A parable of Christianity occurred, for as the two sons sang, they looked at their father full in the face. They lovingly sang a song about God to their dad. Tears started running down my face. Tears started running down the face of everybody at that reception, for we recognized we were watching something very unusual, an Abba-Father relationship pictured on the human level. These mature sons, affectionate, powerful, gifted, musical, and strong, were looking at their dad in love. The height of sonship from a Biblical perspective is to be richly affectionate towards God and strong in one's character and faith, a mature son. One cannot be mature without affection. Maturity without affection is simply crass intellectualism with a thin veneer of sophistication. True maturity is when boundless affection bubbles up within a mature heart in a deep relationship. God the Father has sent the Spirit of God into our lives with a message. He is shouting at us, "You have a Father, Abba Father." He wants you to respond as a mature daughter or son.

> "One cannot be mature without affection. Maturity without affection is simply crass intellectualism with a thin veneer of sophistication. True maturity is when boundless affection bubbles up."

Becoming What God Intended

How does God "guide you by the eye" as Psalm 32:8 says?

Have you ever called God "Daddy-Father"? At first glance it sounds almost irreverent, but this is what Romans 8 and Galatians 4 are telling us. Take a moment now to write out a prayer to God, referring to Him as "Daddy Father," thanking Him for all He has done for you.

The Bible & Psychology

About thirty years ago, Vernon Grounds, a teacher and former President of Denver Seminary, wrote a series of essays on psychology and the Bible. He started out his series of essays by saying, albeit incorrectly, the Bible is not a psychology book, but the Bible contains psychology. After spending the last 25 years grappling with who I am, what the Bible has to say, and what the Bible communicates, I've concluded that the Bible is chiefly a book of psychology; but it presents a psychology of human nature in many different forms of literature so that it is veiled to the unimaginative mind. Because it does not say "Introduction to Psychology" on the cover, one presupposes that it's not a book of psychology. The Bible, on almost every page, is greatly involved with psychology. But the challenge is one of transference - transferring insights from one culture and its literary style over to our own culture. For example, in the Old Testament and in the New Testament, statements like this exist: God will judge your heart and your kidneys. Jesus actually said in the book of Revelation, "I am He who searches the heart and the kidneys (Rev. 2:23)." That's what He said in Greek. When it's translated into English, it appears as "... your heart and your motives," because the translators realized that in our culture, it sounds funny to give a kidney test, except in a medical context. But to the ancient Hebrew, the heart represented conscious awareness; the kidneys represented deep, subconscious motivation. God claimed lordship over the inner life by the use of that imagery. In affect, He said, "I will judge what you consciously determine and what you subconsciously presuppose, for you are responsible for both."

Once we understand the nature of the language that Scripture uses, it is relatively easy to transfer it over to modern psychological jargon. The only problem is knowing how to spot the bridges between Scripture and psychology. One of the very sad things is that Christians are absolutely preoccupied with reading a lot of psychology books (and I also read a lot of them), but they are not preoccupied with spotting the bridges, and recognizing the literary form into which truth was poured it he New Testament or Old Testament, and recognizing how it can be applied across to our culture. Now we'll be looking at an extended illustration of how to do just that.

READING 4 - THE PSYCHOLOGY OF PAUL

Paul took three aspects of ancient culture and presented a psychology of the Christian life. If we walked up to Paul and said, "Paul, I'm really grateful that you wrote Galatians 4:1-11 as a psychology of the Spiritual life," he would look at you and say, "What?!" He never heard of the word psychology; he just thoroughly understood it. He understood the nature of the subconscious; he understood the nature of the conscience. He understood the nature of subconscious determinations. He understood all of that, but when he communicated, he used what the people were familiar with to draw them over to the unfamiliar. He went from the familiar to the very unfamiliar and he did it brilliantly.

Galatians 4 contains Paul's psychology of the Christian life. One will never find that on a heading in any study Bible anywhere, but it is in Galatians 4. He used as example three things with which the ancient world was very familiar: childhood, adult son placement (poorly translated as adoption), and slavery. He used those three things to create a description of what the inner life of the Christian should be like. Taking terminology with which they were familiar, he used it to draw their understanding into new and strange territory. Paul took the nature of childhood, a social institution; he took adult-son placement, a social institution; and he took slavery, a social institution. With these examples, he illustrated a psychology of the Christian life, but he never used the term "psychology." He did exactly the same thing effective communicators in psychology do today. They use illustrations to communicate their lessons. Paul did that in Galatians chapter four.

In Galatians chapter 4, he described what is psychologically unhealthy for the believer. He started out by describing what is wrong in the human family so that it's not replicated in this new family into which we are placed. His entire work presupposed two families that are diametrically opposed to each other. Over and over again, the key to understanding the Spiritual life is to understand how an unhealthy family differs from God's new family, having God as the ultimate and intended Father. In Galatians 4:1, Paul further defines this principle:

And I am continually saying, as long as the heir is a toddler, he differs nothing from a slave even though he is the owner of all.

In his culture, a toddler in the home was treated exactly as a slave even though he was going to grow up and become the heir of everything. In the Greek culture, in the Roman culture, and in the Jewish culture, the toddler was controlled. What is that emphasizing? That the human family is often enslaving. We will soon see that Paul talked about family of origin issues and the new family. Let's continue reading:

But, in contradiction to him being lord of all, he was under guardians and dispensers, or managers, until the set time by the father.

In a wealthy family, the father of the home would say that the son was able to participate in the inheritance and in the family business at the age of twenty (or whatever age he picked). Then the son was recognized as an adult and he was able to buy and sell family property. He was treated as mature. Until that time, he was treated like a slave. Since he was a child, he was not trusted. Why is a person under a guardianship? Because he is not competent. Suspicion is another symptom of the unhealthy family. The two elements present in an unhealthy family are control and suspicion. Now, verse three:

Thus also we ourselves, when we were toddlers,...

This shows that Paul was speaking of spiritual things, and this was something that Paul said continually. Paul used this illustration continually because he wanted to emphasize a point:

Thus also we, when we were toddlers, we were under the rudimentary principles, the basic principles of this world, [for] *we were being enslaved under the basic principles of this world. -Galatians 4:3*

The Greek word for rudimentary principles is ***stoikia***; have you ever heard of Stoikiometry? It's the study of basic elements. ***Stoikae*** are the basic building blocks of life in Greek philosophy. Paul said that when we were toddlers in the spiritual sense, we were kept under very basic elements. What are these basic elements? According to Colossians, the three basic elements of the world are: you earn what you deserve, obtain God's pity by putting yourself in pain, and don't touch, it might be dangerous. All of these are from the latter part of Colossians chapter two.

Three basic statements reveal how the world believes religion works. First, you earn what you deserve. That's absolutely contrary to Christianity. If you want to earn what you deserve, you'll go to Hell and you'll miss the best part of life, which is free: God. Biblical reality is that we are given freely what we have never deserved.

Second, if you put yourself in pain, God might feel sorry for you. That is very wrong. If you are in pain, God feels sorry for you already. If you're sorrowing, God sorrows with you. He is a treasury of compassion. We do not have to talk Him into pity. He pities the poor and needy. The superstitious person says, "If I inflict pain on myself, maybe God will pay attention to me." The biblical person already knows God is paying attention to him or her.

Becoming What God Intended

The third statement is: don't touch, it might hurt. The thought is that if we stay away from the good things of life, avoid sexuality, avoid certain foods, avoid doing things on certain days, and then maybe we can control God's blessing. Paul equated these rules with slavery. Notice how this is put in Galatians 4:3:

Thus also we ourselves when we were toddlers, we were enslaved under the rudimentary principles of the world.

Do you notice that word enslaved? We were dependent. We were dependent upon somebody else to tell us what to feel, to think, and to do. We were slaves. In the Old Testament and in Greek literature, a slave was a tool. The Old Testament said if you want a man to be a slave, you beat him. If you want him to be a son, love him (Proverbs 29:19-21). God has decided that He wants sons, so He loves us into submission. If you want a slave, you beat him into submission. After you beat him, you tell him, "Don't think, don't be mature, just do what I say." That's the Old Testament definition of a slave. The master made sure that he kept him at an emotional distance. The orders were kept simple, and if the slave didn't obey, he was beaten. What Proverbs describes is how the culture of slavery worked. It doesn't recommend it; it simply describes its existence. Paul is saying that when we were toddlers in Spiritual things, we were left with an inflexible family atmosphere, a controlling family atmosphere, and a suspicious, untrusting family atmosphere. That is slavery.

All of these things can be translated into psychological categories, particularly in family therapy. Dependent slavery is unhealthy. The person is a mindless drone to somebody else's authority.

The Holy Spirit defines our psychological relationship to God (Galatians 4:1-11), and these social categories are used to define psychological categories. What are the social categories? Our relationship to God is not supposed to be child-like, leaving us controlled, untrusted, and dependent.

Were fear and suspicion elements that were present in your family of origin? If so, how have they affected your relationships in the present?

Have you ever felt like you were being treated like a child, though you were an adult? How would you describe the difference in attitude between one who is treated like a child and one treated like an adult?

READING 5 - ADULT SON & DAUGHTER PLACEMENT

Now let's step over to a mature relationship. Look at Galatians 4:4:

.. and when the fullness of chronological time came, God sent out His mature son.

In this translation, the adjective "mature" was placed before "son," hence a mature son, because *huios*, the Greek word, is in contrast to *napeoi*, toddlers. One rule of linguistics is that terms become more specific and concrete when they are set in contrast. Paul is contrasting the mature son with the toddlers:

"Maturity is a deeply emotional relationship with God the Father filled with character."

God sent forth His mature son, having come out of a woman, having come under the law, in order that the ones under the law should be bought out, in order that we should receive adoption or placement as adult sons and daughters. -Galatians 4:4-5

What's an adult son placement? Eliminate everything you know about modern day adoption. My wife and I have two wonderful adopted children. We took both of them home when they were two days old. However, this modern type of adoption has nothing to do with that of the ancient world. In the ancient world, usually they did not adopt babies. If the ancients wanted a baby, they just went out to the hillside and picked up one of the abandoned babies left to either starve or be eaten by the wild dogs. A large surplus of babies existed in the ancient world. The people of Paul's time rarely legally adopted babies. Instead, they adopted adults, and it was called *huiosthesia*, the placement of a mature son - adult son placement. In adult son placement a childless couple entering into their old age solved a problem. Rome did not have social security. They needed somebody to take care of them.

They found a fine young man and they placed him as their son with the family name and authority over the family property to participate fully in the family business. Such was adult son placement. Great trust was demanded, because the older couple was putting their future in that son's hands. That son would determine their destiny. That son would determine what would happen to the family business, and that son was given a mature responsibility and a mature relationship of trust.

Adoption in the modern sense did not happen; this is a mistranslation and a misunderstanding. A public rite was connected to this custom. The couple found the mature man and then took him out into the public square. They put a robe on him and said, "This is my *huios*, a mature son."

> "God trusts you more than you trust yourself. God has far more confidence in you than you'll ever have in yourself."

Sometimes a Caesar, an emperor of Rome, did not have a trustworthy natural son. The senate of Rome would say to him, "You must have a *huiosthesia*, you need to place a mature son who's not of your lineage, but who you can trust as your heir, because your natural sons are weaklings and immoral." *Huiosthesia* was a well-known technical term during that time period.

Notice what Paul says here about us, in Galatians 4:5:

> *... in order that the ones under the law should be purchased out, that we should receive adult son placement, and because you are mature sons, God is not viewing you as toddlers or slaves, God sent forth the Spirit of His mature Son into your hearts shouting, "Daddy-Father."*

What's the epitome of maturity? Maturity is a deeply emotional relationship with God the Father filled with character. Maturity is a relationship with Abba-Father where the son or the daughter of God feels warmly about God and is a person of integrity entrusted with the family business.

God trusts you more than you trust yourself. God has far more confidence in you than you'll ever have in yourself. God knows you have a gift. God knows you have ability. God knows you can have character through the fruit of the Spirit.

What's the difference between a mature son and a child? A child says, "Don't give me any responsibility; I can't do anything." A mature son says, "Trust me. I have confidence and I'll handle it." The child says, "I don't understand anything; I'm unsophisticated." The mature son says, "I understand and I'll do what's right." The slave says, "Beat me and I'll move." The mature son says, "I'll trust and I'll do." The mature son says, "I am delighted with this Abba-Father." The slave says, "I am cringing with fear and I'll move when he hits me."

Paul contrasted the mature son versus the protected child and the slave so that we might understand the psychology of the spiritual life and the psychology of the mature life. God has not called us to be beaten like slaves. Unfortunately, what do we do sometimes? We turn to God and we say to God, "Make me feel and do!" God turns to us and He says, "Trust Me. Trust Me today, trust Me tomorrow, trust Me the next day. Trust Me the day after that. Trust Me in the dark. Trust Me over how much you are worth to Me. Trust Me for many days and you will feel like you have never felt before. I'm not going to inject you with emotions nor am I going to turn you into a robot. I don't beat slaves and I don't inject mood-altering chemicals into My children. I will have a mature relationship with you."

> "He speaks to us as to a mature adult, "Based on the evidence of the cross, and the Spirit of God as my down payment, trust Me- but it's up to you to trust."

We trust and the Spirit of God gives the fruit of the Spirit, but it's not a mood altering drug. We are placed in a mature father/adult-son relationship. Slavery beats people into activity. Parents manipulate children into doing right. What do we do with a child when we want to train him? The child is walking towards the stove and we tell the child, "Look over there." As he looks away the child is manipulated. What did the ancient world do with the slave? They abused him. What do we do with the person we really respect? We reason with them and we give arguments. God has given His arguments and then He speaks to us as to a mature adult, "Based on the evidence of the cross, and the Spirit of God as my down payment, trust Me - but it's up to you to trust." He does not manipulate us because the heart of childishness is manipulation. The heart of slavery is cringing fear. The heart of adult-daughter and adult-son placement is where God says, "I respect you too much either to manipulate you or to beat you. Let's have a relationship of trust."

Spiritually and psychologically the difference is critical - it's the difference between co-dependency and maturity. Co-dependents manipulate each other. Dependent slaves hurt each other; they are victims and victimizers. Mature sons relate out of a heart of loving trust.

The Spirit of God wants us to respond as mature sons; since we're worthwhile, we're treated responsibly, we are given true freedom, we're treated gently, and we're trusted. Thirdly, we are affectionately regarded. Why? Galatians 4:6 says:

> *. . . and because you are sons, God has sent out the Spirit of His Son into our hearts shouting 'Abba-Father.'*

In Galatians 4, the Spirit came in shouting, "Daddy-Father." In this text, He's not shouting to God the Father, "Daddy-Father." He's shouting to you, "You've got a dad in heaven, you've got a father in heaven!" He is shouting, continually shouting. Coming into our hearts, the Spirit is shouting, "Daddy-Father, Daddy Father, Daddy-Father."

Is There A Lady In The Trinity?

A question is often asked, "Where is mom in all of this?" A correct understanding of Genesis 1 shows that God has masculine attributes and feminine attributes that are poured into the male and the female. The female is a feminine reflection of who God is, and the male is a masculine reflection of who God is. Male and female are needed to accurately reflect God as a Father. You need both. Both male and female are made in the image of God. The woman reflects the feminine attributes of God. Interestingly, in the book of Isaiah, God says He is like a nursing mother (Isaiah 49:14-16). He doesn't even hesitate to say,"I'm a nursing mother." He also says, "I'm like a mighty warrior looking for a fight." Now that is a pretty bold image. That's an interesting dynamic. That dynamic is present since God actually has feminine and masculine characteristics.

Also the presence of a Father, a Son and the Holy Spirit immediately communicated a message to the ancient polytheistic world, a world of many gods and goddesses. The Christian Trinity will not enlarge itself the way the gods of the Greeks, Romans, and other ancient religions did where the gods practiced incest or rape. The Trinity will stay eternally the same and lovingly stable. Yet the Trinity certainly does have feminine characteristics as well as masculine.

Saying this another way may bring more clarity: <u>God is more nurturing and relational than the most relational and nurturing of women, and God is more purposive and courageous than the most courageous and purposive of men.</u>

So, we are given worth, we are treated responsibly, we are affectionately regarded. With Galatians 4:8, the contrast is not to be slave-like. Unfortunately, the Galatians have regressed to a sub-Christian state. Those who are free have allowed themselves to be enslaved. A slave is always under compulsion. A slave has weak and beggarly resources and a slave runs by simple rules, "Do that or I'll hit you!"

> *But then, on the one hand not knowing God, you were enslaved to the things by nature which were not gods; but now having known God, but rather having become known by God, how could you turn again unto the weak and beggarly elements.* [Those basic principles: How could you turn to earning what you deserved, to throwing yourself into pain to get God's pity and to obeying the touch-not, taste-not, handle-not mentality? How can you do it?] *Which things again from the beginning you desire to be enslaved? Days you are keeping, and months, and seasons, and years. I fear lest somehow I have labored to exhaustion emptily among you.* -Galatians 4:8

This passage fits beautifully into a description of family therapy, as it's called in the United States. It says that manipulative relationships, such as children are involved in, have to be rejected. Dependent relationships that are slave-like, and those in which people are victims, have to be rejected. God wants us to be involved in mature relationships where He first trusts and loves us and puts the destiny of His program in our hands. We have to choose to trust and love Him as a response. He adopts us as mature daughters and sons. We must choose to participate in the joy of his affection, and in the character that He believes we can produce. What is in Galatians 4:1-9 is what the Spirit of God is trying to drive home. God is never going to manipulate any one of us into happiness. Happiness is a derivative of trust. Joy is not an injectable fluid. God will never manipulate us into joy, into a deep emotional response, nor will He beat us into it.

There are neither slaves in heaven, nor are there manipulated kids in heaven. Only those who have been placed in an adult-son and adult-daughter relationship are in heaven. Because that is so, we have a part, and our part begins with a trusting response to His love.

How do you demonstrate to someone that you trust them?

How can we respond to God as a mature son or daughter?

SUMMARY OF THE CHAPTER 5

What are the three take home lessons?

1. You have a heavenly dad. You have a heavenly Father.

2. God the Holy Spirit is a down payment to us.

3. God the Holy Spirit not only wants to impress on us that we have a Father in heaven, but that this Father has sent the Holy Spirit to define our psychological relationship to God as an adult-son and adult-daughter placement.

This is neither child-like nor slave-like. Instead, God has given us a principled relationship with Him based upon a bond of deep affection and ever-growing character on our part.

TO REVIEW:

What are one or two key insights you've been challenged with this week?

Take a moment to pray and thank the Lord for what He has taught you this week.
Lord, I am thankful for:

6 | ACCEPTANCE & TRUST

CHAPTER SUMMARY: We will explore how trust plays a central role in the spiritual life. The Trinity functions by trust, and trust brings us into that circle of love. Trust or faith has three false forms and one true form. We must know how they differ.

READING 1
TRUST IS IMPORTANT IN GOD'S FAMILY

Trust is Important in God's Family

After I became a Christian, the concepts of trust and justification by faith* didn't make much sense to me. Throughout high school and college, and even after I entered the pastorate, I wondered and struggled over those concepts. I believed in them blindly because that was what the Bible said - trust was central to Christianity, and faith was what made us right with God. Those were the marching orders, that's what the Boss said, so that's what had to be.

For years I struggled, and then the reason I couldn't grasp the full meaning of trust and faith finally hit me. My family background made those concepts confusing and difficult to understand. **Every word I used derived its meaning from the home life I experienced as a child.**

When you grow up in a home that is haunted by a compulsive behavior such as alcoholism, every word you hear becomes tainted by that unhealthy background. The real meaning of every word is contradicted by its emotional environment.

When you grow up in a family that runs on shame - where people are controlling and inflexible - critical and ungrateful, you feel worthless. You must be worthless, you reason, because people are treating you so badly. Deep irrational suspicion becomes part of the air you breathe. Levels of distrust are so high that the very idea of trust is incomprehensible.

Because of my background, trust, in my mind, meant another person might be occasionally reliable. In those earlier years, what I meant by trust was, in fact, a lower level of suspicion. That is not the biblical definition of trust, but it is the definition of trust that many people know because it's all they have experienced.

> *Theological Jargon Box* Justification by faith: This refers to how a believer, through trusting the Gospel, is all right with God forever.

> "In God's family, trusting is a normal, common thing to do every moment."

They have never experienced the affectionate consistency of a loving person. Yet if a person's family background is unhealthy, that does not mean the person should stay that way. Growth toward trust is important.

Why is trust so vital to daily life?

Trust and God's Family

In biblical Christianity, the Trinity runs on trust. God's family trusts each other every day and every second. Trust is the very air breathed. For many people, this is a totally foreign atmosphere. God's family is gentle; true freedom exists; the possibility of success is ever present with the confidence that failure will not alter your relationship with the Father. No one in God's family is ever accepted or rejected based on their performance. The slave mentality of fearful, black-and white thinking is eschewed. No slave mentality exists in the Kingdom of God's dear Son. In God's family, people feel worthwhile. They accept one another with their weaknesses and they trust.

Transitioning From Distrust to Trust

Individuals who have grown up in an atmosphere of suspicion and distrust find the transition to a religion built on trust difficult. People who come into God's family from an environment of suspicion and abuse only need to exercise faith as small as a grain of mustard seed* to trust Jesus as their Savior and be justified forever. At that point they have breathed in some air from heaven. They have become spiritually alive.

> ***Theological Jargon Box**
> A mustard seed: The smallest seed visible to the naked eye. It represented the smallest amount of faith we could muster. The smallest amount of faith can achieve the greatest results, salvation.

In regard to the permanence of salvation, it really doesn't matter biblically or theologically if we ever trust God again until the day we leave this life, because we are dealing with a God who is always consistent. If we are faithless, He remains faithful. He is not going to deny His character just because we fail. If we trust in His Son just a little bit, He justifies us forever and He happily takes us home to heaven because we have taken His Son seriously. He is so thrilled about our choice of His Son that He will share His home with us forever.

The first year of my conversion, I trusted God twice, and it felt so good that I thought it was enough to last the whole year. Then I slid back into depression. I didn't even realize I was depressed, because it was normal for me. Then over a period of years the truth began to dawn. If I tried to trust God at least once a month, or even once a day, it might change my life. But the experience of consistent trust seemed strange, because I wasn't used to it. In God's family, trusting is a normal, common thing to do every moment.

> "In those earlier years, what I meant by trust was, in fact, a lower level of suspicion."

Trust is critical to spiritual growth. Being confident in another's consistency is part of the fabric of a normal family, but it is foreign to the unhealthy family. If you are coming from a stressed out, unhealthy family, your definition of trust is probably incorrect. Finding out what trust really is and practicing it as a recreational activity will revolutionize your life.

How was trust exhibited (or not) in your family of origin?

☐ There was a high level of trust and respect.

☐ There was an occasional level of trust.

☐ Trust in our family meant "a lower level of suspicion."

☐ Other, explain briefly.

Trust & Justification

In Romans Chapter 4, Paul shows how we become involved with the justification process by trust. He shows us this principle of trust through the example of the two most important characters in the Old Testament - Abraham and David. Trust is pivotal to God's way of doing things in the Old Testament and is pivotal to what He is doing in the New Testament through His Son. Romans 4:1-3 speaks of Abraham.

> *What then are we saying that Abraham, the forefather of us according to the flesh, has found? If for the sake of argument Abraham was justified directly out of works, he has a basis for boasting; but not before God. For what is the Scripture saying?'And Abraham trusted God, and it was accounted to him for righteousness.' -Romans 4:1-3*

God counted Abraham righteous because Abraham believed God. Verses 6-8 speak of David.

> *Even as also David says concerning the blessing of the man to whom God reckons righteousness apart from works: Oh the blessed ones whose lawless deeds have been forgiven, and their sins have been hidden. Blessed is the man to whom God will absolutely never reckon a sin. -Romans 4:6-8*

This passage is saying God will never keep a record of sins or judge a man for sins He has forgiven. In Greek, a double negative is the equivalent of never. The double negative used in Greek in verse 8 means <u>absolutely never</u>.

Paul is showing here that in the story of salvation, trust is crucial. If you want to be alive to God, you have to trust Him. When trust is employed, the most powerful psychological reality that exists is tapped. The path into your life, and the foundation of any personal relationship, is trust. You cannot enjoy a sustained relationship with another person unless you trust. Long-term relationships cannot be bought by bribing people with how nice you are and how many things you do for them. The great gift is trust.

Trust is the most powerful force in our psyche, and yet it is probably the least addressed force in modern psychology. In Christianity, conscious change is the only change that matters, and without trust we go to Hell. Without trust we cannot have relationships. Without trust life doesn't begin. Without trust we are dead while we are living. Christian or non-Christian, we are dead if we don't have trust.

Trust is at the center of what Christianity is all about and is the most powerful psychological force today. Conscious choices are connected to trust; it is always a gamble, it drives right into the center of your heart and determines every response you have to life.

What part does trust play in our relationship with God?

READING 2 - GOD TRUSTS US

God The Father Trusts Us

In God's family the members of the family trust one another. God trusts His children. God trusts you far more than you trust yourself. Before you get around to trusting God, focus on the fact that God has already trusted you immensely. God wants us to learn trust by seeing how He has already trusted us. He is not like the unhealthy father who turns to us and says, "Perform well and I'll love you and give you some responsibility and entrust things to you." God the Father teaches us trust by choosing to trust us before we ever get around to trusting Him. If God is really healthy, if the Trinity is a model of the perfect family, if the Trinity is really the pattern for relationships that we are supposed to follow, then the Trinity really must run on trust. If we are part of this new family, then suspicion and critical attitudes must be left behind.

Personally and psychologically, this is a difficult truth to learn. To help those he was working with to understand, Paul took the social institutions of his time to explain the new set of relationships into which the Christian has entered. He used those social institutions to deliver a phenomenal message, that when people trust in Christ even a little bit, God is ready to trust them a lot. The heir of heaven is the heir of trust. Look at Galatians 4:1-3.

> *I am saying, the heir* [in any family] *is a child through the entire time and he doesn't differ from a slave, even though he is the lord of all. But he is under trustees and managers until the time determined by the father. -Galatians 4:1-3*

Paul used childhood to illustrate the psychological relationship of dependency and manipulation. A young child in a poor or rich family is essentially treated as a slave. Paul used this example to define what life was like before Christianity. For children, such treatment is not a bad thing. If you have young children, you realize they are absolutely dependent and if you don't manipulate them at times, they will not survive.

> *"God the Father teaches us trust by choosing to trust us before we ever get around to trusting Him."*

After this negative example, Paul went on to the defining illustration for our new relationship. Notice how in Galatians 4:4-6, Paul used the concept of adult son adoption or placement to describe the psychological relationship we are supposed to have with God now. He was not describing our position in Christ, but the nature of our relationship.

> *When the fullness of time came, God sent out His Son, coming out of a woman, coming to be under Law, in order that the ones under Law He should buy out of the marketplace of slavery, in order that we should receive the adult son placement. And because you are mature sons and daughters, God sent the Spirit of His Son into our hearts shouting "Abba Father" (Daddy-Father). -Galatians 4:4-6*

I have used the words "adult son placement" instead of adoption, because adoption as we understand it today doesn't give the full meaning of this passage. In the ancient world, adult son placement happened when an older couple adopted an adult into their family because they had no children. They turned their entire business over to him, they turned over to him the right to buy and sell things, and they stated publicly that he could participate in the family business as an equal. He then had a position of authority and responsibility. Everything was his—now that is trust! Paul used a social relationship from the ancient world to describe how God is in the process of treating us. Just as the aged couple entrusted the family business to their newly adopted adult son, so God is allowing us to significantly participate in the family business of Christianity.

Other parts of the Bible illustrate this also. In the story of the prodigal son*, a very significant detail is in the text. When the father saw his son coming home, he ran to meet him. The prodigal son said, "Let me be a slave." The father replied, "Bring sandals, because no son of mine is going to walk barefoot like a slave." In those days, free men wore sandals and slaves went barefoot.

The father also put a ring on his son's finger as a token of his trust in him. The son could take that ring and stamp it into some ink for a deed of sale. Through the use of the seal, he was an equal and full participant in the wealth of his family. That's how the father treated the prodigal son. No slaves would be among his relatives. When an immediate relative was a slave, the Jewish family was shamed. The father's treatment of his prodigal son illustrates some of the truths in Paul's use of the custom of adult son placement or adult adoption.

> ***Theological Jargon Box**
> The Prodigal Son: A story of an extremely wasteful person. This individual took his part of the family fortune and wasted it. After recognizing what he had done wrong, he returned to his family home and, to his surprise, found forgiveness.

In the ancient world, adult son placement implied two things: maturity of relationship and depth of affection. Healthy relationships are mature and affectionate. Maturity has the twin marks of reliability and affection. Paul defines the type of relationship God has given to us as one of adult son placement, where He trusts us, likes us, and wants us to like Him in return.

In that sense, Christian love is always responsive. Love never starts out with us. If it starts out with us, it will not get beyond us. If it responds to Him, it will be powerful.

Becoming What God Intended

Then Paul goes on to say in Galatians 4 that the psychological relationship as illustrated by the social institution of slavery - that is, a relationship of victimization - is not for us either. Look at what he says in Galatians 4:7-11.

> So that no longer you are a slave (property) but a mature son, and since a son, also an heir through God. But then, on the one hand you were enslaved when you did not know God, to things by nature not being gods. And now, having been known by God, how can you return again unto the weak and the beggarly, cheap elements? Do you desire to be enslaved (as at first)? Days you keep, and months and seasons and years. I fear that somehow I have labored to exhaustion pointlessly among you.

When Paul wanted to describe this new responsible relationship to God, he used a custom from the ancient world. Then, through the Spirit of God, he thought, "I've got it! Adult-son placement! That will do it!" Our relationship to God is graphically illustrated by it. God treats us as mature people, adopts us into His family, and on the day of our adoption He gives us every right in the family business and He develops a relationship of affection with us. We carry the family name, we inherit the family property, and we are trusted with everything. Whether you like it or not, God trusts you as an adult. Many times we feel like children, and we wonder how people can trust us with things like jobs, important projects, money or charge cards.

Yet the practical principle is; trust cannot be taught if it is based on suspicion and the expectancy of failure. God gives us the adult daughter and son relationship so that we can grow into it. He prompts responsibility from us by treating us in a responsible way.

If you were notified by an attorney that you have been made an heir to an elderly friend who was quite wealthy, and your portion of the inheritance was equal to the man's own children, how would you feel about that man?

What does that say about that man's feelings for you?

God the Son Trusts Us

The Gospel of John records Jesus' great plan for our part in the family business. He told His disciples that He had to die on the cross, but afterwards He would meet them at a mountain in Galilee after His resurrection. They all agreed, but they were so confused and frightened after Jesus was arrested and killed that they all went into hiding. The resurrected Savior had to go around town collecting them. This is so true to life! When Jesus finds His disciples, they don't even recognize Him. They think He's a ghost. Notice what Jesus told them in John 20:21.

"He prompts responsibility from us by treating us in a responsible way."

> Jesus said to them again, "Peace to all of you, even as the Father has sent me, even so I am sending you."

Jesus trusts us to be His representatives. In His absence we are the physical presence of Christ in the world. His character, His ability, and His gifts have been poured into our lives so we can represent Him on a massive scale. He breathed on us and said, "You receive the Holy Spirit." He endowed us with the power to carry out His plan and simply said, "I'll turn over my whole mission to you. I'm leaving. You can do it." He gave us resources and then left the planet.

Mark chapter 16 tells us what Jesus said to the people who stood watching as He ascended into heaven. After being raised from the dead and ministering to them on the earth for 40 days, He said, "You can evangelize the world. I'll go to heaven and represent you."

My wife and I have never left our two young children at home alone. When they were young, we didn't trust them to be at home alone together. They were together one day, and my sweet little daughter flipped my athletic son around and broke his collarbone - while we were present! God, on the other hand, has trusted us enough to turn over the family business to us, and this family business is to bring people into God's enjoyable circle of love. The assignment is to enlarge that circle to include those who will admit they are needy. Only those who know they need God can be a part of the family of God. If you are not needy, if you are not a broken person, you cannot participate in the beauty of what God is doing. If we cannot find people who know they are sinners, we will not find people who will want to become saints.

> **T**he Son trusts us as His representatives in God's great hobby of helping people - not like a codependent rescuer, but like a father who is looking for his wayward children.

I have always thought that it is absolutely ludicrous that God would turn the evangelism of the world over to the likes of us, until I realized what He was up to. He was perfectly willing to gamble on us that we would not give into Satan's lie that we are a bunch of incompetents. We may be dolts, but we are Spirit-indwelt dolts. We are dolts with a spiritual gift, we are dolts with a Bible, and we are in the Body of Christ. He was willing to gamble on us and say, "I will hand over the business to you because it is the only way of communicating to you that you are worth a Son. And the family business of transforming people is so much more fun when we are doing it together." Trust begets trust. I thought it was ludicrous to turn the evangelism of the world over to us because I instinctively believed I was ludicrous. I needed to repent* of that, as all of us need to repent of our poor, pathetic view of ourselves. When we turn back to God, God puts sandals on our feet, a signet ring on our hand, and says, "Welcome to the family business."

> ***Theological Jargon Box** Repent: A religious term referring simply to a deep change of one's mind and heart.

God the Holy Spirit Trusts Us

The Father trusts us as adults, and the Son trusts us as representatives. In addition, the Holy Spirit has entrusted Himself to us as shown in Ephesians 4:30. The Holy Spirit is with us, and therefore if we aren't living our lives correctly, He, being a sensitive soul, feels pain.

> *Now all of you stop putting the Holy Spirit of God in deep pain. In Him you were sealed unto the day of full redemption. Every variety of bitterness, and outburst of anger, and slow burn, shouting and stupid talking, let it be taken from you with all evil. Be kind to each other, act mildly, be emotionally involved, be ones who freely forgive each other, even as God in Christ has previously forgiven you. -Ephesians 4:30-32*

From Ephesians 4:30-32 How do we stop the Holy Spirit from experiencing pain?

How do we allow those negative qualities or moods in the verse to be taken from us?

Becoming What God Intended

When our speech comes from the negative moods of the flesh, the Spirit of God feels pain. But even so, the Holy Spirit has entrusted Himself to us. God treats us as adults. He has joined Himself to us. Because we all suffer from varieties of spiritual insanity, we don't quickly see the implication. He is modeling trust so that we will trust back. He recognizes that modeling is the most forceful way of teaching. God does not manipulate us the way a dysfunctional person would. He doesn't say, "Produce and I'll be nice to you. Do what I want, and I'll do unto you."

That is unhealthy. God, being a good Father, has started out by saying, "I will trust you, I will ennoble you, I will treat you in a principled way, and I will be faithful to you forever because you have trusted me a little bit. As you understand that kind of love, I will melt you into a human being. I won't hurry the process, because My children get melted into humanity, not beat into humanity." He is willing to take the time to win our hearts by treating us nobly. God trusts us.

READING 3 - WE NEED TO TRUST TOO

Trust is the basis of any healthy relationship in life. You will only enjoy life as you trust other people. The raw excitement of trust is worth the inevitable experience of being disappointed by people. At least we have lived, because the person who doesn't trust, doesn't really live. You may end up divorced, you may end up killed, but at least you have lived because you trusted. God, who is the ultimate model for all that is healthy, has made trust the central fact of Christianity.

Trust Affects Our Righteousness

Trust is also at the core of what we can become. Notice Romans 1:17.

For a righteousness of God by the Gospel is being revealed out of faith as a source back into faith, even as it has been written, and the righteous person shall live out of faith, and shall go on living out of faith.
-Romans 1:17

> "If I am correctly trusting, I will have every variety of joy and peace. The process occurs over time, but it does occur. Such strong emotions cannot be injected. Don't ever let yourself off the hook by saying, "I'm just an emotionless person."

This verse is saying that there are two ways to be righteous: either be a perfect human or participate in the righteousness that flows between God the Father and God the Son. A human righteousness depending upon perfect obedience exists. The righteousness belonging to God, however, is defined by the quality of relationship between God the Father and God the Son. When you exercise faith in the person and work of Jesus Christ, no matter how little faith you can muster, God gives you the righteousness of God in Him.

That is the definition of justification by faith. Our standing before God is not based upon our working to earn it. It is based upon relationship. God the Father is perfectly willing to treat us the way He treats His Son, if we will do one essential thing - trust His Son. God is not suspicious. He is not dysfunctional. He trusts us instinctively.

This does not mean we trust God at the beginning and then to maintain our place with Him we become like tomato canners on His production line. We can't keep His love by canning a lot of tomatoes or doing repetitive religious works.

God Invites Us Into A Relationship Of Trust

God invites us into a relationship of trust, and when we bring our little works into it, He says, "Why are you ruining the party? Take that out of here. It is out of faith, into faith. Out of trust into trust. I gave my Son for you. Get those works out of here. If you want to bring flowers to the party, bring flowers to the party because you are in love with the people at the party. But don't come in the door and start working just because you think you need to work to stay in heaven."

What role does trust play in our righteousness?

Trust Affects Our Emotions

We need trust for justification, but it is important to remember that we also need trust for emotional maturity. I am a firm believer that we should always allow our emotions to tell us where we are. All of us have listened to very well known men of God who insist we should not trust our emotions. But look at Romans 15:13.

And may the God of hope, fill you with every variety joy and peace in the process of believing, unto your abounding in hope by the inherent strength from the Holy Spirit. -Romans 15 :13

As far as I know, joy is an emotion. Once, while team teaching a group of new seminary students with our staff psychologist, he said something like this, "When you have an emotional difficulty, you have to use spiritual means to solve that emotional difficulty."

"You have just said nonsense," I chided him. "Nobody here knows what you have just said, and I'm not quite sure you know what you have said."

The word 'spiritual' means nothing in our circles. Spiritual is just a buzzword. If I asked a room full of people to define 'spiritual,' I would get a room full of different answers. The word spiritual doesn't mean anything anymore because it has been overused.

What my friend should have said was, "If you have emotional problems, you should use Scriptural means leading to very specific, positive emotional results."

Scripture describes some very specific ways of affecting our emotions. The most powerful way is to trust. If you say to me, "I have trusted and I don't feel a thing,"I will say, "You are deceived." I have worked with enough people to know that correct trust in biblical realities leads to a positive emotional explosion.

However, I see three problems with using Scripture to solve emotional problems:

1. Misunderstanding the doctrine (being poorly taught).

2. Having an evil conscience (adding our own little pious works to the work of Jesus Christ).

3. Confusing our family of origin with the new family of God (not sorting out how the new family works differently than the old family).

In order to understand biblical trust, we have to know where the problems originate, and we have to know what new realities exist. If I am correctly trusting, I will have every variety of joy and peace. The process occurs over time, but it does occur. Such strong emotions cannot be injected. Don't ever let yourself off the hook by saying, "I'm just an emotionless person." If you are, get a physical check up, because something is wrong.

Emotions are the music of the soul. They tell you what you are really thinking. When God created music, He created emotion to be its counterpart within us. Like a beautiful melody that accompanies lyrics in a song, emotions are the background music for our thoughts and beliefs. If our beliefs are poor, our emotions will be also. If our beliefs are healthy, our emotions will be powerfully positive.

> The New Testament says in effect: emotions do not authenticate truth,
> but emotions do authenticate our understanding of truth.
> We can often tell where we are by the emotions we feel.

The absence of emotion is a profound indicator of great stress occurring somewhere in the life. God is emotionally involved with us. We do not serve a cold Greek philosophic god. We serve the warm, kind Hebrew God who is similar to the image of man. He feels. For example, look at 2 Corinthians 1:3-4.

Blessed be the God and Father of our Lord Jesus Christ, the Father of tender mercies and the God of every variety of encouragement; the encourager of us concerning every particular pressure with the goal being that we will be able to encourage those in every variety of pressure, through the encouragement with which we have been encouraged by God. -2 Corinthians 1:3-4

Becoming What God Intended

God is encouraging. He has tender mercies. God desperately wants us to be melted into humanity, melted into a puddle of positive emotion by responding to His love.

What role does trust play in our emotions?

What does the statement "emotions do not authenticate truth, but emotions do authenticate our understanding of truth" mean to you?

READING 4 - FALSE KINDS OF FAITH

If what is felt is the product of what I understand and believe, I had better be very concerned about faith. Even more importantly, Scripture not only demands a trusting response, but in its text, four kinds of faith are present. Three are bad; one is good. The New Testament spends some time differentiating among several varieties of faith.

In the English language the words "trust" and "faith" are terms that we don't subject to close scrutiny. We don't make close distinctions about types of trust, probably because our culture does not preoccupy itself with the experience. In some ways, American culture is deeply suspicious. In the biblical culture, trust is at the very heart of everything. Much more care is taken to understand true trust.

Whatever a particular ethnic group or culture preoccupies itself with, will determine how much vocabulary and thought is poured into the use of words. For example, the Eskimos have many words for varieties of snow and the Bedouin Arabs have numerous terms for types of sand. There need to be distinctions in the worlds of snow and sand. I do some skiing and I have learned to make distinctions about types of snow for skiing. I never made such distinctions before I took up skiing. The world of the Bible is not preoccupied with rolling dunes or with ice, but the air of that world is trust. Since trust is so crucial, necessary distinctions are made among the types of trust. Most of the distinctions exist to show what real trust is and is not.

Pointless Faith

The first kind of unacceptable faith or trust is pointless faith. We call this intellectual assent. I Corinthians 15:1-2 explains this.

And I am making known to you, brothers, the Gospel which I have preached to you, which also you have received, in which you permanently stand, through which also you are being saved, by which word I have announced the Gospel to you. If and since you are holding it fast, unless you have believed __pointlessly.__
-1 Corinthians 15:1-2

It is to agree with an intellectual concept, without allowing the intellectual concept to grab hold of one's life. For example, there are many non-believers who can and do write volumes regarding the nature of God, but they have had no personal experience with God. Their faith is a pointless faith, because it does not lead them to the ultimate conclusion which is to trust in that God. The Gospel tells us that if we believe in the Lord Jesus Christ, we will be right with God forever. What does that mean? I turn to God and say, "I trust Your Son, I gamble on Your Son. Either He gets me to Heaven or I don't go. If I go to Hell, it is His problem. He told me to trust Him. So I believe with a point. I trust Him and He produces." If He doesn't produce, we are the losers. If He is not faithful, we are doomed. We don't hold onto the Rock, the Rock holds on to us. His faithfulness guarantees our security. We must have a sense of the daring gamble where all our chips are placed on Him - either we win or everything is lost. We are the ones who say either Jesus saves or we go to Hell. We believe so we can keep ourselves from going to Hell, and so we can get into heaven and be right with God forever. A point exists to our faith.

Faith Without Substance

Another form of bad faith is faith without substance. Look at I Corinthians 15:14.

And if then Christ has not been raised, then our proclamation is empty and your faith is too.

Literally in the Greek it says, "For the sake of argument, if Christ has not been raised, EMPTY is our proclamation!" If that is true, our faith is without any content, without anything in it, an empty bucket. Faith without substance is the opposite of faith without a point. A person with a pointless faith, intellectually understands the content of the faith, but has not allowed the implications of the content to transform his or her life. Faith without substance would be the person who says, "Yes, I believe in Jesus," but has absolutely no idea who He is or what Jesus did. They know the words, but there is no content or understanding behind the words. On the contrary, the Jesus we believe in is not a banner without words. Jesus is the one who has died. He is the Son of God. He is the Eternal God. He is God who has become man. The glory of the Gospel is that God humbled Himself to become man. He died on a cross, was raised on the third day, and is now up in heaven. We believe what God has told us according to the Scripture. Our faith has substance.

So our faith must have a direction, a point, and content. Biblical faith is based on Christ and purposefully expects Christ to follow through with His promises.

Faith Without Results

The third kind of false faith is faith without results. I believe there is a mistranslation that has become historically accepted: *faith without works*. But in Greek it is: *faith without concrete results*, effects. Faith from Paul's perspective and James' perspective is a profound psychological reality, because in biblical faith we gamble on a Person. This is not intellectualism. We gamble on a very specific person. We gamble on someone we have never seen. I did not see a video of the resurrection of the dead. God hand-selected 500 witnesses of Jesus' resurrection, but that is the limit of the evidence He provided.

I do not believe that you have to convince every non-believer of the reasonableness of Christianity. I believe we should draw a line and say, "God has given His Son for you, and if you are not satisfied with the evidence, then you may inherit Hell." This is a trust proposition. God has given enough evidence to satisfy the reasonable person, but He has not given enough evidence to make it 100 percent provable. Enough information is available so that you almost know what Jesus smells like, but He still leaves us with the responsibility of trusting. The greatest compliment you can pay anyone is to trust him. God gives us the privilege of trusting Him because He has trusted us with His Son.

How would you define the following:

1. Pointless faith:

2. Faith Without Substance:

3. Faith Without Results:

Our faith has substance, and part of that substance is its powerful inward work in our hearts. Notice how faith has a massive psychological effect, according to James 2:14-20.

What is the benefit, my brethren, if you should say a certain one has faith, and not effects. Now is that faith able to save him? For example if a brother or sister being naked and being destitute or needing food, and if a certain one from among you should say go in peace, get warm and get filled, and you do not give to him the things necessary for the body, what is the profit? Thus also faith, if it should not have results, is dead being by itself. But one will say you have faith and I have results, show me your faith apart from the results and I will show you out of my results, the faith. You yourself believe that God is one, you do well, also the demons are continually believing and their skin is shuddering with fear. And do you desire to know, O empty man, that faith apart from results is useless?

Becoming What God Intended

In the particular Greek words James uses, he emphasizes faith as a producer of visible results. James wrote this passage to a synagogue of Christian Jews. Their previous religion of Judaism had two main tenets, one pertaining to God and one pertaining to a man, Abraham. The first is that God is one, and the second is that Abraham started the religion when he was justified by faith.

Believing in one God is the fundamental confession of Judaism. However, Biblical faith is more than just acquiescing to information, for James says that even the demons believe God exists. Their faith affects them emotionally, so much so that their skin, if they have any, would shudder. They cannot trust God for salvation, because no gospel has been extended to them. Using the strange illustration of the demons, James wants to underscore that the most basic truths need to affect the life. Intellectualized data alone is not enough.

This is where we have to be really careful with ourselves and not cheat. Properly exercised biblical faith produces an emotional result in our lives, because faith shifts us from the safety of deep suspicion to the gamble of trust.

> To trust in the consistency of another is to shift from independence and withdrawal to dependence and association.

The assumption here is that faith without results cannot save, because faith without effects is unbiblical as James explains in verse 20. The word usually translated vain actually means to be empty; the person is empty of faith. Nothing is within the person because true faith has not been exercised, so the inner life has been left unaffected.

READING 5 - HEALTHY FAITH

Saving Faith

Paul approached the subject of faith in a similar way to James. He viewed faith as a producer of genuine psychological effects that always result in a changed life, no matter how few and far between the changes occur. Hebrews 11:1-2 gives us the definition of this kind of faith.

Faith is the foundation of things being hoped for, and it is the certain conviction of things not being seen. For by this the elders were witnessed to (in a positive way by God). *-Hebrews 11:1-2*

Biblical faith suddenly opens up the unseen world. No longer is the person's life solely restricted to what he or she sees. The heart now has its own unique way of knowing.

I have had lots of people say to me, "I'm afraid I'm going to lose my salvation." Or, "I'm afraid I don't have salvation."

So I ask them a few questions, "Do you believe there is a God? Do you believe there is a Jesus Christ? Do you believe He is God? Do you believe He was raised from the dead? Do you believe He is up in heaven? Do you believe every word of the Bible, even if you haven't read it?"

If they say yes, then I respond with, "And you think you are going to lose your salvation? Don't you realize that everything that you have described is evidence of salvation?"

"Too often unhealthy churches turn the proof of our faith into what we do. In Scripture, the proof is what we see with the eye of faith. Then what we see produces results."

Faith is that profound psychological shift that opens up a vast, unseen world which leads you to believe what the world finds unbelievable. You believe in God. You believe it so much that you become afraid of losing salvation. You believe it so much that you shudder with fear. You are all tangled up with it, and yet, according to Hebrews 11:1-2, the greatest proof of salvation is the ability to see what no unsaved person has ever seen. The greatest proof of life in the Bible is light, or not being blind to the truth of the Bible.

Faith Shifts Us From The Safety of Deep Suspicion To The Gamble Of Complete Trust

If we go out on the street and ask the first person we come to if he believes there is a God, he may say he does. If we ask whether he believes in Jesus Christ, he may say, "Yes, He was a good man." If we ask whether he believes Jesus was raised from the dead and that He lives in heaven and prays for us and that He is coming back as a reigning king, the person may look dumbfounded and say, "What?!" If we ask him if he is worried about losing his salvation, his response would be negative. Only those who have salvation can worry about losing it.

In saving faith, we gamble on God and then somehow a whole universe opens up. The ability to see this universe is the greatest proof that we are members of it. We sometimes lose our excitement about that miracle, because Satan comes along to lie to us and steal our joy by saying, "It's not too exciting to have eyes, it's not too important to see. Being aware of God now proves nothing."

Biblical faith is when I gamble my eternal destiny on a person, Jesus Christ, described in Scripture. When I do it correctly, the universe opens up and there is a God and a resurrected Christ in it. This is the evidence, the certain conviction of things not seen. Too often unhealthy churches turn the proof of our faith into what we do. In Scripture, the proof is what we see with the eye of faith. Then what we see produces results. If I really believed I was sitting in a room filling up with water, I would break a window and jump out of the room because I wouldn't want to face the consequence of unbelief - drowning.

With biblical faith, I trust God in order to gain eternal life. My trust is based on what is found in Scripture, and as a result, a whole new world opens up. When I see this world, I respond emotionally and intellectually to it as it exists, and I receive an eternal inheritance from God that no one can take from me. This is God's plan of acceptance and trust.

Putting all the elements together, biblical faith is trust purposefully placed in Jesus Christ. This Christ is defined in Scripture, and we have a full description of His significance. We can recognize that this is biblical faith because our inner person is affected and our outer conduct is changed. The reason faith comes with such impact is because the unseen world is suddenly opened to us. I became a Christian at seventeen. I can remember taking a short bus trip through Buffalo, New York. As we were going up Delevan Avenue, I noticed a wooded area off to my left. The thought sprung into my mind, "Evolution did not make those trees, God did!" I looked at the trees in a completely different way. They were now "magical." The unseen world was opened up and I had concerns I never had before. Now I wanted to please this God and hear His voice of approval and acceptance. And, we find His approval and acceptance through faith.

Answer the following questions:

How does Biblical faith open up the unseen world?

Since becoming a Christian, how do you view life differently?

What is the foundation for your salvation?

SUMMARY OF CHAPTER 6

1. **Trust:** Trust is at the center of biblical Christianity because trust inhabits the heart of the Trinity. Trust is what makes us right with God, and faith brings the emotional power of the fruit of the Spirit into our lives. Each member of the Trinity has entrusted something to us: the Father has entrusted a principled affectionate relationship to us, the Son has entrusted to us His work of taking the Gospel to the world, and the Spirit has entrusted Himself to us.

2. **Faith:** Faith can be confused with false imitations. Mere intellectual assent can be confused with the "gamble" of entrusting ourselves to another. Or faith can be confused with an amorphous, ill-defined religion. Neither is acceptable. Our faith has to rely on the well-defined person of Jesus from the Bible. This is neither child-like nor slave-like. Instead, God has given us a principled relationship with Him based upon a bond of deep affection and ever-growing character on our part.

TO REVIEW:

What are one or two key insights you've been challenged with this week?

Take a moment to pray and thank the Lord for what He has taught you this week.
Lord, I am thankful for:

7 | ACCEPTANCE & OUR IDENTITY

CHAPTER SUMMARY: We will explore how a Christian shares the same quality of relationship that Jesus has with the Father. This is because we are identified with Christ by being placed in union with Him. Acceptance of this truth gives us the freedom to have an open and heart-warming relationship with the Father. Our relationship does not depend upon what we have done or how we view our past. Our personal friendship is based upon what Christ has done for us and God's view of us as joined to Him.

READING 1 - WHAT IS IDENTITY?

When a person realizes that the problems of his life, his addictions, or wrong habits, have become too difficult to handle by himself, he or she may seek out a professional for counseling or therapy. A difference exists between the two.

Counseling is wise advice, but therapy tries to help a person rearrange their basic instinctive reactions to life by redefining their relationship to their family of origin. Most therapists assume that parents and families are the most crucial formative influence on a person. Often they try to separate a person from the negative influences of the past that are damaging them in the present.

The thought that growth is directly connected to drawing a conclusion about the negative influences of one's family of origin and embracing a new perspective of oneself is not new. Christ spoke about repudiating the unhealthy aspects of the family of origin in Matthew 10:34-36.

Don't begin to think that I have come to bring peace upon the land; I have not come to bring peace, but a sword. For I have come to divide a man against his father, and the daughter against her mother, and a bride against her mother-in-law. And the enemies of the man will be those who belong to his own household. -Matthew 10:34-36

Becoming What God Intended

Christ said He is coming with a sword to cut us free from the effects of our family of origin - no matter how good it is, how mediocre it is, or how bad it is - because it can never compare with His new family. Jesus demands a division between us and our family of origin. A new complete revolutionary allegiance to God the Father and his Son Jesus Christ is called for. Without a conscious rejection of the negative influences of the family of origin and a very positive acceptance of the qualities of the new family, biblical Christianity cannot have its proper place. In Matthew 10:37, Christ emphasizes this point:

The one who likes [in Greek this is ***phileo*** or family affection, not ***agape***] *father or mother more than me, is not worthy of me; and the one liking son or daughter more than me, is not worthy of me.*

Jesus says, we have to take ourselves out of the trans-generational experience and find a totally new identity in relationship to Him. The force of this demand is underscored by its comparison to accepting crucifixion in verses 38 and 39:

And who does not take up his cross and follow me is not worthy of me. The one finding his soul shall lose it, and the one losing his soul on account of me shall find it. -Matthew 10:38-39

Why is Jesus calling for such a radical response to our family of origin? Because it is the family of origin that forms the image we have of ourselves, and this image is oftentimes in direct conflict with the image God has of us. We have a perception of who we are based on the way our father or mother perceived us, the way our siblings perceived us, and the way other relatives perceived us. We have already discussed the issue of self-worth in Chapter 2.

> "Counseling is wise advice, but therapy tries to help people rearrange their basic instinctive reactions to life by redefining their relationship to their family of origin"

We stripped away the word self from self-worth and said that worth really is the value that others place upon us. In the same way, self-image is not really an image that comes from myself, but it comes from how I believe others have perceived me over a period of time. That period of time was when I was most vulnerable to the opinions of others, the time when I was being raised.

Self-perception based upon how others perceive us has a strange power in our lives. When the self-perception is positive, it gives freedom to the heart. When it is negative, it may lead to depression and fear. As we begin to perceive ourselves the way God perceives us, it will have an incredibly powerful positive impact upon us.

Let me give several illustrations of the influence another person's perception can have. Have you ever been called into your boss' office? As you head toward the office, you regret the fact that the office door is not glass but wood so you can't get an inkling of what is facing you. You knock on the door and hear somebody say, "Come on in." You open the door, and the first thing you do is check out the boss' face, because you want to know if he is smiling. At that moment it doesn't matter how you perceive yourself, it only matters how your boss perceives you. If the boss smiles at you, you will be vastly relieved. If the boss snarls at you, you will feel stressed. Your emotional response is triggered by how you are perceived. Self perception is based on how others perceive us.

I realized this one day when I drove my children to school. On the way, I happened to get pulled over by a motorcycle policeman on the road to my daughter's school. All her friends gawked as they went by. As the policeman walked up to my window, I had an insight into the reality of self-perception. At that point how I perceived myself did not matter. Whether or not I got a ticket would be the result of how the policeman perceived me. He perceived that I deserved a ticket, and my 12 year-old daughter was humiliated by the whole incident. When I suggested lightheartedly that she wave hello to her friends as they passed by, she indicated that I wasn't funny at all.

Self perception or self-image is a composite of the views of one's father, mother, siblings, and other relatives, which then becomes one's view of one's self. Depending upon how unhealthy the family may be, if it is suspicious, critical, ungrateful, shaming, controlling, inflexible, or driven by compulsion, the self perception may be profoundly out of variance with reality.

One of the privileges of having been a dean of a seminary is that I dealt with some very brilliant people. Strikingly, the perspective of some of these bright individuals is much like that of a nine year-old child. They lack confidence, work like dogs to secure acceptance, and are often emotionally feeble, so that with the slightest bit of criticism one can almost see them dissolve. Yet when their pedigree is examined and they open up, they are very impressive people. Who they are is profoundly out of "sync" with how they perceive themselves. When I begin to talk with them honestly about how I perceive them as being impressive, brilliant, creative and clever, the words are like rubber bullets hitting a steel tank. They have no impact. In a critical (sometimes Christian) home, where shame and put downs were a normal part of the environment, a sophisticated person may learn to view himself as a bumbling child on the inside. Even though a person may be in his or her 30's, 40's or 50's, critical aspects of their self-perception may be back at the developmental stage of a 6 or 7 year-old.

I know a lady who is statuesque, attractive, wonderfully articulate, and extremely perceptive, but she assumes that she is unattractive and not worth anyone's interest. When one hears how she feels, one thinks, "How startling. How could that be?" Yet when she articulates, and speaks, those about her think, "How striking and impressive she is." If she is complimented, the expression on her face registers that the compliment is meaningless because she has a view of herself that makes her invulnerable to a compliment. As she said once, she does not have the enzyme to digest a compliment. Why? She grew up in a home where compliments and appreciation were intermittent and random, and unexpected criticism often occurred.

I've seen this in my own life as well. I grew up in an alcoholic home. Looking at that home from the outside, one would have seen a group of high achievers, going to colleges and universities, rising up in management positions and doing very clever things. But if our hearts were examined, depression would have been uncovered. The family members lacked the ability to have close relationships. The gap between what could be seen on the outside and what was actually happening on the inside was immense.

How has your own family of origin influenced how you perceive yourself?

Christ has come to cut us free from our families of origin, whether they were good or bad. What is your reaction to this statement?

How is life in the family of God different from your family of origin?

READING 2 - IDENTITY & THE FAMILY OF ORIGIN

Our family of origin creates an image for us that we will often unconsciously accept. Simply put, if there is not a time in adult life where we repudiate that image, that image will be worn over our heart until the day we die. Without a time in our conscious life where we discover and repudiate that image, we cannot embrace Christianity the way we ought. A sword brought by Jesus Christ should cut off the individual from the family of origin so that the affections of the believer are totally caught up with the new family. If there is not a separation from the perceptions of the family of origin, not the persons, but the activities and the ways of approaching life, and if new ways are not embraced, dissonance and a sense of dissatisfaction will always be present. The person will be trying to mix two families that don't fit very well.

Have you ever left home and then returned at a much later time? Upon your return, you notice the constraining emotions of the past suddenly surface. After you walk into the living room, it feels like your feet are as heavy as lead and your mind is slow. A very predictable set of words have to be said to your father, mother and siblings. If somehow this instinctive pattern is not followed, one almost senses that the known universe will collapse.

What happens is that the negative feelings and identity of the past surfaces in full-force. Not only that, but the family often expects the members to function within that set of past feelings and identities. One of the rules of an unhealthy family is blind loyalty. The more unhealthy the family, the more it demands blind loyalty and blind habits or patterns. God doesn't even ask for that. Look at Romans 3:10-12.

> *Even as it is written there is none righteous, not even one, there is no one who continually understands. There is no one who continually seeks God. Every one has gone out of the way. Together we have become useless. There is not one continually being kind. -Romans 3:10-12*

Notice the phrase at the beginning of verse 12: "Everyone has gone out of the way. Together we have become useless." For many the family of origin creates an unhealthy system. The system doesn't work and is useless. In the midst of family, the children develop a perception of themselves that will dominate their adult lives.

Sometimes people will spend their entire adult life proving to their parents, who might even be dead, that they are not worthless. What may be driving a lot of people to perfectionism is trying to satisfy someone who may not even be on the earth anymore. At some point in their life, that significant person convinced them something was wrong with them. With a desperate desire to refute that belief, they spend their adult life trying to satisfy somebody who probably didn't even care to begin with.

> *"What may be driving a lot of people to perfectionism is trying to satisfy someone who may not even be on the earth anymore."*

Since learning about your new identity in Christ, are there any self perceptions that have proven to be false? If so, what are they?

What are some habits or patterns that stem from your family of origin? What principles from your new family may be applied?

READING 3 - IDENTITY & THE FATHER

In the view of the Bible, our self-perception should be based on how God the Father perceives us. As we accept His perception of us, a powerful new dynamic will be introduced into our life. Before psychologists ever created the idea of self image, the New Testament already addressed the issue. In the New Testament, the image we are supposed to have of ourselves is God's view of us after we accept Jesus Christ as Savior.

How does God view the person who has trusted Jesus Christ? Galatians 3:24-25 tells us what we have received:

So that the Law was our child guide in order that we should be justified out of faith. Having come to the faith, no longer are we under a child guide.

A child guide, translated "schoolmaster" in the Authorized Version, was a Greek slave who was responsible for taking the master's son to the teacher. For the Jew, the Old Testament law was simply a slave that led a child to a teacher. The slave was supposed to protect and guide the child and then hand him over to the teacher - the Messiah, the Christ - to instruct him. The Law was never the teacher; it was simply a guide that led to the teacher.

Why aren't we under a child guide any longer? Why aren't we being treated like children? Verses 26 and 27 give the answer by introducing how God perceives us:

For every one of you are mature sons of God through faith in Christ Jesus. For you were immersed into Christ. We have clothed ourselves with Christ. -Galatians 3:26-27

Before Christ, we were treated like kids being told to do this or do that, don't touch this or don't do that. But under Christ we are viewed as mature sons and daughters of God. Now why is this so?

Baptize, Baptism

The word "baptized" in the Bible means to be immersed. Water is not necessarily involved. The word simply means to be immersed or fully sunk into and identified with some element. The element is understood by the context. A very clear New Testament illustration is found in I Corinthians 10:1-2. The event alludes to the time when Moses led the Hebrew people out of Egyptian bondage.

> *For I desire you not to be ignorant, brethren, that our fathers, that is our Jewish fathers, were under the cloud and all passed through the sea, and all were baptized into Moses in the cloud and in the sea. 1 Corinthians 10:1-2*

The Hebrews followed Moses and the cloud through the Red Sea. They weren't immersed into the sea, but they went through the sea. They were immersed unto Moses through the cloud and through the sea. They were totally identified with Moses. The only ones who were immersed with water were the Egyptians and they were drowned. As one can see the word baptism does not demand water, but it does demand some element or person to be placed into or with which to be fully connected.

Galatians 3:27 explains that we were immersed into Christ Jesus, so when God the Father looks at us, He sees Christ. He sees His mature, godly, perfect Son. Every time he looks at Christ, He smiles. Every time He sees us He feels good. He doesn't see us related to our family of origin, but totally immersed into Christ, or identified with Christ. Galatians 3:28 expands upon this idea. God has provided the identification of the new family.

There is neither Jew nor Greek [all religious identification is gone], *there is neither slave nor free* [all social identification is gone], *there is neither male nor female* [all gender identification is gone], *for you yourselves are one person in Christ Jesus. And if you are Christ's then you are descendants of Abraham and heirs according to the promise. -Galatians 3:28*

The old family of origin had a tremendous impact on every person. The new family of origin should have a greater impact. We have a choice to make. We can spend our life trying to find out what was wrong with our family of origin, or we can pursue a new family as we sort out the baggage of our backgrounds. If we are wise,

Becoming What God Intended

we should spend twice as much energy pursuing the new family of origin, so that we have the emotionally rich resources to address the issues connected with the old family. One of the real problems with therapy is that those who begin an archaeological dig into their family background, may not be able to handle what they find because they have no resources. They are defenseless, except for the resources of a very human therapist who now has to be a substitute father, mother, or god. Instead we should become more emotionally identified with this new family than we were with the old family of origin. Tremendous spiritual power will be unleashed.

Immediately following this description of how we have been immersed into Christ is a depiction of the psychological relationship we have as heirs of God. Galatians 4:1-5 shows how any dependency or manipulation is set aside in this new relationship. The mentality of a victim is rejected. We are in Christ, God views us as mature sons, and our responsibility is to choose to consciously identify with this new family and with God's view of us.

Let's discover why God views us the way He does, what it means, how to emotionally derive benefit from it, what this means to us, what it means to God, and how it can become a most powerful force in our lives, particularly in the breaking of obsessive and compulsive habits.

Our identity with Christ means that we are clothed with His achievements. Paul tells us that through a personal knowledge of that reality we can break the power of sin in our lives, with its moods and desires to do wrong, and with its enslaving obsessive and compulsive drives. Notice in Romans 6:1-3 the phrase, "Do you not know?"

> *"If there is not a separation from the perceptions of the family of origin, not the persons, but the activities and the ways of approaching life, and if new ways are not embraced, dissonance and a sense of dissatisfaction will always be present."*

> *What then are we saying? Should we continue in sin in order that grace might increase? May it not be! We are such that we have died to sin, how yet should we live in it? Or do you not know experientially that whoever was baptized into Christ Jesus was immersed into his death? -Romans 6:1-3*

Paul says we break the cycle by knowing that we have a new identification, by knowing we have a new self-image. For, from a scriptural perspective, it is the old self-image that keeps us enslaved. This new self perception will help us to break free from guilt, sin, shame, desire, temptation, and wrongdoing. How we view ourselves will determine our ability to handle sin.

This is why I believe that self-image is a critical reality. How you view yourself will determine the quality of your moral life. Paul continues this idea in verse 4-6.

> *In order that just as Christ was raised from among the dead through the glory of the Father, the display of God's splendor, thus also we, in a new kind of life, should order our existence. For if we have become joined with Him in the likeness of His death, also we are joined with Him with the likeness of His resurrection, this personally and continually knowing that the old man of us has been crucified with him in order that the body containing sin might be rendered inactive, or nullified. -Romans 6:4-6*

Our old identification, our old relationship to the family of origin, otherwise known as the Adamic identification, has been crucified with Christ. The Christian basis for morality is all together different than what might be initially expected. Paul asks, "Do you know how to handle the problem of sin within?" Then Paul answers, "Have a correct self-perception of who you are." Most of us already have bought into how our parents and friends view us. We might as well buy into how God views us. If we buy in with a resulting emotional effect upon our lives, a basis for a totally different moral response to life will be present. If we understand how God views us (and if we make it a substitute for how we have been viewed by others), we will be able to deal with the issue of personal wrongdoing, and our compulsive and obsessive enslaving behaviors.

Notice how Romans 6:7-11 continues.

> *So that you are no longer enslaved to sin, for the one having died has been justified from sin. And if we have died with Christ, we believe that also we shall live with Him, knowing that Christ having been raised out of the dead no longer dies; death over Him no longer rules as a lord. For that which He died, to sin He died once for all; and the life that He lives, He lives to God. Thus also assume yourselves to be like corpses on the one hand to sin, but continually alive on the other hand to God in Christ Jesus. -Romans 6:7-11*

God enjoys His Son. God decided to do Himself a personal favor. Every time a person trusts in Jesus Christ, God does something that gives Him a kick. Ephesians 1 says it gives Him pleasure. He feels good because He likes His Son. Ephesians 1 says that joining us to Christ gives Him joy. Not only are all Christians identified with His Son every moment; but every time He glances at them they are going to be a reminder of His Son's death on the cross, His burial and resurrection. Because God's noble Son died willingly for the mass of humanity, God decided to "paint" the universe with His Son. Every time a person trusts in Jesus Christ, God the Father takes the "paint" that contains the person of His Son and covers the new Christian in His Son and He says, "Here is another reminder. This makes Me feel good. I'm going to identify them in such a way that they remind Me of the death, burial and resurrection of My Son."

Reminders of Someone You Love

A few months after my mother died, I was in a Safeway grocery store. I was walking through the aisles and I thought I saw my mother. She was a little old lady, white hair, overweight, big nose, and not particularly attractive to anyone else but her five sons who idolized her. I started walking toward her and I was going to throw my arms around her and say, "Mom what are you doing here?" Then I looked again, and realized that my mind was playing tricks on me. This was not my mother. But because I had identified this woman with Mom, I still wanted to walk up to her and hug her. She reminded me of someone I love. At that moment I would have done anything for her, because she reminded me of a beloved person in my life. A great sense of joy welled up within me upon seeing her. When someone physically reminds you of someone you love, it does the same thing to you.

If you have trusted in Jesus Christ, God puts you into Christ so that He can enjoy looking at you. He not only puts you in Christ, but He puts you in Christ at Christ's greatest moment in history. In a wonderful way, you have been immersed into the activity of Christ's life at its peak moment: His death, burial, resurrection, and ascension. Every time He looks at you He feels wonderful. As a result, He says, "I'll treat you maturely. I won't treat you like a slave. I won't treat you like a child. I'll treat you like My Son." We have the righteousness of God in Him. Why? Simply because it makes God happy.

What is our responsibility? Look at verse 11:

Thus also you, assume yourselves on the one hand to be like corpses indeed to sin, but continually alive on the other hand to God in Christ Jesus. -Romans 6:11

What does that mean? I'm to assume that I am absolutely alive to God. I need to do nothing, because I'm accepted in the Son. When the Father looks at me He sees the Son. He sees me accepted in the Son. He sees me as a reminder to Him of the Son's greatest works. You may say to yourself, "That is mystical." You may be already overpowered by a false identification from the family of origin. But we have nothing to lose by taking God's identification seriously.

Why is it important to spend more time becoming integrated into our present family than digging into the roots of our family of origin?

How could God's view of you with His warm feelings toward you change you when you are down, depressed, or struggling with a particular sin?

Becoming What God Intended

List the three most emotionally significant events in your life. List three events that you believe your parents would write down. Then list the three most significant events from God's perspective.

Your List	Your Parent's List	God's List
1.	1.	1.
2.	2.	2.
3.	3.	3.

Now on God's list, write:

    1. Suffered with Christ.

    2. Died with Christ.

    3. Alive with Christ.

Answer this question: Does God have as much right to His list as you do to yours? Explain your answer.

READING 4 - CHRIST'S IDENTIFICATION WITH US

Another exciting aspect of this new identity or position is seen in Ephesians 2:1-7.

And God being rich in pure mercy on account of the great love with which He loved us, and we being corpses in our shortcomings, He made us alive together with Christ. By grace you are permanently saved and you are raised up and seated in the upper heavens in Christ Jesus in order that He might display in the coming ages the super abundant wealth of grace and kindness upon us in Christ Jesus. -Ephesians 2:1-7

We are raised up and seated with Christ in the heavenlies. When God turns to His Son who is seated in the heavenlies and looks at Him, He sees us! God has not hidden us in Christ so that we are unseen; instead He has given us a new family identification. When He looks at us on the earth, He sees His Son. Why is He doing that? Because God is into family identification. He wants all of His sons and daughters to bear the impress of the Christ. But also Christ bears the impression of us; He is identified with us.

In Christianity the most powerful force in life is identity. Christ has come to separate us from the family of origin. God the Father has sent the Holy Spirit to totally immerse us into Christ, so that we have a new identification. The biblical assumption is that as we take this new identification seriously, it will deal with obsessive-compulsive acts of wrongdoing, otherwise known as sin, and the shame that always seems to accompany sin.

I was listening to an interesting debate between John MacArthur and Frank Minirth, two Christian radio personalities. In the middle of the debate, Dr. Minirth said something profound, "Psychological research has shown that the driving force behind obsessive-compulsive behavior is shame - the refusal to be open with others as to who I am, and what is going on within me." The driving force behind repetitive sinful activity is shame. What Paul wants to tell the believer is that no basis exists for shame. God accepts and welcomes us each and every moment in the same way He accepts Christ. He is willing to listen to us and communicate with us even when we are unwilling to communicate with Him.

How does this new identity become the basis for character change? We have a striking example of how Paul uses our identity in Christ as the basis of profound character change. Imagine that you are going to the Apostle Paul for counseling, and you are going to share with him that you have gotten into the habit of regularly going to see prostitutes. You are scared to death of what Paul is going to say to you. You are ashamed and humiliated.

But Paul is going to tell you exactly what he told the Corinthian Christian men. A group of men were regularly going to prostitutes. They were enslaved by their addictive behavior, and the first thing Paul does is explain to them that wrongdoing is enslaving. Paul does not begin with a scolding but with an explanation. Notice what I Corinthians 6:12-13 says.

> *Everything to me is lawful, but not every thing builds up. Everything to me is lawful, but I shall not be put under the authority appetite. Food is for the belly, and the belly for food; and this and these things shall God nullify. The body is not for sexual immorality, but for the Lord; and the Lord for the body.*

If you went to Paul's counseling office and told him, "I have a problem, I'm ashamed, embarrassed to death, but I am day by day, week by week, wasting my money on prostitutes. I am sexually obsessed!" Paul would look at you very compassionately and say, "The first thing you need to understand is that even if you regularly eat food you can become enslaved to it and become overweight." You might look at Paul and say, "Wait a minute, I came in here to get yelled at, and you are explaining to me about weight reduction? You're telling me that if I get enslaved to food, I'll get fat?"

Paul starts out with a general principle: succumbing to any appetite repetitively can lead to enslavement. It creates an addictive pattern. After dealing with the general idea of compulsive eating, he says that the same thing applies to sexuality.

In an effort to help a person overcome addictive behavior, a lot of Bible teachers and preachers say, "If you are absolutely sincere, determined to obey God, and perfectly willing to be obedient, you will be delivered." Also they add guilt-inducing comments to motivate us negatively. Paul did not use those tactics. Notice the next thing he says in verse 14 and 15.

> *The God who raised the Lord shall also raise us up through His power. Don't you know the information that your bodies are the members of Christ? Therefore, then should I take the members of Christ and I shall join them with a prostitute? May it not be! -1 Corinthians 6:14-15*

Paul's solution to repeated wrongdoing is to apply how God views us in Christ. Paul helped these Corinthians change their view of themselves by saying, "Please remember that your body is owned by God and is claimed as the members of Christ. Take it seriously."

The two previous readings described how we were dead, buried and raised with Christ. As you read them, you may have asked yourself, "Does my identity with Christ continue to exist even when I sin?" Yes, it is true, even when the believer joins himself to a prostitute. God sees it - He sees His very own Son joined to us as we do the wrong! Think it through. Since the believer is joined to Christ, what does God the Father see?

The New Testament describes this union with Christ in various ways. God sees the believer immersed into Christ.

- We have been plunged, so to speak, into His person so that we are surrounded with Him (Gal. 3:27).

- We have been clothed with Christ so that we, so to speak, wear His identity as a garment (Gal. 3:27).

- We have been grafted together with Him in the likeness of His death and resurrection (Rom. 6:5).

- We are commanded to assume that we are continually alive to God in Christ Jesus (Rom. 6:11).

Only God can see or be aware of this reality, and that is why Colossians says that our life is hidden with Christ by God (Colossians 3:3). Ephesians expresses it by saying that we are members of His body (Ephesians 5:30). Union with Christ is the Heavenly reality that God the Father is continually conscious of and sees. That reality does not cease when we sin. He can even see those in union with His Son joining themselves with a prostitute. God the Father, who gave his perfect Son for us, has joined us to the Son so that our members are His members even down to the intimate details. Of course this does not mean that Christ is committing wrong, we are. But just as Christ identified Himself with our sin by becoming sin for us according to 2 Corinthians,

"Paul's solution to repeated wrongdoing is to apply how God views us in Christ."

> *"He who knew no sin became sin for us that we might become the righteousness of God in Him.*
> *-2 Corinthians 5:21*

Becoming What God Intended

Christians who sin implicitly identify Him with our sin, but He does not sin. Now notice what else Paul says about this sexual sin in verses 16-20.

> *Or do you not know that the one joining himself to the prostitute is one body, that is the two shall become one flesh. The one joining himself to the Lord is one spirit. You flee sexual wrongdoing. Every sin a man does is outside of the body; but the one committing sexual immorality, against his own body sins. Do you not know the information that your bodies are an inner sanctuary of the Holy Spirit which you have from God, and you are not your own. For you have been bought with a price; therefore glorify God in your body.*
> *-1 Corinthians 6:16-20*

An intimate physical relationship is created with a prostitute. The prostitute becomes physically close to the man, but because the man is joined to the Spirit, he is still closer to God. At the deepest part of who the man is, his spirit, he is connected with God.

When we sin, we do drag God into our wrong. First, we whose members are owned and identified with Him should not take His members and do wrong with them. Further when we sin, we also drag the person of the Spirit of God into that experience. That is why Paul says that we should not put the Holy Spirit into deep pain by outrageous behavior because we are sealed with Him until Heaven (Ephesians 4:30). The Holy Spirit does not sin along with us, but He is unwillingly present when we do. We are joined to the Spirit of God and that connection continues. The great news is that God does not abandon, disown or disconnect His own; the bad news is that due to the Trinity's loyalty to us, when we sin, we sin against their presence, identity, connection, and grace.

I Corinthians 6:19-20 continues with the three things Paul says are effective against addictive behavior involving sexual sin. The first is simply recognizing that wrong behavior is enslaving. The second is identifying with Christ. The Christian is so profoundly identified with Jesus Christ that even in an act of sexual immorality, God sees His own Son involved with him. We are so joined to Christ that even in the most intimate details of our life, God the Father sees us in Christ, and that bond cannot be broken no matter how heinously we sin. Therefore, no matter how far we fall, our foundation, our union with Christ, is firm so that we can repent and return to God. The third reality is that we are worth a Son to God. God looked at me at the most wretched point in my life and said, "That person, hidden underneath all that slavery, underneath all of that bondage, is worth a Son to me. He has been bought with a price."

Knowing how God views us, that we are joined to Christ, should become central in our lives. What was central prior to Christ? It was how our family viewed us. If our family viewed us as a failure, or as worthless, why not become involved with a prostitute, because that's how worthless people act. But if instead I am joined to the Son, I will eventually be constrained to do what is right and clean and good.

The ultimate reality behind this truth is that Christ does not "disappear" on His friends when they do wrong. We are never abandoned! No matter where we are, we can instantly start relating to God the Father and obtain deliverance. God is so infinitely satisfied with His Son's suffering for our sin, He sees no reason to abandon us, nor dissolve our union with His Son when we sin.

How would you respond to a person who confessed a particularly heinous sin to you?

How does God view that person?

94

Can you think of one area where your wrong behavior is enslaving you? Take a moment to picture in your mind Jesus Christ Himself sitting in on your 'wrong behavior.' He throws His arms around you and tells you how much He loves you. How do you suppose you would respond?

READING 5 - IDENTITY AND WRONGDOING

There are three basic truths that Paul emphasizes as the Christian means of breaking addictive behavior. They are: recognizing the behavior is enslaving, recognizing our profound identification with Christ, and recognizing how much we are worth to God even at the greatest point of human weakness.

How does this knowledge set us free from wrongdoing? One of the most powerful forces in life is the imagination. It is not what we see that controls our lives, but what we imagine that controls them. As we picture these things to be true (and they are) and we choose to view them from God the Father's perspective, an emotional and spiritual power is unleashed in our lives (if we really trust them to be so). We will feel the truths and act on them.

What will happen to the Corinthian Christian men? If they allow these truths to percolate through their being, they will no longer put blinders on and blindly walk in shame to the prostitute's house. The blinders enable them to follow the desire to do wrong, like a dog after a bone. They are the blinders of shame. The one thing that will allow repeated acts of wrongdoing is the refusal to communicate to others and to admit the wrongdoing. What they should say as they are walking down to the prostitute's house is, "God sees me in Christ. I am as alive to God the Father as Christ is. There is no reason for me to hide this from Him. I have been bought with a price. I might as well tell Him. Father, I am going down to the prostitute's house. Father I want to go there. Come along." Then as time passes, a powerful emotion will well up within me saying, "What on earth am I doing?! God sees me in Christ. I don't have to live out of shame. I don't have to live in the dark. I don't have to crawl under a rock. God sees me in Christ. I am worth a Son."

The only way a person can continually commit sexual sin is to isolate himself from relationships. That is the only way. We have to close ourselves in and stop communicating to ourselves and to others, which leaves us able to simply feed off the lust.

> The second we take our eyes off the lust and recognize we are fully accepted by the Father, that He sees us in Christ, suddenly our whole life is opened up to a new perspective. At that point shame disappears. Shame is critically needed to do wrong.

What was the first thing that happened after the fall with Adam and Eve? Their perception was changed and they became ashamed. They clothed themselves in fig leaves to hide their embarrassment and shame from each other, and they hid in shame from God in the bushes. **Shame, not guilt, is the primary emotion of the fall (Gen. 3:1-11).**

The first effect of sin is a refusal to communicate so that we can feed on our desires and lusts. If I can recognize God's perception of me, and if I recognize what I am worth, I have a sufficient reason to turn to God and say, "God I am thinking about doing wrong. I am driven with lust. Let me tell you all about it." What happens when we do that? The Spirit of God goes to work. Our perspective will change. We are opened up to a whole new perception of who we are and how to live our lives. The effect on our moods and desires is powerful. The reason to hide under the rock and do wrong has disappeared. We are accepted by God in Christ. Even if I should do wrong, He sees me in the Son, and I am worth a Son to Him. Those images must become rich emotional values. The power of those images energized by the Spirit of God frees us.

Becoming What God Intended

Scripture tells us that a new perception of self leads to a new personal life of power. If that is true, then the old perception of self must lead to slavery, which is exactly what Romans 6 says. Our old union with Adam led to slavery, our new one leads to freedom. How we perceive ourselves is the step to that freedom. If we perceive ourselves the way God perceives us, and that becomes a powerful emotional value in our life, we will have sufficient strength from the Spirit of God to break obsessively wrong behavior, because we will no longer hide ourselves from His light.

A practical way of illustrating this is to imagine telling a dirty joke to God. Try it sometime and you'll notice that at the end of the joke you won't laugh. If you tell a dirty joke to God you will realize, "This is ridiculous. I'm talking to God. I can't tell Him a dirty joke."

> **I**f we want to deal with addictive behavior in our lives, start by sharing it with God. He already knows about it anyway. But as you assume your identification in Christ and are open with Him, there will be a new power in your life to change.

On the one hand, we have to recognize that we need to repudiate the influence of the family of origin, even if it was good, because nothing can compare with our new family position. Certainly we should take the best and leave the rest. On the other hand, we have to consciously pursue God's view of us. In my mind, one of the great problems with therapy is that it focuses on an archaeological dig and gives nothing to build on. Just the opinion of the therapist is not enough; he doesn't qualify as God. Christianity says it is all right to do an archaeological dig, but be sure to pour twice as much energy into believing and pursuing the new identification in Christ. If we pursue a wondrous and beautiful relationship with God, as that is sorted out, we will have the encouragement and strength to take an honest look at the past and an enjoyable look at the future. We won't be blackmailed by the past, because our new family will powerfully override the influence of the old family.

If you are in therapy, as you pursue an understanding of your past, make doubly sure that you are pursuing an understanding of your present. Make doubly sure that you are believing God's view of yourself. Make doubly sure that you are emotionally caught up with the beauty of being worth a Son to God. Make sure you are richly living off of God's perception of you. These archaeological digs can be fatal if the only equipment provided is a shovel. But if the cross is the basic piece of equipment, one need not be afraid of anything dug up in the past. With our identity in Christ, we will have the courage to look at anything!

Why is shame the primary emotion of the fall?

What is the danger of being driven by shame?

How can we prevent our emotions and desire for wrongdoing from overcoming us?

SUMMARY OF CHAPTER 7
1. Our new identity in Christ gives us the courage to deal with our past.
2. Our new identity in Christ allows us to experience a full range of rich emotions.
3. Our new identity in Christ gives us the power to overcome addictive habits and behavior

TO REVIEW:

What are one or two key insights you've been challenged with this week?

Take a moment to pray and thank the Lord for what He has taught you this week.
Lord, I am thankful for:

8 | ACCEPTANCE & MOODS: WALKING BY THE SPIRIT

CHAPTER SUMMARY: We will explore how walking by means of the Spirit addresses the moods and appetites of the flesh. We will note the negative power of this twin threat. We will find having a healthy relationship with the Trinity delivers us from the power of lusts and moods and provides us with the spiritual resources to manage our moods and appetites.

READING 1 - IDENTITY AND OUR MOODS

Abiding in Christ: A Prerequisite for Walking by the Spirit

Biblical Christianity involves all three members of the Trinity at the same time. We relate to the first person as to a wondrous Father; we rely on the Identity we share with the Son as the definition of the quality of relationship we have with the Father. As we bring the circle of our lives into the relationship with the Father God, we are empowered by the Holy Spirit.

Our Identity with Christ is absolutely critical to the spiritual empowerment we receive from the Holy Spirit. Jesus underscored the supreme importance of our identification with him in what he told His disciples in John 15:1-5.

> *I am the true vine and my Father is the vine dresser. Every branch in me that does not bear fruit, He lifts up. And every branch that bears fruit, He cleanses it. You are already clean because of the word that I have spoken to you. Abide in me and I in you. As the branch cannot bear fruit of itself unless it abides in the vine, so neither can you unless you abide in a living relationship to me. I am the vine, you are the branches He who abides in me and I in him, bears much fruit. For apart from me you can do nothing.*
> *-John 15:1-5*

The passage shows how complete our identity with Christ is. It says that we are like branches in a vine. Christ is the vine. We are to abide in that vine, and apart from the vine we can do nothing. What needs to be remembered is that this illustration is a metaphor. In actual fact, of course, we are not branches but the metaphor illustrates how important it is to be connected to Christ. Branches do not have a choice, but we do have a choice about abiding.

This passage is often misunderstood, but it provides the key to bearing fruit in the Christian life. Many versions of the Bible translate the words "He lifts up" as "He takes away," creating a possible misunderstanding. In the cultivation of vines, the gardener must make sure that a vine never touches the ground or it will not bear fruit. Lifting it up keeps the dirt of the earth from ruining the growing of the fruit. In addition, the vines must be kept clean. In the ancient world, the vine dressers took sponges from the sea and literally washed the branches free of debris, bugs, dirt and dust, in order that they might bear more fruit. In our case, it is God the Father who keeps us off the earth and in His care. In this delightful picture we are in union with Christ like a branch is joined to a vine. The Father lavishes the same kind of care upon us as He does upon the Son because we are in union with the Son.

Jesus used this illustration of the vine to show us we cannot do anything in the spiritual life without recognizing our unity with Him in three areas: Identity, Participation, and Replication.

First of all, we have been identified with Christ in His propitiation for our sins. According to Romans 3:25, we are told that through Christ, God is satisfied concerning the issue of sin, and He is delighted to justify anyone who trusts in Jesus Christ.

Secondly, we have unity with Christ because God the Father used His Son to establish what we are worth to Him. To the Father we are worth a Son. In Romans chapter 5 we are told that the Father publicly demonstrated how important we are to Him by having His Son displayed openly on the cross. He took our penalty of death upon Himself.

> "We have been placed into Christ so that when the Father looks at us He sees Christ."

Thirdly, Romans 6 says that we have been placed into Christ so that when the Father looks at us He sees Christ. When He looks at Christ, He sees us. This seems like an odd reality, but it is actually very biblical. All through the Old Testament significant individuals were used to create an identity for entire nations. For instance, Jacob was used to create the identity of the entire nation of Israel.

Esau was used to create the national identity of the Edomites. In Romans 5 we are told that Adam was used to create the identity of the entire human race, and that the last Adam, Jesus Christ, is used to create the identity of all those who are in the body of Christ.

The Father looks at His Son seated next to Him in heaven, and sees you. And when He slips His arm around Jesus in heaven to give Him a fatherly hug, He hugs you also. Then, when He looks down upon you on the earth, He sees His Son. He enjoys what He sees, because He sees you crucified, dead, buried and raised with Jesus Christ. You are a reminder to Him not only of His Son, but also of His Son's greatest moments. Remember this is a two-fold identification: Christ has humbled Himself to freely be identified with us, and we have the supreme privilege of being joined to Him according to the Father's perspective.

As we absorb that identification in our minds, as we create it imaginatively within our emotions, and as we reckon it to be true, we grow in this new identity. We can assume these realities and make them the basis for a loving relationship with God the Father. At the doorway to salvation is the Son. The purpose of Identity, participation in Christ's greatest moments, and the recapitulation of Christ's life is to help us to live intelligently with the Father of our new family. In this relationship with the Father, we have infinite and total acceptance. As we seek the Father in an open-hearted, honest, truthful relationship of personal trust, based upon the acceptance we have through Christ, the fruit of the Spirit will begin to be manifested in our lives.

This is what the Bible calls "walking by means of the Spirit." As we build our life on the foundation that Jesus Christ has provided, in a living relationship to the Father, we can then order our entire life around spiritual qualities. Based upon what the Son of God has done, the power of the Spirit of God is unleashed. This power yields the fruit of the Spirit, creating an atmosphere of godly character within our hearts. Our relationship to the Father produces the tree, so to speak, the identity with the Son provides the roots, but the power of the Spirit of God produces the fruit. We aggressively abide in Christ and God powerfully works with us. We can't produce any spiritual fruit by ourselves.

Becoming What God Intended

According to the metaphor in John 15:1-5, how does the fact that God "lifts up" the branches encourage us to produce spiritual fruit in our lives?

Since we can't produce 'spiritual fruit' by ourselves, how can it 'grow' in our lives?

"A Personalist Theology"

We call this a Personalist Theology, because it assumes that at the absolute center of Christianity is a relationship of acceptance with God the Father, created through the Son and empowered by the Spirit of God. In this Triune relationship, character growth flows out of our interaction with the Persons of the Trinity. All of the moment-by-moment values and blessings come from relating to God as a Father through what Christ has provided. Christianity does not work when it is reduced to a mere system or religion.

READING 2 - THE PROBLEM OF SIN

Romans chapter 1 describes why we don't walk in the Spirit. Sin is the culprit continually driving our culture to the edge of collapse and causing the moral failure of mankind. Sin is not simply an act: it involves a false identity, a misuse of one's inner life, and the acting out of damaging relationships leading to a cultural collapse. Evidence of the moral collapse as given in Romans 1:26-27 is homosexuality and lesbianism because they defy the definition and limits of humanity. Sartre, the great French existential philosopher, was fascinated with homosexuality because he believed it was the ultimate philosophic expression of pure will. In his eyes homosexuality made absolutely no sense. Human will was choosing a deviant life style against every possible bit of evidence given by nature.

Paul the Apostle did not view these aberrations in human sexuality as alternate lifestyles, but as the ultimate expressions of chaos. They contradict the original plan of God to make male and female human beings in His image.

Abandoning a clear image of God leads humanity into personal chaos, for our God defines who we are. But when our identity and God's identity become confused, it leads to savagery. When God is turned into a toad (as the ancient Egyptians did when they worshipped toads), is it any surprise that we act like frogs? Notice how Romans 1:23-26 describes this.

And they changed the glory of the incorruptible God into the likeness of the image of corruptible man and birds, and four-footed creatures, and reptiles. Wherefore God gave them over in the desires of their hearts unto uncleanness (in this context it is sexual uncleanness) *for the dishonoring of their bodies among themselves. They were of such a nature that they totally changed the truth of God by the lie, and they worshipped and they served the creature* (idolatry), *rather than the Creator who is blessed unto the ages, Amen. On account of this, God gave them over unto dishonorable passions. For their females changed the use of nature with that which was against nature. Likewise the men changed the use of nature by their desires.*

So sin is more than just choosing to do wrong. Sin is also participating in a false identity, being driven by mismanaged moods and desires, and mindlessly creating false alternatives to the true God. The phrase "in the desire of their hearts," is pivotal to biblical psychology. When men and women have ceased having any relationship to God, all that is left is a desire that needs to be fulfilled - not a relationship to fulfill, but a desire to fulfill.

Moods and Desires: The Strategic Weapons of Sin

The women went into lesbianism and the men went into homosexuality based upon two internal forces - sinful desires and moods. These two forces are the great weapons of the flesh*. Romans chapter 1 says God has turned humanity over to moods and strong desires, because they wanted no part of God. Since they wanted no part of Him, He left them alone with their own insides. The worst thing that can be done to a person is to leave her or him alone with what is inside without a relationship to the great God outside.

> ***Theological Jargon Box** The Flesh: The New Testament uses the term 'flesh' to refer to the human body or to describe the negative influence of painful moods and uncontrolled appetites. Instead of managing one's moods from the mind in the spirit of love, moods and desires drive the person. This is what is meant by "the flesh".

These moods and desires are what enslave people to addictive patterns. Most of us are aware that lusts lead to sins. Scripture is more sophisticated. Underneath every desire to do wrong, the Scripture points out, is a troubling mood or a troubling passion. A cycle of obsessive-compulsive, addictive behavior keeps a person repeating the same set of sins over and over again. This pattern is created by moods and leads to sin and back again to negative moods and strong desires.

Recognizing when we are being tested by a strong desire to do wrong is not difficult. What we don't understand is that our problem is not the desire to do wrong, but the oceans of negative moods sweeping through us. The desire to do wrong comes from the sea of negative moods that engulfs us. The desire to do wrong becomes more attractive because of its ability to kill the pain present in those moods.

What is a mood? Our hearts create an enveloping atmosphere within based upon our shortcomings, deprivations, jealousies, and other negative feelings. These moods are also often aggravated by laws and rules. Rules amplify moods powerfully. The Law does not enrich the spiritual life but it does create guilt, shame, and a sense of failure. God nullifies these negative moods not through rules and law but through the forceful delights of the fruit of the Spirit. In Galatians 5:22-24, Paul says that the fruit of the Spirit, which is the by-product of an effective relationship with God the Father, is beyond the Law and its resulting moods and desires to do wrong.

The fruit of the Spirit is:

- **Love**- an internal disposition of delight in God and people
- **Joy**- unmistakable satisfaction
- **Peace**- absence of inner turmoil
- **Long-temperedness**- patience with people
- **Kindness**- an attitude of wanting to be beneficial
- **Goodness**- an attitude of wanting to be helpful
- **Faith**- the ability to believe
- **Meekness**- the ability to not assert one's rights
- **Self-control**- the ability to control bodily appetites

. . . against such things there is not a law. And the ones who belong to Christ Jesus have crucified the flesh (as a system), *with its moods* (the passive moods that envelop us) *and the desire to do wrong.*
-Galatians 5:22-24

Sin's most critical weapons are moods and desires to do wrong. These moods enveloping us are called *pathema*, derived from the Greek word *pathos* meaning something churning around within and producing powerful pain. These moods come upon us and we are passive as they envelop us. That's what happens to us inwardly, while the strong desires or lusts lead us to act outwardly. Paul says that those who belong to Christ have crucified the system of the flesh with its weapons: moods and strong desires. We do not need to hand ourselves over to them.

> Moods like anger, discontent, fear, shame, and guilt are exactly opposite to the fruit of the Spirit, which is love, joy and peace - tranquility before God.

Describe what a false identity would look like. Why is it a sin to participate in a false identity?

Can you identify which moods and negative feelings have caused you to sin the most? Do you have any idea where the underlying pain is coming from to drive those moods? Take a moment and ask the Lord for clarity, wisdom and power to sift through these thoughts. Write down your experience.

READING 3 - WHAT TO DO WITH MOODS

As believers, we are not only responsible before God for what we do with being tempted to do wrong and what we do with the desire that produces the temptation, but we are also responsible before God with what we do with our moods. In Colossians 3:5 Paul exhorts the Colossian Christians:

> *Put to death then the members of your body which are upon the earth as far as they are involved with fornication, sexual uncleanness, moodiness, evil desire and greed, which is idolatry.*

Notice how Paul puts moodiness right next to evil desire. Moodiness and evil desire are a word pair - they go together. When Paul mentions one, he mentions the other, and in combination they are a significant spiritual problem. I Thessalonians 4:4-5 also speaks of moods:

> *Each one of you should know how to manage your own vessel* (body) *in sanctification and honor, and not in the moodiness of evil desire.*

Before adultery ever takes place, discontent or a negative mood must reside in the heart.

> Tempting easy-going, happy people is very difficult. On the other hand, tempting the discontented, the guilty, the anxious or those who feel worthless is extremely easy.

Tempting is very easy, because the atmosphere of the heart is already primed for moral collapse. They are in pain already, and out of their discontent they see an object (another person's spouse) and they think that knowing that person, getting sexually involved with that person, will kill the pain. The pain will be killed, but the death of marriage will also take place. The force of the moods within and the appetite embracing the other woman without clouds the mind from seeing the relational peril.

Desiring to do something wrong serves as the short-term solution for the unhappiness of the heart. The unhappy person desperately needs wrongdoing, because it is a quick fix for pain. On the other hand, happy people find great difficulty in doing wrong. They don't need it.

The book of Romans gives us an interesting description of addictive behavior or put another way, continual sin triggered by discontent. Romans 6:12 tells us how sin rules over us:

Don't then let sin reign as the king in your mortal body by continually listening to your desires to do wrong.
-Romans 6:12

Paul is saying we need to stop allowing sin (the sin principle within us) to reign over us as a king - in our mortal bodies - within our frames - by listening to our desires. The Greek word for listen is *hup-acuo*. *Hup* means under, and *acuo* means acoustic or hearing.

Paul has a very sophisticated model of how sin works. Sin within will produce a mood of discontent. Out of discontent will come a desire to do wrong so as to produce pleasure and kill the pain of discontent. The desire will be a pain killer and a pleasure-giver. The end result is sin. After the act of wrongdoing, the negative mood will eventually return giving a powerful thrust to the lust when it arises again. Soon the lust or appetite will become a habit and appear right after the corresponding mood is present. Sinning is an endless circle, and Paul calls it slavery.

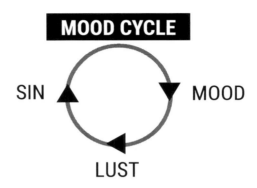

This description of addictive behavior is as up to date as tomorrow's newspaper! A triggering mood causes a person to look around for something to kill the discontent. Then he finds an object to focus on to get his mind off of the mood. This generates a quick thrill and nullifies the mood producing the sin. That is the cycle. As people become more and more enslaved, the cycle becomes more and more powerful.

Why Sin Is Sinful: A Person's Worth Versus A Mood's Power

Have you ever wondered why sin is sinful? Why does God hate sin? Something is really nasty about it. Some of the women and men reading this book have been sexually abused. Some have probably been raped. They were raped because the rapist loved evil desires more than he or she cared about the person being hurt. The person was more interested in the few moments of satisfaction than the years of damage inflicted on the victim. The deed and its results are absolutely disproportionate.

> "Desiring to do something wrong serves as the short-term solution for the unhappiness of the heart."

Why does the killer kill? The person he wants to kill is seen as meaningless.

The person Christ died for is valueless in the killer's sight. What is important to the killer is the short-term thrill he gets out of watching somebody die. He is desperately discontented. Killing somebody, he has found, gives him a jolt, a thrill. The person he kills is far less important to him than satisfying his evil desire. The act and the result are deeply disproportionate.

The person who sins, who does wrong, will damage another in order to satisfy a transient mood and lust. The other individual simply becomes a target to satisfy a desire. Sin is sinful because a horrible ratio is created between the infinite worth of a person and a transient mood.

We can examine any of the different sins and find the same story. If I satisfy a mood of anger by having a desire to hurt, and I lash out, I get the jolt of revenge. But the person who is the target of my revenge is shattered. Moods and desires are totally non-relational. Someone who is seeking for illicit sexual satisfaction is not interested in the other person, but only that person's body.

For the preceding reasons, the Bible warns against sex before marriage. If young people practice self-control before marriage, they prove that they are interested in their partners for who they are, not just what they can get from them. Sexual abstinence proves that they value each other more than they value the satisfaction of their own moods. Ultimately, God calls fornication sin, and that is why it is wrong.

Becoming What God Intended

From God's perspective, it is unacceptable to make another person a mere instrument to satisfy a desire. Using that person to deal with the mood of discontent is a terrible wrong. Reducing a person that Christ has died for, a person made in God's image, to mere chattel, someone to be used in order to satisfy a mood and a lust, is unacceptable. The world is collapsing around us because of this pattern of sin. Moods and strong desires have become more important than persons.

Negative Moods: Idolatry for the Christian

In Philippians 3:19, Paul describes people who are living to satisfy their own moods:

Their end is destruction, their god is their belly, and they glory in their shame, and they are merely understanding the things of this world.

The critical phrase here is that their god is their belly. In Hebrew and Greek psychology, the belly represents moods and appetites. Paul says that two different types of people exist: those who have God as their Father and those whose god is their appetite. The person whose god is his appetite has decided that human beings don't matter. They are just fodder or feed to be consumed.

It is of great spiritual importance to notice negative moods effecting spiritual growth in our lives. Too often we notice a wrong desire but forget to deal with the internal environment, the negative moods creating the basis for the wrong desire.

How does a mood differ from a wrong desire?

The next time you have a desire to do wrong, what kind of strategy can you enlist to uncover the underlying mood causing the desire and to expose that mood to God's healing power?

READING 4 - MOODS & THE LAW

Romans 7:5 says something astonishing about moods and how they relate to sin and the Law. Paul described the unsaved, non-Christian individual as totally encircled by the governing principle of the flesh. Yet when law was considered, the internal state actually worsened. When Paul described the Christian's relationship to the flesh, he spoke of Christians chasing after the flesh and not being governed by it, as he indicates here for the non-Christian:

For when we were continually surrounded by the flesh, the painful moods that belonged to sins were continually working through the law in our members for the bearing of fruit to death (separation from God). *-Romans 7:5*

The powerful negative force of the Law produces these moods. Paul says the Law is spiritual, just and good, but the rules of the Law do not produce character. Rules produce guilt. Nothing can make one feel as rotten as guilt. Nothing else can amplify and empower the enslavement to lust as guilt, worthlessness and shame.

What is the source of endless guilt, worthlessness and shame? The Law. What makes us feel like dirt? The Law. What makes us feel painfully guilty? The Law. What makes us feel ashamed to the point we don't even want to look in the mirror? The Law.

Sin loves Law, because sin needs moods to give urgency to the appetite. As the moods preoccupy the mind, the appetite becomes even more central to stop the pain of negative moods. Only one thing is more appreciated by sin than rules, and that is more rules. Ironically, when the preacher gets up and starts teaching the Ten Commandments, sin just sits there and says, "Thanks! Preach another one! Tell them how they have fallen short! Tell them how they are no good! Tell them how they are failures and wicked! Come on, GIVE THEM MORE RULES! Look how they are beaten down! They can't look each other in the face! Great! I've got them now!

The Pain of the Law #1: Guilt and Fear

Law produces three types of pain. The first is guilt. The Greek equivalent to "guilt" in the New Testament is **phobos**, fear, or **deilia**, cringing cowardice. Notice the word **phobos** is used in 1 John 4:18,19.

There is no fear (guilt, fear of punishment) in agape (love), but mature love casts out guilt (fear), because fear has the expectation of torment. The one continually fearing has not come to maturity and agape love. We love (in a mature way) because He Himself first loved us. -1 John 4:18-19

This use of **phobos**, or fear, refers to guilt because fear has the torment of certain, expected punishment. How do we get rid of this fear? Focusing on how much God has loved us will make this fear disappear. As we focus on the love exhibited on the cross, propitiation, and our position, fear will go. If we merely focus on the law, the first thing we feel will be a sense of guilt, a fearful expectation of judgment.

The Pain of the Law #2: Worthlessness

The second kind of pain arising from a preoccupation with rules is a deep sense of worthlessness. Did you ever say to yourself as a Christian that you felt like garbage? Sometimes we feel like garbage when we discover how weak and guilty we are.

How does one break free? Paul shows us a way in 1 Corinthians 6. Paul strongly presented three truths to a group of men from Corinth who were enslaved to sexual sin. He told them to: recognize that sin is enslaving, to focus on the image of themselves as being in Christ, and to recognize their worth. Why did he do that? He knew that what leads people to act wrongly and surrender to appetites is viewing themselves on the level of animals. When a person has a deep sense of worth, their backbone straightens out, and their courage develops. They know how to say no to sin. Paul says in 1 Corinthians 6:20:

Remember what you are worth, you are worth the blood of the Son of God. You have been bought with a price.

If we get preoccupied with the rules instead of what the Father and Son have done,
a sense of worthlessness is generated.

The Pain of the Law# 3: Shame

The third type of pain is shame. Paul said the ultimate solution to sin is to accept the Father's perspective on us (what we have in Christ) and then use that in a living relationship with the Father, so that we are open and honest with Him.

After Paul described our position, notice what he says in Romans 6:10-11.

For the death which He (Christ) died, to sin He died once for all, and the life which He lives, He lives to God. Thus also reckon yourselves to be corpses on one hand to sin, while continually being alive to God in Christ Jesus. -Romans 6:10-11

This passage describes how Christ died on the cross for sin once for all. He was buried. He rose from the dead, and He ascended to the right hand of God the Father. He is now seated immediately next to God the Father. He is alive to God, and Paul said we should assume the same for ourselves. The answer to shame is knowing and understanding our position in Christ.

Becoming What God Intended

Frank Minirth had a key insight based on psychological research: shame drives addictive behavior. Shame will cause me to refuse to face myself or anyone else. I will even refuse to share myself with God. I will just hide. In the misery and loneliness of hiding, I will look for something to ease the pain. The quickest way to ease the pain is addiction or compulsive behavior. The addiction can be food, drugs, alcohol, sex, or hurting people. All addictions give some kind of high. In my shame, living in the reality of non-relational moods, I will reject any relationship with a person I might victimize. I will even reject any relationship to myself, and any relationship to the living God.

What does God the Father do to free us from shame? He puts us in Christ and says, "In Christ you can tell me anything. In Christ you can talk to me any moment of the day. In Christ you are absolutely, infinitely accepted. Say anything you will. Feel anything you want. Share anything you can imagine, and you are still accepted." This is His answer to shame.

If you would like to test how rules amplify wrongdoing, try this experiment.

Let me give you a rule: **Do not think an evil thought for the next ten seconds.** If you take me seriously, you may well begin thinking all sorts of evil thoughts, and soon you will become so uncomfortable, weak and embarrassed with yourself that you will hide from God, from others, and even from yourself. Shame occurs as a result of breaking the rules.

The Freeing Power of Acceptance

A relationship to God the Father based on our absolute acceptance in Jesus Christ unleashes the Spirit of God. This is what Romans 6:12-14 says.

> *Don't let then sin reign in your mortal body as a king, by continually listening to your lusts. And don't keep giving your members over to unrighteousness as weapons. But quickly, go mentally stand around God, like one who is just resurrected from among the dead, and quickly present your members as instruments of righteousness to God. For sin shall not be your Lord, for you are not under law, but under grace.*
> *-Romans 6:12-14*

This is a dynamic truth. We can get submerged in moods. Out of those moods will arise a flood of desire taking us captive. If we assume ourselves alive to God the Father and work on a trusting relationship with Him built on responsive love (He loved us first), and hang out in His presence, sin will not be our boss. This slavery will be broken.

"The answer to shame is knowing and understanding our position in Christ."

The heart of the matter is where our mind is focused. We can plunge our mind into a mood, and we will be drowned in wrongdoing. Or we can turn our mind's attention off the mood, off the strong desire to do wrong, and on to God, talk to Him about it, share ourselves with Him, sort it out, think it through, and trust Him, and the power of the Spirit of God will be unleashed in our lives.

How does the Law aggravate our moods?

As you have considered your own personal struggle with sin in the past or present, has anything kept you from coming to God?

In light of today's study, what can you do when the struggle with sin arises?

READING 5 - THE THREE-STEP APPLICATION

How can you get the power of God to be unleashed in your life? Three steps must be taken. The <u>first </u>step is to understand Christianity: God has loved us first. The <u>second</u> step, as we build our understanding, is to create positive images that both define the personal relationship we have with God the Father, and make the truth about God come alive in our hearts. The <u>third</u> step is building a relationship with God.

Step 1: Understanding Christianity-God has Loved us First

Our love is always responsive. We do not generate it out of ourselves. We respond to being loved. When we recognize that Christ is our satisfaction before God, that we are worth a Son to God, that we are identified with Christ and we bring delight to the Father because we are joined to the Son, when we understand God's heart of love, and when we feel the magnitude of God's love for us, then we will instinctively respond with love.

Step 2: Creating Positive Images to Define a Personal Relationship with God

Filling our minds and emotions with positive images will tear down the destructive images we carry from our past. The study of psycho-linguistics, the psychological aspect of language, postulates that vocabulary comes out of a context. Our definitions of words came out of the context of our growing-up years. Let me explain this concept with an illustration from my childhood.

After I became a Christian, for some time the phrase "God loves you" was meaningless to me. I scratched my head and thought, "Why are these people excited about the idea of God loving them?" Then I had a sad insight. When I visited my parents (until the time of their death), I would say to my mother, "I love you." I learned to say those words as a Christian. She would look at me, blush, and look around and say, "I love you too." My father only used those words when he was drunk. Before becoming a Christian, I despised him for humiliating me by being slobberingly affectionate only when he was inebriated. That explained to me why the phrase "I love you" didn't mean much. Images or pictures from the past give the meaning to words.

As I explained in chapter Three, one of the great questions for me after I became a believer was, "Where was God when I was being humiliated and scared to death?" I only thought about the question late at night when I didn't have enough conscious energy to push it aside, because it hurt me too much. But one day, when I read in Colossians about God's wealth of compassion, an image burst into my heart. What I saw was an image of an eight-year-old boy being hugged by a drunken dad, an image of an eight-year-old boy who was scared of what was going to happen next. At the edge of this scene God the Father was weeping for this eight-year-old boy. This picture had an instant impact.

God's love finally meant something to me, because I could replace my old image of love with the image of a God who was concerned about me. I had a new image of a Father, and when that image hit me, a deep transition to a feeling of being loved went on within me. Images give vibrancy to words. Images give context to words. We all have images for the language we use.

That is why the Bible runs on two tracks: a propositional track and a poetic track. These tracks have loads of information and tons of images.

I**f you just run on information, your life will be sterile, because the images are what grab the heart. God created a forceful image in the crucifixion of His Son. He didn't just tell us we were worth dying for; He gave us a powerful image of our worth to preoccupy our imaginations.**

Becoming What God Intended

As we further understand things, each one of us has to become an image crafter. If we counsel people, we must become image-crafters for ourselves and the people we counsel. If you are a Christian, you need personal images for propitiation, worth and your position in Christ. As you are seeking to understand these truths, work with them in your mind to produce pictures touching the heart.

Image of Propitiation

Here is the image of propitiation that works for me. Picture a totally black afternoon, the afternoon when the Son of God is dying. All of the heavens and earth are shrouded in blackness. God has made His Son a sacrifice. I, being the religious over-achiever that I am, crawl up the hill of Golgotha with a sack.

Stumbling into total pitch-blackness, I work my way through the crowd until I get to the center of the hill by the cross. Following the sounds of pain and groaning, I find my way. I open the sack. I really want to be accepted by God. Taking out a devotional booklet, "Our Daily Bread," I drop it at the foot of the cross. I turn to God and say, "Your Son plus my devotional booklet makes me feel accepted." In the darkness, the earth quakes. "Something is going wrong here," I say to myself. "I had better stick my hand into the sack again." Pulling out my church contribution and putting it next to the devotional booklet, I look up to the heavens and say, "God, won't you accept me now. Here is my devotional booklet and my money in addition to your Son." The ground shakes even more, and I think I had better grab a few more things out of my sack. Reaching in again, I pull out my good works and begin to put them at the foot of the cross. A few drops of blood from the cross fall down onto my hands. The ground shakes even more. I think, "He is not happy." So I take my booklet, the money, and the good works and put them back in the sack. The ground quits shaking. Tying up the sack, I swing it around my head and throw it as far as I can. Suddenly three o'clock in the afternoon occurs and the light breaks into the darkness. God wants nothing to be added to the death of His only Son. When an evil conscience forces us up Golgotha to dump our religious works at the foot of the cross, the ground shakes because God is offended. He only had one Son and we will not improve the character or sacrifice of that Son by our works. Do you get the image? Does it do something with your emotions? I shared with you my best image of our worth to God in chapter two. I pictured God's reaction to the worst sin in my life, and then I saw Him taking me to the foot of the cross at that very moment and saying, "You are worth a Son to Us even during your worst possible sin." Take the biblical truth, turn it into a picture, and meditate in your heart until you respond emotionally. Your emotions* will tell you if you are on target.

My image for identity is seeing God the Father looking on us and seeing us in Christ. Just imagine yourself seated next to God the Father in heaven. Picture that he turns to you, puts his arm around you and says to you, "You can tell me anything you want because when I look at my Son I see you, and when I look at you I see my Son. You are accepted. Don't be ashamed. Share yourself with Me."

> ***Theological Jargon Box**
> Emotions: Feelings do not authenticate truth, but feelings authenticate our understanding of truth.
> Feelings are the heat of thought. They tell us when we have really grasped something. In that way love, joy, and peace tell us where our hearts are with our God.

Step 3: Reckoning Ourselves Alive in God: Getting to Know God Personally

According to Romans 6:11, we must assume, or reckon, ourselves to be continually alive to God the Father in Christ Jesus. Then we can begin to relate to Him.

The three critical moods, or types of pain keeping us from sharing our life with God are: guilt, worthlessness and shame. These moods will lead us to desires that will thrill us so we can forget the moods. They will generate sins that make us feel more guilty, more worthless, and more ashamed. In order to destroy these moods, we must be more preoccupied with Christ's propitiation than with our own guilt. We must become more preoccupied with the worth of the Son than with our own sense of worthlessness. We must become more preoccupied with our position in Christ than with our shame.

We can use our identity in Christ as a basis for a living relationship with God the Father, because we have an adequate reason to look Him in the face and share our life with Him. When we do that, the foundation under our strong desires to do wrong will be taken away. The fruit of the Spirit, the "Big Three," (love, joy, peace) will replace them. A contented, happy person will not want to go out and brutalize somebody for a thrill.

We can manage our moods and nullify our desires to do wrong. This is possible through Christ. We manage the negative by a positive pursuit of our relationship. Christ gives us permission to begin the pursuit.

Why is it important to have feelings in response to truth? Isn't it enough simply to know the truth?

Do you have an emotional response to the phrase "God loves and accepts you" or do you simply accept it intellectually?

What image comes to your mind when you hear the phrase "God loves and accepts you"? If no image or a negative image comes to mind, think of a positive image that illustrates unconditional love.

When you have feelings of guilt, worthlessness or shame, take the time to call upon the positive image of God's love. Meditate upon the image until you can feel His love. As you do this, the negative feelings and moods will gradually dissipate and be replaced by the fruit of the Spirit. Write down your experience.

SUMMARY OF CHAPTER 8

1. Walking by means of the Spirit addresses the moods and appetites of the flesh.
2. We can bring our struggles to God immediately and He will help us sort them out.
3. A healthy relationship to the Trinity delivers us from the power of lusts and moods and brings to us spiritual resources.

TO REVIEW:

What are one or two key insights you've been challenged with this week?

Take a moment to pray and thank the Lord for what He has taught you this week.
Lord, I am thankful for:

9 | ACCEPTANCE & FRUIT: WALKING BY THE SPIRIT

CHAPTER SUMMARY: We will explore the different ways in which the Spirit of God ministers to us. At the same time, we must recognize how radically different His ministry is versus that of the flesh. We are commanded to walk by the Spirit, to be led by the Spirit, to have the fruit of the Spirit in our lives, and to take individual steps into life by the Spirit.

READING 1 - RELATING TO THE FATHER

God enjoys His view of us. Because He sees us joined to Jesus Christ, and immersed into Jesus Christ, He does not see us as sinful, weak, failures. While viewing us as joined to the Son, He sees the Son joined to us. In this union, we bring Him delight.

Imagine a little child running towards a father, and the father throws out his arms to embrace this little child. The emotions of the dad are the feelings that God has about us. What He feels about his own Son, He pours upon us. A corporate identity exists between those who have trusted in the Gospel and the Son of God. The Father absolutely loves God the Son. As a result, He is filling up the Universe with reminders of the Son. God the Father created that corporate identity to increase His joy. He is continually creating a larger family. In addition, we are a continual reminder to Him of His Son's noble death (the most wonderful thing to happen in the history of the Universe), of the Son's burial, and of His glorious, victorious resurrection. God's joy over this shines in the reading of Ephesians 1:3.

> *Blessed be the God and Father of our Lord Jesus Christ, the One having blessed us with every spiritual blessing in the upper heavens in Christ* (that is in unity with Christ), *even as He chose us in relationship to Him before the establishment of the world, to be holy and blameless before Him in love.*

An ocean of blessings is poured upon those in Christ. All of this comes from God's love. Love is subjective; it's a feeling. The pleasure God feels is alluded to in the next several phrases:

Having predestined us unto adoption as mature daughters and sons through Jesus Christ unto Himself according to the good pleasure of His settled desire. -Ephesians 1:5

Note the phrase "*according to the good pleasure of His settled desire.*" Joining us to Jesus Christ gave Him great pleasure. He thought it was a wonderful idea. According to Ephesians 1, it is the purpose of the ages, the absolute center of God's plan.

Not only are these realities important for our future, they also have significance for the present. How He looks at us gives us the opportunity to be liberated from the power of sin. Romans 6:9 says that the Christian life works out of relationships-a relationship with God as a Father.

And knowing that Christ Jesus was raised up from the dead, no longer He will die, death no longer rules over Him, for the death He died, He died to sin once for all. And the life He lives, He lives presently to God Thus also, assume yourselves to be corpses on the one hand to sin, but continually living to God in Christ Jesus. -Romans 6:9

If I recognize how He perceives me as being joined to Christ, nothing should hinder me from sharing my life with Him. Not the taint of my insides, nor the corruption in my character, nor feelings of shame should prevent me from turning to Him in a living relationship. What I'm feeling and thinking doesn't determine how He looks at me. How He sees me in Christ determines all.

Since all of this is true, I can relate to God the Father with the same quality of relationship that the Son has with Him. God as a Father is the pivotal figure. The Son has laid the foundation of the relationship and defined its quality.

All of us have run into crabby, critical, negative types who could only find nasty things to say about us. After we've gotten away from those people, we have also run into people who have liked us. They treat us with dignity and respect.

The Symptoms Of Love

In human terms when people are in love, certain symptoms are present. They choose each other for a relationship; their thoughts are positively intertwined; they want to be in each other's company. All of the elements of a great love affair are present in the story of God and the church of His Son.

He has personally chosen each of us as a companion of His Son; the element of choice or commitment is present. Though with God the choice was exercised before the earth was prepared for us. He also is endlessly positive about His love in the blessings He speaks upon us in Heaven.

All the elements of a great love affair are present:

1. Commitment through choice (Eph. 1:4).
2. Passion through expressed love (Eph. 1:3).
3. Friendship through positive thoughts (Eph. 1:5).
4. Passion through personal desires (Eph. 1:5).

Like kids with doting grandparents, we almost quiver in place with joy. Isn't it one of the greatest pleasures in life to be liked by somebody who is open-hearted and loving? Romans 6 and Ephesians 1 both say that this is how God treats us in Christ. He is not negative, critical, or nasty. Since He welcomes us warmly, the Bible commands us to share our lives with Him:

Continually count yourself alive to God in Christ Jesus. Don't then let sin reign like a king in your mortal body by listening to its lusts to do wrong. -Romans 6:11-12

We are not to take our mind and submerge it in the lust sin produces within, nor submerge our brain in the shame sin generates, nor the guilt, shame and sin that the law foments, nor the sense of worthlessness sin and Satan create. Instead, we are to relate personally to God the Father.

What does it mean to count ourselves alive to God the Father? Let me give a personal illustration. My wife and I don't argue all that much. In earlier years we had big arguments, and then we gave up on those because of the pain. Sometimes though, we went to freezing each other out. When a person is frozen out, this is how it's done. My wife would be in the kitchen. I walk into the kitchen. She's two feet away, and she knows I'm ignoring her. I am counting myself and assuming myself to be alive to the cupboards or the refrigerator, and dead to my wife. I am dead to her and alive to the refrigerator. I look in the refrigerator, pick up a soda, and close the refrigerator. I'm alive to that refrigerator and the soda, and I'm still dead to her. I froze her out.

This is what Romans 6:11 is about. It tells us to take our attention off of the strong desire that might be compelling us to do wrong, and turn our attention to God as a Father. We must not submerge into the desire to do wrong, but instead turn our attention to God as a Father, and begin to talk to Him.

The more we recognize how positively He views us, the more open we'll be about our problems. Facetiously, I advise that the next time you plan a burglary, include God the Father in your plans. Discuss the details with Him. Be alive to Him, and two-thirds of the way through the planning, the Spirit of God will take away any desire to commit burglary. Romans 6:13 expresses it this way:

And stop presenting your members as weapons of unrighteousness to sin.

Paul assumed sins work this way: we feel discontent, guilt, worthlessness, anxiety and we notice a desire within to do something wrong. That desire is attractive because it will preoccupy the mind from those other pains. I say in effect, "Let me put my hands into some of the strong desires to do wrong. Let me sink my hands, my head, my person into those moods and those strong desires. I know where it will end; in wrongdoing."

Paul says, "Don't do that, but instead quickly and immediately present yourself to God as one living from among the dead." Almost as if we've just popped out of a coffin, we turn to God and say, "I owe nothing to the past. I am alive to you, here I am." Then, I stay around His presence.

Why does God feel delight when He looks at you? What do you think is going through His mind?

Look at the elements of a great love affair. Do you feel like you are experiencing the "symptoms of love"?

Isolate a mood or a strong desire to do wrong with which you struggle. Take your attention off the feelings and talk about them to God the Father. Notice that the longer you share with the Father, the more the moods and desires dissipate. Do this several times today! Write down your experience.

READING 2 - WALKING BY THE SPIRIT

When we walk out of our problems, moods, and desires, and walk into the Father's presence, we begin to sort things out in a personal trusting relationship with Him. Then the Spirit of God supplies the fruit of the Spirit called self-control. He supplies the positive, basic virtues of the Christian life: love, joy and peace. The Spirit does this as he sees us relating properly to God the Father.

Now we are going to look closely at the Spirit of God's place in this process of Christian living. The process that the Spirit of God introduces is called walking by the Spirit. In Romans 6:4 it says:

> *... that as Christ was raised out from among the corpses through the glory of the Father, thus also we ourselves should walk in a new kind of life.*

The phrase ". . . in a new kind of life" refers to a life built on how God sees us, as opposed to a life built on what we feel. Our past was consumed by the negative effects of sin; our present should be based upon how God sees us.

Go over to Romans chapter 8, and we find that the phrase, ". . . we should <u>walk</u>" occurs again. Notice in Romans 8:4-5, we are told that this walking is done by means of the Spirit.

> *In order that the righteousness of the law should be fulfilled among us, the ones not walking according to the flesh, but according to the Spirit. For the ones walking according to the flesh, the things of the flesh are understanding. But the ones walking according to the Spirit, the things of the Spirit.*

What are the things of the Spirit? They are our position in Christ and the new relationship with our Father. They are the things described in chapters 3-6 of Romans. Romans 8:6 says:

> *For the understanding or perspective of the flesh is a state of death, non-relationship, and the understanding or perspective of the Spirit is life and peace.*

How do these three things work together? God the Father sees me in Christ. That's the positive picture. That's how He sees me. I turn to Him, and I begin to reckon myself, assume myself, to be alive to Him as Christ is alive to Him. I begin to share my thoughts, my feelings, my fears and my anxieties in a trusting relationship. As I do that, I can then take a positive step into life. As I take that step, the Spirit of God will empower me. Out of a positive relationship with God the Father, I can take that step by the Spirit, and not by the moods and the lusts of the flesh.

Walking by the Spirit is feeling the effects of the Spirit's presence and arranging how I'm living relationally in this world. The act of walking is by the Spirit's power, and it is under girded by my relationship with the Father and my identity in Christ. The steps that I take as I properly relate to the Father will be empowered by the Spirit of God.

How does this work out practically? Philippians 4 has an illustration. Are you ever afflicted by anxiety? Paul gives advice for handling anxiety in verse 6. Literally, he writes it this way: "Stop being anxious in relationship to anything." Anxiety is a horrible mood. Anxiety feels like somebody is continually stabbing you with a little knife. First, Paul says to recognize that anxiety is a spiritual issue. We have to decide to talk to God about it. Now will God look at me through my anxiety, or will He see me in the Son? My anxiety doesn't interfere with my relationship to Him, because He sees me in the Son. Therefore, I can turn to Him and describe everything bugging me.

I can go to God the Father, tell Him all about it, and make very specific requests for help. I can ask for help; it doesn't matter how irrational it is. He's my Father, and He likes me. With thanksgiving, I can talk this out with Him.

As a facetious example, if you are genuinely afraid that an army of red ants is going to invade your home and begin consuming you, if that's a fear in your life, tell God about it! He'll accept your openness as a compliment. Then you thank Him, that even if they chew you alive, He'll see you through the pain, and you have a home in glory. Talk it over with Him, with thanksgiving, because you know that God is with you.

What is the Spirit of God's place in Christian living?

Becoming What God Intended

As you let your request be made known to God, (Philippians 4:7) the peace of God comes from the Spirit. The peace surpasses all understanding. The peace protects your heart the way a garrison protects a city.

Analyze the threefold relationship. <u>First</u>, I'm in Christ. That's the basis of my relationship to the Father. <u>Second,</u> I relate to the Father through my position in Christ. <u>Third</u>, as I deal with the problems of life, the Spirit of God will empower me as I focus on the Father and live out of my union with Christ. This will be an empowerment in the practical affairs of life. Romans 8:4-6 tells us that this is called "walking according to the Spirit." The walking is the end result of practicing Romans chapter 6 and 8.

Isolate several of your favorite anxieties and do the following:

1. List them.

2. Describe them to God.

3. Ask for His help in general.

4. Ask for His help in specifics.

5. Thank Him specifically that He is bigger than the problem, and that He is with you through the difficulties.

6. Pray until you are PEACEFUL (Phil 4:6-7)

What are one or two key insights you gained from this exercise?

Observation

One of the major problems in many evangelical theologies is they do not have a theology of the Spirit. Many times they will have a theology of the Son, but they will not have a theology that unifies how the Father, Son and Holy Spirit interact in our lives. It's disjointed, so that we're not quite sure how to relate to the Father, how we relate to the Spirit, or what "in Christ" means.

The New Testament shows how each member of the Trinity relates to one another and to us. A lot of bad theology addresses the Spirit of God but does not say how the Spirit of God relates to the Son or the Father, or they emphasize the Son while excluding the Spirit of God and God the Father. The biblical view is that we are immersed into the Son (Romans 6), and we count ourselves alive to God (Romans 6:11) in a living relationship, assuming we have the same quality of relationship that Christ has with the Father now. We work out of that relationship, and the Spirit of God will empower us to walk with character.

The critical point is our relationship with the Father. That's why we have to make sure that we are not confusing God the Father with our family of origin. The quality of our spiritual life will be directly related to how we understand the Father's view of us. A relational reality exists among the three members of the Trinity. We are in Christ, so we can relate to the Father with the result that the Spirit of God empowers us to handle the affairs of life.

This is good, sound, New Testament theology, but it is also good, sound psychology. Psychology says one of the biggest problems in life is dealing with the family of origin. The solution is to be adopted into a new family, and the Trinity provides one.

Now this empowerment is positively emotional and mentally enabling. The place of emotions is critical in properly understanding the empowerment of the Spirit of God. God the Spirit does not produce abstract philosophers, but lovers.

How do you view the role of the Spirit of God in your life?

Practice relating to the Father in prayer. Focus on what Christ has done and is doing, and cooperate with any positive healthy impulse the Spirit may provide. Since the devil does not influence by love, joy, and peace, you can be confident that the positive desires and insights are worth following.

READING 3 - WALKING & THE BOOK OF GALATIANS

Galatians has a very lengthy development addressing how to walk by means of the Spirit and how to oppose the problems coming from the flesh. Galatians 5:16 uses the phrase "walking by the Spirit" again. Paul wrote the letter to the Galatian Christians telling them to avoid the promises of the false teachers, the Judaizers. After dealing with the Judaizers and their beliefs, he told them in 5:16:

And I am saying by the qualities from the Spirit continually be walking [ordering your life] *and a lust of the flesh you will never complete.*

This is a great promise. If we order our life in such a way that we allow the Spirit of God to minister to us, the lust of the flesh will not be satisfied. We may feel tempted, but it will not be completed.

If we allow the Spirit of God to emotionally meet the need represented in that lust, the power of the flesh will be broken. The opposite of lust will appear: happiness, love, contentment, and self-control. When those emotions are present, the force of the flesh with its moods and desires loses its power.

Verse 18 continues:

And if by qualities from the Spirit you are being led along, you are not under law.

As we relate to the Father, we can bring the large circle of our lives under the influence of the Spirit of God's ministry, which is known as walking by means of the Spirit. Within the larger circle of the Spirit's ministry are specific things He does for us. One of those is **Spirit leading**. In **Spirit leading** we are positively prompted by emotion and insight to love people and trust God. Our responsibility is to respond to being tugged along, being led by the Spirit. When we are being led by the Spirit, we are not under law. Our preoccupation should not be with rules and regulations. Instead we have a father/son relationship based upon the emotions, feelings, and perspectives that the Spirit of God produces.

> *"The Spirit brings life and joy, the flesh brings chaotic and confusing moods and desires. These moods and desires harden into habits of the heart and life called the works of the flesh."*

This wonderfully enriching life is directly opposed to the life lived in the flesh. While the Spirit brings life and joy, the flesh brings chaotic and confusing moods and desires. These moods and desires harden into habits of the heart and life called the works of the flesh. These are individual habits people become addicted to in their lives. In Galatians 5:19-21 he explains what the works of the flesh are.

And the works of the flesh are manifest. These are of such a nature as fornication, uncleanness, gross sensuality, idolatry, sorcery, hating, divisions, jealousy, (there's nothing as emotional as jealousy), *outbursts of anger* (notice how emotional these are), *fractions, splits, party spirit, envying, drunken bouts, banquets* (parties that are thrown just so people can have illicit relationships) *and things of such a nature .*
-Galatians 5:19-21

From this list, notice the powerful emotions involved in the works of the flesh. People who are caught up in adulterous affairs, people who are trying to break habits of fornication, people who are sexually obsessed, and people who have been living off of hateful relations are dealing with emotional dynamite.

"Strongly emotional" is an understatement when describing the works of the flesh. Now it's quite interesting that Paul uses the word "works." When moods and desires are fulfilled, they produce the works. Moods produce a pain-killer which is the desire to do wrong things. The desire to do wrong things becomes a lifestyle producing habits or works.

Becoming What God Intended

Paul is describing basic counseling problems. His solution is a radical change in the emotional state of the person with these problems. Let's continue reading verse 21:

And things like these, which I was telling you before, even as I have told you, that the ones who are continually practicing such things shall not inherit the kingdom of God. -Galatians 5:21

God is not going to throw parties for illicit sex in heaven. Heaven is not going to have fornicators. Heaven is not going to have haters. Nobody in Heaven is going to be in that state.

This is the pattern. Paul says sin produces moods; passive states of anxiety, fear, worthlessness, shame, and guilt. Out of that atmosphere arises desires or lusts to do wrong things. These desires produce a lifestyle that revolves around the works of the flesh. These works also involve a mindset. The mindset or perspective of the flesh is relational death. The person is not oriented to God or others. The orientation is to one's own insides: persons do not matter. All of this is called flesh.

Opposite to that, Paul says, is another way of living, called "walking by the Spirit." If we walk by the Spirit, we will be tugged along by the Spirit. If we succumb to the tugging, we will have the by-product of the Spirit's presence (the fruit of the Spirit in our life). Sorting out our emotional lives in a living relationship to the Father is called walking. As we do that, the Spirit of God will start giving us peace, love, and joy. As we allow ourselves to be pulled along by those feelings, they produce an inner-atmosphere and a perspective of mind, or inner-character. This fruit, all of which is profoundly rich feelings, is described in the next section.

Galatians 5:19-21 describes the habits enslaving individuals. No one person engages in all of these works, but it is common to have more than one habit. Those who are engaged in these habits are actually in emotional bondage.

Look at the list of the works of the flesh, and for each work write down two emotions that may be working in the person who is captured by the habit.

1. Sexual immorality

2. Sexual impurity

3. Idolatry

4. Strife

5. Envying

6. Drunkenness

How can the Spirit of God address these powerful emotions?

READING 4 - THE FRUIT OF THE SPIRIT

The fruit of the Spirit is *agape*. These are the characteristics the Spirit of God produces in a life. *Agape* is a delight in people, an enjoyment of people.

Agape love is wonderfully emotional. It is more than love, but it is also to genuinely like others, it is something that pulls our entire being into a profound unity of enjoying people, because God enjoys us. We love because He first loved us. When we respond correctly, it will be *agape*, a love that enjoys.

Joy

Another way of putting it is deep satisfaction with life. That's what joy is. When we look at life and we think, "this is wonderful," that is an attitude of joy. The perspective that life is a gift is joy. Joy is a deep satisfaction with life. It is not based on perfect circumstances, because Christ gives joy in a way that is different from how the world gives joy. The world calls winning a lotto prize joy.

Real joy is when we have poor circumstances, and we're still enjoying ourselves.

If we have 800 reasons why we are not satisfied with life, we need to sort that out with the good Father. Trust this good Father. We need to look at ourselves through His eyes. In His presence, joy is forever more. People carry an atmosphere with them. God carries an atmosphere with Him. As we walk into His presence and are open with Him and trust Him, He'll share joy with us. We will live in His atmosphere.

Peace

Peace is absence of inner-turmoil (I'm phrasing it differently, because we are used to the religious sounding words). The gospels describe Jesus as walking on the water. Peter saw Jesus on the water and wanted to join Him, but the tempestuous waves frightened him. To the tempestuous waves, Jesus said, "Peace be still." Peace means a person's emotional life is not driven and tossed. Having an absence of inner-turmoil though is not a vacuum. A positive sense of well-being is present because the heart is relaxing in the goodness of God.

Primary Christian Emotions: Love, Joy, & Peace

Love, joy and peace are primary Christian emotions. They are the birthright of every believer. They are the "Big Three." Not based on circumstances, they plunge deeper than the pains of life. The Christian's promise is that God can bring a peaceful strength deeper than the pains of life. "Blessed are those who are mourning, for they shall be comforted" (Matthew 5:4). Comfort penetrates deeper than the pain of mourning, because we are comforted by a Father who is the God of all comfort (2 Corinthians 1:3-5).

The "Big Three," love, joy & peace are the birthright of every believer.

The Fruit: Love, Joy, & Peace

Love, joy, and peace are the fruit. The roots of the tree, so to speak, are our position in Christ. The trunk of the tree is our relationship with the Father. The fruit of the tree is how we take our life and bring it into conformity with the Father. Love, joy, peace will begin to grow in our life, affect our perspective, and affect our responses.

In Galatians 5:24 Paul gives the critical, theological principle. Those who belong to Christ Jesus have crucified the flesh as a principle. Our new spiritual realities have resulted in the flesh being crucified with its moods and its strong desires. No need exists to live within the system of the flesh. The moods are the enveloping atmosphere of guilt, fear, anxiety, shame, discontent, and the lusts are those feelings that make us feel we've got to chase something to kill the pain.

Moods are passions which engulf us; lusts pursue external targets. Christ has crucified any reason to live within those domains. All that's left is the experience of strong feelings and negative emotions, but the principle of living according to the flesh has been nullified. We have the Spirit of God within; we're in Christ; we have a Father. We can handle the crucified enemy.

Becoming What God Intended

Contrast the world's definition of love, joy, and peace with God's definition of these terms.

Analyze the "tree" in your life. On what area do you need to concentrate or better understand: the roots (your position in Christ), the trunk (your relationship with the Father), or the fruit of the Spirit of God?

READING 5 - STEPPING BY THE SPIRIT

So far Galatians has used the most inclusive term of all, "walking," to describe the over-all work of the Spirit. A part of walking is Spirit leading. That is when we respond to the influence of the fruit of the Spirit-love, joy, peace, and other positive qualities in our lives. Another term appears in Galatians 5:25 that deals with particular, concrete circumstances we need to address spiritually. That is called "Spirit stepping." Now verse 25 says:

And if we are living by the Spirit, also by the Spirit, let's keep in step. -Galatians 5:25

Now that word for step is *stoikeo* which is different than the Greek word for walk. *Stoikeo* refers to an inch-by-inch, short step-by-step keeping of principles. Walking refers to organizing our life. With this word *stoikeo* we make sure that each step we're taking is in harmony with love, joy and peace. We must apply the ministry of the Spirit to each of our relationships in life. Love, joy and peace should be carried into every aspect of our dealings with people. So if we face a difficult phone call, or an uncomfortable conversation, or a stress at work, we need to be sure we are "putting our best foot forward," in this case it is our spiritual foot.

> *"The presence of the fruit of the Spirit (the essential elements are love - a delight in others, joy - a deep satisfaction with life, and peace - an absence of inner-turmoil) keys us into the fact that we're relating properly to God."*

What this means is that spirituality is a highly subjective business. We've got to be in touch with our emotions. We've got to be able to recognize what a negative mood is, what guilt is, what shame is, we've got to view it as an enemy, we've got to view it as a spiritual issue that we have to take to God the Father. We have to recognize that He views us through the Son, and not the way we feel. We have to stand outside of our emotions and stand in Christ relating to God the Father.

Now why is it so important to be sensitive to what we are feeling? The works of the flesh are highly emotional and the fruit of the Spirit is powerfully emotional. We need to know the source of the different feelings floating through us.

If we went to a psychiatric emergency ward, having an emotional collapse, the first thing they would want to sort out is, can this person stand outside their emotions and describe what's going on inside? Or have they just become one big emotion? If one can still stand outside and describe it, they'll say, "there is hope for this person." In the psychological world, being self-observant is important. In spiritual realities, being self-observant is also critical.

When the person becomes the negative emotion, then the counseling profession will consider using medicines. The brain has become submerged in negative emotions. Spirituality begins when we stop living by negative moods and lust. Life needs to be lived out of a relationship to the Father.

The flesh works with negative feelings. The Spirit leads us along by positive feelings. Being a Spirit-led person simply means that we're habituated to live off of the "Big Three," love, joy and peace.

The maturing Christian who is becoming familiar with the Spirit's leading knows how to apply, in a detailed way, love, joy and peace to all the relationships of life. The growing person knows how to take a negative mood, like discontent, that comes from the flesh, and knows how to dissipate it by having an intelligent, spiritual conversation with the Father. All of this revolves around emotions.

The flesh has an atmosphere of its own that we need to be able to recognize, and we need to be rather tough with ourselves. We may not be able to shake these things fast, but we've got to be straightforward with ourselves. The flesh produces moods, passivity, negative emotional atmospheres, and strong desires to do wrong. It also produces a perspective. Romans 8:7-8 tells us that the flesh, over time, will produce a perspective:

Therefore the perspective, or the understanding of the flesh is death for it is not subject to the Law of God.

That word 'perspective' is the mindset. The flesh will produce a vague, hopeless, passive, negative mindset, that says this is all that life has. The person will be imprisoned in the moods and the strong desires of the flesh, with a limited mindset where God really doesn't exist practically. God is not included, so that perspective of the flesh has to be challenged, radically and bravely challenged.

Then the flesh produces works (Galatians 5:19-21). The flesh will produce ways of handling life. For instance, people will handle relationships by becoming sexually active or hating people.

A Christian has to become an expert at spotting the moods of the flesh and skilled at transitioning to the fruit of the Spirit. The presence of the fruit of the Spirit (the essential elements are love - a delight in others, joy - a deep satisfaction with life, and peace - an absence of inner-turmoil) keys us into the fact that we're relating properly to God. If you say to yourself, "I'm not satisfied with life, I'm not peaceful and I really don't like people," I would say your understanding of Christianity and of God as a Father is deficient. You have an improper understanding of who God the Father is, and how God views you in Christ. None of us have a perfect understanding, but we should have a growing understanding.

How do we access this in an emotionally rich way? We first have to understand the doctrine. Christ satisfied God. Secondly, we are worth a Son to this Father. Thirdly, we are in Christ. On the basis of those realities, we can begin to bring the circle of our lives under the Spirit's ministry. As we do so, the Spirit will lead us by emotional promptings, and loving insights. Going through life, we need to learn how to meet individual, concrete problems as we are influenced by the Spirit. This is called taking steps by the Spirit.

"The Spirit leads us along by positive feelings. Being a Spirit-led person simply means that we're habituated to live off of the "Big Three," love, joy and peace."

Is it okay for a person to be controlled by emotions? Why or why not?

Do you know someone who actively displays the qualities of love, joy and peace in their life? What is this person like? How do you feel when you are around them?

SPIRITUAL REALITIES TO REMEMBER
1. Walking by the Spirit (is the largest term for the Spirit's work in our lives) 2. Spirit Leading (is the positive prompting of the Spirit) 3. Fruit of the Spirit (is the character the Spirit produces as we do the above) 4. Stepping By the Spirit (is when we apply these truths to a particular, concrete situation)

Think of an area of life where you are struggling, and take a specific spiritual step into that area. If it deals with your job or your church or family life, or friendships, or your sex life, or your hobbies, what ever it is, apply the following:

1. What is the Spiritual Challenge?

2. Share it with the Father in detail, and trust Him for His help.

3. Search the Bible for what it says you should do.

4. Seek godly counsel and advice.

5. Specifically think and pray through:

- What should your perspective be?

- What emotions from the fruit of the Spirit should you have?

- What specifically should you say or do?

6. In <u>faith,</u> follow through with your plan.

10 | ACCEPTANCE & PRAYER

CHAPTER SUMMARY: We will discover how our relationship with God the Father is expanded through prayer. Prayer is based neither on the investment of time nor the multiplication of words. Instead our prayer life is based on a set of issues we must face daily. These issues determine how we relate to God as a Father and the world about us.

READING 1 - THE ISSUE OF THE FATHER

In Scripture, the Christian life follows this pattern: our spiritual foundation is in Christ, on the basis of what Christ has done, we personally relate to the Father as the 'Abba' Father, the Daddy-Father, and as a result, the Spirit of God, who is a person, ministers to our character, and supplies spiritual ability to us. As we step out into life, we can proceed in a spiritually powerful way.

Even more simply put, the Christian life works this way. God has done something for us in Christ. We respond to what he has done for us in Christ. He initiates, we respond, and as we respond correctly, the Spirit of God responds to us. God has initiated with the cross of Christ, and we respond to what God has done through Christ in a living relationship with the Father. **As we properly respond to the Father, the Spirit of Christ responds to us.** So it is initiation, and response. In true Christianity, God always is the starting point, and we in amazement and awe respond. As we properly relate to the Father, we can step out into life and be empowered by the Spirit of God.

Prayer is based neither on the investment of time nor the multiplication of words.

Prayer has a major place in the Christian life. The way we communicate the daily issues and needs of life to God is prayer. Christ taught His disciples to pray, and what He taught them has great meaning for us. His teaching addresses five areas or issues. Five areas exist that need to be sorted out on a daily basis with God the Father in order for the Spirit of God to have a

> "The flesh will produce a vague, hopeless, passive, negative mindset, that says this is all that life has."

powerful ministry in our lives. Those five areas are in the Lord's Prayer from the Sermon on the Mount in Matthew 6. A careful look at the Lord's Prayer will isolate five critical spiritual issues in relationship to God as a Father. Those five issues will determine the quality of relationship to God as a Father, and secondly, they will determine how effectively the Spirit of God will minister to us.

Look at Matthew 6:5:

… and whenever you pray, don't you be as the hypocrites, because they really like to be standing and praying in the synagogues and on the street corners.

One of the beliefs of the Pharisees was that prayer should occur three times a day. This was their approach: they would time it so that they would be walking through the market place at noon. When the sun was directly overhead, the Pharisees would stop and look up to heaven, with eyes wide open, and arms up, and would pour forth memorized prayers out loud in the midst of the crowds. That was Pharisaic praying, designed to draw attention to themselves. They prayed by the clock: in the morning, at lunchtime, and in the early evening. Christ said not to be like the hypocrites. Don't set your clock in such a way that you strategically place yourself in order to be seen by men. Christ went on to say, "… they are receiving their wage doing that sort of thing."

> "Don't set your clock in such a way that you strategically place yourself in order to be seen by men."

Т**he first thing Christ taught his disciples was to turn to God the Father and say, 'Our Father, the One in the heavens.' That's revolutionary!**

The alternative he recommended is in Matthew 6:6:

Whenever you pray, enter into a quiet inner room and lock the door. Pray to your Father in secret and your Father, the one seeing in secret, shall pay you a wage.

God the Father is in heaven. No one can see Him from the earth. He's not terribly concerned that anyone should see Him anyway. He's not overly impressed with Himself; He's merely God. He doesn't have to make a display out of Himself, so why should His children make displays out of themselves? Then it goes on:

… and your Father, the one seeing in secret, shall pay you a wage. And don't be continually praying using nonsense words even as the Gentiles, for they are thinking that in their many words, they shall get a hearing. -Matthew 6:6b-7

What is Christ referring to with his reference to the non-Jews and their verbal volume? The Greeks, who had the Dionysian cult, got drunk and drugged and they would babble incoherently for hours on end. In doing so they believed they were turning themselves over to a demon, which in their religion was a minor god, a demigod. The mark of being possessed by the god was babbling incoherently at great length. Since Greeks were in Jerusalem, and the Dionysian cult was throughout the Mediterranean, Christ was aware of their practices. They thought their volume of words would get them in touch with the supernatural. Christ said, "Don't be like them."

So a biblical relationship to God is not based on time. Nor is it based on the amount of words, or fasting. Matthew 6:8 goes onto to say:

And don't you ever then become like them, for your Father knows the needs you have before you ask Him.

Another truth about prayer is that it is not need-based. What Christ eliminates from prayer is fascinating. The first thing He eliminates is time. The second thing He eliminates is a lot of verbiage, a lot of words. The third thing He eliminates is a grocery list of needs. He simply says, that God already knows what your needs are. That's not the pivotal issue in prayer. So if it's not time, if it's not words, and if it's not my needs, then what is it? What it is are those five issues from the Sermon on the Mount and its prayer.

The very first issue is simply God as our Father. The first thing Christ taught his disciples was to turn to God the Father and say, "Our Father, the One in the heavens." That's revolutionary. The phrase, God the

Father, only occurs two or three times in the Old Testament. At the very beginning of Christ's teaching on prayer, notice the critical issue He selected. Having a picture of ourselves as a child of God and a picture of God as Daddy-Father, our Heavenly Father, is very important. The truth of the Fatherhood of God cuts two ways: God is our Father, and so, we have a relationship of an adult son or daughter to Him. The very first issue in prayer is how God looks at us as His child and how we look at God as a Father. Do we view God as a kind, generous-hearted, emotionally involved, compassionate, absolutely loyal God, who wants our best, who delights in our company, and wants us to be in heaven with Him forever?

The phrasing of the prayer is meant to create a spiritual crisis because we're supposed to be able, through faith, to look at God and say, "You are my Father. You are personal, you're emotionally involved with me, and you view me as a mature son or daughter in Christ. You do not view me as a slave, you do not view me as a kid, but you view me through the person of Jesus Christ. Therefore, I have to respond to you not based on a relationship of rules and fear, but on a relationship of affection and principle."

What's the difference between a child and an adult? A child responds based on black and white rules. An adult should respond based on principle.

God wants us to respond to Him maturely, and to view Him as an affectionate, emotionally involved God. Psalm 103:10-14 is a critical passage for our understanding of God. In the next verses, the word "healthy" was added so the contents made more sense in our culture.

He has not dealt with us according to our sins, nor does He pay us back according to our lawless deeds. For like the height of the Heavens above the earth, thus did His loyal affection prevail over those who respect Him. Like the distance from the East to the West, so far has He removed our transgressions from us. Like the tender pity of a healthy father over his offspring, so Yahweh has tender pity for those who respect Him, for He personally knows our form while remembering that we are just dust. -Psalm 103:10-14

These referred to those who have a respect for Him. The respecters of God respond the way He wants them to respond. They don't add their works to God's grace, but they take God at His word in faith. That's how to respect God both in the Old Testament and in the New Testament. One doesn't add to what God has done. We trust His word and rely on Him as a person who needs His help. For He Himself knows our frame, and He is mindful that we are but dust. The first spiritual issue in prayer is to sort out that we have a Father who is emotionally involved with us. He sees us in Christ, and we're totally accepted as Christ is accepted by Him.

In one seminar a person made this comment, "If prayer is supposed to be issues-oriented, I don't think I'll get beyond the first issue for the next year and a half." If it takes a year and a half to sort out the relationship with God as a Father, that's fine. He won't mind. To have a clear view of God, the effort is worthwhile.

The first part is understanding God as a Father. The second part is making the reality a rich source of emotional strength within. This is done by picturing it. A most effective way to minister to our own emotions is to <u>first,</u> understand the doctrine biblically, out of the text. Next, we take emotionally significant images and play those images through the mind, using the imagination to view God as an affectionate Father.

So in my own mind, I view God the Father as a Dad who is running to meet His children, and He's smiling, and He's grabbing them up into His arms, and He's dancing with them, He's enjoying them. When I see a healthy father responding in a gracious and kind way to his children, I take that image and I play around with it and I say, "That's what God is like." We need to feel these emotionally rich truths.

That's what language is supposed to do. Language is supposed to feed the imagination. We need to function like poets, using the imagination to grapple with truths. When we're delighted with what's in our imagination, we should turn to God and say, "I'm grateful that you're like that."

The intended use of the imagination is to view the world as God sees it.

Our culture uses the imagination for entertainment and for creating untrue stories. But the Bible has greater uses for that gift of God. The intended use of the imagination is to view the world as God sees it.

Becoming What God Intended

The Hebrew word for imagination, *yetser*, illustrates what we do in the mind. It is related to the word *yotser*, which is a potter, a person who forms things out of clay. The word for imagination is simply the things formed in our own mind, and what we form in our own mind is like a work of a potter.

Our imagination is one of the several abilities we are supposed to use for meditating. We are not supposed to meditate abstractly, but to actively create images. These images should describe this great and good God in a way that is true to the Biblical text, and in a way that fires our emotions. When we find an image that we really enjoy, we should play it over and over in our mind and connect it with God. We need to make sure it is Biblically accurate, and then use it to feed our heart. Then in the midst of a positive emotional response, we turn to God and say, "I'm glad you're like that."

This is important particularly if a person comes from an abused background. Already we have an image of what a father is like. That's why the word father has no positive meaning for many people. So we have to be kind to ourselves, and take the Scriptural picture of God as a Father, and recreate some positive images in our hearts. Many say, "I have a flat response to God as a Father." The reason for it is background. Sometimes all the images our imagination has are negative. The way we minister to our own heart is to meditate using our imagination and to create pictures.

Often adults who have had troubles while growing up don't realize they can change the powerful and controlling pictures from the past. Having walked out of their families of origin, they carry with them a family picture album, not under their arm, but in their heart. The pictures of conflict and disappointment often dominate the adult life. That can be changed. As adults, many times we don't realize we can open the album, choose a harmful picture and consciously choose to cover the negative image with a powerful new picture of God as a Father, Christ as a brother, and the Trinity as our new family.

A pastor, who is a dear friend of mine, told me a story. He met with a lady who had been sexually abused by her dad. He was trying to communicate to her that God was her father. She responded as people normally do in that situation saying, "The word 'father' just repulses me." My friend said to the lady, "Do you have any memories or images of adults who have treated you well?" Looking my pastor friend in the face, she said, "I don't have any recollection of an adult treating me well while I was growing up." Now frankly, that is sad, but it isn't unusual. For a lot of hurt people, life has been a jungle.

My pastor friend went on to describe, through Scripture, what this good God was like. An hour passed as he did that. The lady did not react. Leaving his office, she sadly drove through town, through the suburbs. As she slowly drove along, she saw a dad helping a young daughter, about 4 or 5 years old, learning how to ride a bike. As the dad helped the daughter learn, she looked at him, watched the scene, and thought to herself, "That's what God wants to do for me. He wants to help me to learn the simple things. He will keep me safe as I learn them." She pulled over to the curb, her head falling against the steering wheel, and she sobbed. Now the truth of Scripture had a meaningful image. When the truth comes with a poetic image, it comes with power. That's why the Bible was not written like a geometry book. Images fill the pages that feed the imagination. One of the things we can do for ourselves is when we hear that God is a Father, we must flesh out that meaning by taking images that are meaningful to us and then relate them to God.

The images of God as a Father will help us with the crisis the prayer in Matthew 6 creates. The Lord's Prayer is written in such a way that we have a crisis on our hands; we have an issue on our hands. If we take very seriously the phrase, "Our Father, the One in Heaven," the way the New Testament takes it, where the Father is the ultimate and intended Father for every human being, then we're not supposed to call any person on earth our father. No one else is the ultimate source of our reality, the definer of our relationships. The Heavenly Father has that position. Realizing and living that truth is the crisis.

"Often adults who have had troubles while growing up don't realize they can change the powerful and controlling pictures from the past."

How is this explanation of prayer different than your own understanding?

Take a few minutes and create two pictures in your imagination illustrating what kind of Father God is to you.

READING 2 - THE ISSUE OF THE FATHER'S WILL

The second crisis is created when we honestly turn to God as a Father and we say to him, "Let your Name be sanctified." The word 'Name' refers to the character, works, and reputation of God as a Father. Then we say, "Let your kingly authority come." In Scripture, the word 'kingdom' really should be translated 'kingly authority.' That gives deeper meaning to the word 'kingdom.' In the ancient world, when a person thought kingdom, he thought king.

In our world, when we think kingdom, we think of England with a queen, but the queen has no power. In the ancient world, they took the issue seriously.

When a kingdom was mentioned, the first thing they said was, "Who is the king?" So when we turn to God the Father and say, "Let your kingdom come," what we're really saying in the context of the ancient world is, "Let your kingly authority reign over us." We are also saying to God, "Let your authority as a ruler come as in heaven also upon earth."

This is the second issue, the second crisis: our willingness to accept His desire for our lives. After we say He's a good father, the very next issue is His desire for His children. We turn to Him and say, "May your desire for our lives, and for the people around us, and for our church, come to be. As your desire is fulfilled in heaven, may it be fulfilled in our lives." That's an issue—that's a crisis. As believers, we need to sort that out in prayer. As a normal part of our day, we need to turn to God and say, "What you desire for me, let it come to be, specifically and generally, may it come to be."

Now that may take some emotional energy. But please remember that we're dealing with a Father who has given His Son on our behalf. Nothing about His will ever ultimately hurts. His will only heals, bringing character and joy. Nothing about the Father's will should instill anxiety. Now Satan will tell us that the Father's will is harmful because he is desperately trying to assassinate the character of God. Nothing is wrong with the Father's will.

To see the positive elements of His will, let's take a look at how it works. Look at Matthew 11, and notice what Jesus has to say about following Him and also about knowing God. In Matthew 11, Jesus Christ had to deal with the Pharisees. He had to deal with those who were putting religious weights on the people of God. In verses 28-30, Jesus described what it means to have a relationship to Him and a relationship to God through Him. Notice what He said:

Come to me, every one of you who is continually worn down by religious labor and weighed down by religious obligations. -Matthew 11:28

In the context, religion is what he is talking about. The Pharisees placed religious obligations and religious labors on people. Turning to the people He said in effect, "Come to me. If you're worn out by religion, try Christianity."

If our Christianity has worn us out, we may have the wrong brand. That's not the religion of our Savior, Jesus Christ, and not the religion of God the Father. It's fake; it's false. Why? Let's look at this.

> "Now Satan will tell us that the Father's will is harmful because he is desperately trying to assassinate the character of God. Nothing is wrong with the Father's will.

And I shall cause refreshment for you. -Matthew 11

He shall refresh us, and He shall relax us. The word is *anapouso*. *Anapouso* means to become relaxed, refreshed. The word "pause" is derived from it. Knowing Jesus as He really is should be refreshing to the spirit, a relaxing experience.

W̶e must evaluate our own emotional life.
If our Christianity is harried, hurried and harmful, it's not Christianity.

Some form of religious Pharisaism has overtaken us. Knowing Jesus actually relaxes the heart. **Anything else is a substitute, and we can tell it's a substitute by the emotional effect. If it wears us out emotionally, it's not biblical Christianity.** With biblical Christianity, one can be cast down and not destroyed. Introducing drudgery was not the reason God died on the cross. Let's continue reading at verse 29:

Take my yoke upon yourselves.

Now among the Pharisees, a follower of a Rabbi would say, "I am taking Rabbi So and So's yoke upon me. I am putting myself under his yoke." Using the language of a Rabbi, Jesus said to the assembled crowd:

Come to me and take my yoke upon yourselves and be discipled by me.

Why should we be discipled by Jesus and come to him? Jesus said, "Because I am mild." The Greek word is *prous*, which means easy-going. I am looking forward to heaven because I want to see the response of some of my friends. I've become convinced over a period of studying the Word that God is actually easy going. I know to some that sounds blasphemous. The idea that He's actually easy going is very biblical. I base it on this word *prous*, meaning an emotional mildness and an easy-going spirit. If God said, "I'll separate your sins as far as the east is from the west from you," He can't be a legalist. With such an approach to life, it would be hard for God to be a legalist, a hard-nosed rule-keeper. If He says that He's not going to treat us like kids when we act like children, and He's not going to treat us like slaves when we want to be enslaved, He's got to be a lot more easy-going than we think He is. One of the great joys of Heaven is going to be watching some believers who are presently very scared of God. Watching them run into the God of the Bible in Heaven will be a pleasure.

When they get to Heaven, they won't even recognize Him because of His smile. He'll want to comfort them; He won't be judgmental, or hard-nosed. He'll be reasonable, kind, and gracious, and He'll be thrilled to see them. Some of them are going to say, "This can't be heaven, because God is nice." Notice what it says, *"Take my yoke upon yourselves and be discipled by me, because I am mild and humble of heart."*

Can you imagine the Son, God Himself, looking at you and saying, "Hang around me. I'm humble. I'm just God. You'll be discipled by me and you'll be refreshed. You'll be able to relax because I'm humble of heart."

B̶iblical humility is knowing who we are, being satisfied with who we are, and having no need to impose ourselves on others to feel good about ourselves.

God is depicted in the Bible as humble. Heaven is going to be an absolute delight and a wonder. To watch perfect character displayed in a person, and to think to oneself, "God is humble, God is easy-going. He is not at all like the preachers described Him." Heaven is not a bleeding ulcer. Heaven is a kind, emotionally involved, absolutely Holy God. Holiness in scripture is not poisonous. A holy God is simply a gracious person who maintains His own character as He shows forth his kindness to others. So we are to:

. . . take my yoke upon yourselves and be discipled by me because I am meek and humble of heart and you shall find a refreshment for your souls, for your emotional life.

Growing up, I played a lot of baseball, and two kinds of coaches existed. The first were bad coaches who yelled and screamed and scared the players. So when I went up to bat, I'd be so clenched up and so nervous I couldn't hit anything. I was filled with fear. The other kind of coach was one who knew how to get the best out of people by relaxing them. The first type was much more common then the second.

> *"Emotionally, every one of us has to sort out daily if we really want what God wants for us."*

The secret to holiness is a relaxed heart. God wants to relax our hearts. The will of God should not be frightening. Properly understood, God's will is the best news we'll ever find. He will not begrudge us a second's happiness. He wants us to have far more in this life than we'll ever imagine, beyond what we ask or think. Notice what else He says, Matthew 11:30:

For my yoke is kindly, and my burden is light.

His yoke is kindness and His burden is easy to bear. The second spiritual issue deals with the will of God while the first issue deals with the person of God. Emotionally, every one of us has to sort out daily if we really want what God wants for us. What God wants for us is the best. Now this is upsetting to people who are involved in habitual wrongdoing, in incorrect relationships, drugs, greed, or other such things. Their whole body has become accustomed and habituated to behaviors that induce almost a drugged-like behavior on their part, so God's will is frightening. Their deliverance is embracing what they are afraid of - God's will.

What must be remembered is that His yoke is kindly. John is very straight forward as he tells us about the will of God in 1 John 5:3.

For this is the agape love that belongs to God that we should keep His commandments.

Properly loving God is to recognize that His way is best. And it is! He's not the devil, He's our Father. A proper love of God is to keep His commandments. Notice the rest of verse 3:

... and His commandments are not heavy, are not difficult.

That's critically important. Satan wants us to believe that God's will is hurtful. Early on in the Christian life, we don't know enough about the will of God to be anything else but suspicious. But the way we deal with those suspicions is to remember that He gave on our behalf the person of Jesus Christ. He is the only one who will be loyal to us through all of eternity.

If you want to have the Spirit of God powerfully minister in your inner life, begin to grapple with the will of God in the particulars and in the generalities of your life. Trust Him, love Him, sort it out, and the Spirit of God will powerfully minister to you. The person of the Spirit of God gives the character, the freedom, the joy, and the satisfaction to do His will. So the second issue is the will of God the Father.

What are some of the things that keep people from wanting what God wants for them?

Are there areas of God's will for your life that frighten you? Take a few moments now to list them:

Pray about the list and trust God with each of the items. Write down your experience.

READING 3 - THE ISSUE OF OUR NEEDS

The third issue regarding prayer is our needs. When the order of the Lord's Prayer is examined, something striking is noticeable: before we get to our needs, we've got to take care of our relationship to God as a Father. The Lord's Prayer starts out with the Father as a person, it then addresses His will, and then right after that it deals with our needs. After dealing with our needs and who we are, it continues by addressing our relationships and it concludes by explaining Satan's role, which is to confuse us. The order is quite systematic. The pivotal part is our relationship to God as a Father and His desire for our life. When we deal with Him, we can go on to our own needs. But each of these is an issue, and each one determines what we're going to do with the next one. If I have not come to the conclusion that God is a good Father, how can I cope with His will? If I don't have #1 straightened out, #2 is difficult. If I don't have #2 straightened out, about His will for my life, #3 is going to be hard as I begin to talk about my needs. If I don't trust His will, I'm not going to share my needs confidently with Him. You cannot get to #3 until #2 is taken care of, and #2 won't be dealt with until #1 is addressed.

This is why this is called issues-oriented prayer. Time is not the important reality, but the issues that we grapple with are. If we seriously grapple with these issues, the Spirit of God will be unleashed in our lives. In these five issues, the Spirit of God will generate character as we take these issues seriously. So the second issue is His settled desire for our day and our life. The third issue is our needs, and notice how it is said in the most simple way in Matthew 6.

The cheapest thing to buy in the ancient world was bread. Loaves were a most common commodity. Food was a basic need, but it was easy to get. Bread, in my mind, is used to represent all of the needs that we have. Notice verse 11:

The bread, the one of our existence, give to us today. -Matthew 6:11

This teaches that prayer is supposed to be daily. If I'm supposed to say to God, "Give me my daily bread," how then do I pray? I pray day by day. Prayer is something that should go on day by day, and it should be built around God as a Father, His will, and then the needs that involve that day, from the simplest slice of bread, to the great issues of life.

That loaf of daily bread illustrates, first of all, that prayer should be a daily affair involving the needs of the day, both physical and emotional. For instance, anxiety represents an emotional need. That's a daily-bread issue. If an anxiety occurs during the day, that anxiety should be viewed as a friendly green light saying to you, "You need to pray and trust God about this." Use anxiety like leverage to remind you to pray. Don't be afraid of anxiety; it's perfectly normal. It's a gift from God. He wired everyone with a little bit of anxiety. Anxiety should not push us around, but anxiety should be used to drive us to God the Father to sort out what we're worried about. We must go to the Father, let Him know everything we're worried about, make specific requests, thank Him that He's bigger than the problem, genuinely trust Him, and then allow peace to settle into our hearts.

> "Anxiety should not push us around, but anxiety should be used to drive us to God the Father to sort out what we're worried about."

The only limit set on prayer is the principle of praying until we are peaceful. That could take 30 seconds or that could take two months. But either way, that is the principle that determines the length of effective prayer. We pray until we're peaceful. If we are building our prayer life around a watch, we should throw away the watch and use the spiritual quality of peace as the determiner of spiritually effective prayer.

We need to remember Philippians 4:6-7:

Don't be anxious for anything, but in relationship to everything, by prayer and supplication, let your specific requests be made known unto God with thanksgiving. And then the peace of God that passes all understanding shall guard your hearts and minds like a garrison guards a city, through Christ Jesus.

The peace of God tells us if we've effectively prayed. In the whole Old Testament and the whole New Testament, there is no emphasis on the amount of time put into prayer. The emphasis is on issues, not on time. We pray until we are peaceful.

Anxiety is a daily-bread problem. Anger is a daily-bread problem. If we're ticked off at somebody and it's eating at us, we should pray to God about it, sort out our emotions, and go tell the truth to the person we're angry with. We should not become Christ-like liars, but we need to tell the truth to that person if it's going to help that person to grow. Usually it does, but we must also minister to our own emotions. Anger is a daily-bread issue. Or if we're running on shame and guilt, that's a daily-bread issue. That should be sorted out with God as a Father. We should minister to our own emotions by applying Hebrews 10:22 that roughly says, "Purify your hearts from the evil conscience. Have the fullness of feeling that comes from faith. Don't add anything to the work of Jesus Christ. But instead, allow the blood of Jesus Christ to be the only thing we stand on in our relationship to the Living God." That is a daily-bread issue. Biblically and psychologically, our negative emotional states should be part of the sum and substance of our prayer life.

If we have no affection for people or no joy within, that absence of emotional feeling is a spiritual issue, a daily-bread issue, and that should be sorted out with the Lord on a daily basis. Shame, guilt, anger, lack of feeling, anxiety, emotional issues or physical issues are daily-bread issues. The simple stuff is important to God because our concerns are important to Him. If it causes anxiety in your life, it causes emotional concern in the heart of God. Remember, Peter says,

> *"If God knows when a pigeon is hungry in the park, is He not far more concerned about you?"*

"Cast your cares upon Him, for it is a concern to Him about you." -1 Peter 5:7

Some may be concerned that we are over-humanizing God. We are not humanizing God, God is humanizing us. We're made in His image, and if it is a concern to us, or provokes anxiety in us, it's an emotional issue to Him. He's a good father. If we have children, don't we want our children to share their fears? If our child is scared, wouldn't we want our child to run to us? Wouldn't we want our child to open his or her heart to us? Absolutely we do. Well, we're evil, I'm evil, and I have that motivation for my kids, so how much more should God want that from us?

The third issue is simply our needs, both physical and emotional. That loaf of bread represents the simplest of needs. Christ is using a Rabbinical device called **kal wahomer** or 'light and heavy.' Many believe that was the most common Rabbinic teaching device. The Rabbi would examine something insignificant, such as bread in this case, so as to recognize a truth about truly significant things, all our important concerns. The bread is something unimportant, but he's using the bread to represent all of the issues of life that are important to us. Christ uses the same technique when He says (Matthew 6:25-27), God knows when a pigeon is hungry in the park. If God knows when a pigeon is hungry in the park, is He not far more concerned about you? Christ goes from something unimportant to the vastly important. He continued to say, "*If God has so clothed the lilies of the field, will He not be concerned about our clothing?*"(Matthew 6:30) So the concerns and anxieties of our lives are spiritual issues.

How can grappling with these issues of prayer release the Spirit of God in your life?

Are there issues in your life that overwhelm you? Take a few moments now to list your anxieties:

Share them with God, and trust Him with them. Thank Him that He is greater than these threats. Ask Him specifically what you want Him to do with those threats. Pray until you are peaceful. Write down your experience.

READING 4 - THE ISSUE OF OUR RELATIONSHIPS

Now let's go to the fourth issue. We transition from our needs to our relationships. In Matthew 6:12, God is concerned about our relationships. If we want to have a powerful spiritual life, we have to sort out our relationships in prayer. In verse 12, we say to God:

And forgive us our unmet obligations.

Now that sounds like a good deal. I don't begrudge God if He takes away my unmet obligations. Now notice the phrase following:

As also we have forgiven the obligations of those who are obligated to us. -Matthew 6:12

Remember this prayer is written in such a way that it creates a crisis. Christ phrased it that way to scare us. He phrased it that way to drive something home. If we are children of God (which means we are breathing in the air of forgiveness), after having been forgiven by God the Father, we turn to a brother or sister and say, "I won't forgive you; you've not met your obligations to me," we anger God. If He has forgiven us, we must share the same with others.

A while back, a couple of friends of mine did some hurtful things to me. Nothing is as hurtful as being betrayed by friends. How I proceeded was to work through the five issues in the Lord's Prayer. Every time I got to this fourth issue, I practically choked on it. The emotions in my heart were so deeply hurt and resentful, it would just tear me up. The emotions of resentment and anger were so strong within me, that I was no longer rational. In fact, that's what a few friends said to me, "David, you've hit the irrational level about this." I even assured them that I had. So day by day, I faced this issue. I talked to God about how I felt. A month passed before I was actually peaceful.

Finally I was able to turn to God and say, "I am at the point where I can honestly say to you, my Father, that their unmet obligations to me are gone. I accept the pain they caused. I will no longer dwell on it. Their unmet obligations are forgiven." That felt good. It's not easy, but prayer involves issues. Not time, issues. It may take a month of time, it may take six months of time, but don't allow these issues to be skirted. Don't worry about the time it requires, be concerned about the issues. God's concern over our relationships is that we don't go around saying to others, "I don't forgive you your trespass." The word in Greek is actually an unmet obligation. Those unmet obligations are the only things that Christ commented on in this prayer. In verse 14 He says:

And if you forgive men their trespasses (unmet obligations)*, your Father in heaven will also forgive you. And if you do not forgive men, neither will your Father, the one in heaven, forgive your trespasses* (unmet obligations)*. -Matthew 6:14*

How does this work? Normally sins that people commit in churches do not blow churches apart. It's when Christians say to one another, "That person should have done this . . . and those people should be more spiritual . . . and those people should give more money . . . and those people should give more time . . . and those other people should be more friendly . . . and those people should invite me home . . . and this other group should be more gracious." Everybody's going around talking about what the other one should do. It would be easier if they just sinned against each other. Resentment will fill the church when Christians go around saying, "Oh, let me tell you about another unmet obligation. This church has not met that need, and they should have." What rips a church apart are people who are preoccupied with what other people should have done.

We should notice that the Lord's Prayer is different in Matthew and Luke. In Matthew, the word "debts" is used, in Luke, it's "sins." **We can do wrong two different ways: by not doing what we ought, and by choosing to do wrong.** In Matthew, Christ emphasized **unmet obligations**. He said, that forgiving others their unmet obligations is a spiritual issue. Life is so simple when we decide to forgive others their unmet obligations. The heart, the head, and the relationships are cleaned up. Then we won't go around being bitterly disappointed with people.

List as many unresolved and hurtful relationships as you can think of, particularly those in which individuals have disappointed you. Be honest!

Now in prayer accept the pain they have caused you, and send away the obligations and resentment you have towards them. Do that because of the cross. Write down your experience.

Does it matter whether or not you feel like forgiving someone their unmet obligations? What should you do if you don't feel like forgiving them?

READING 5 - THE ISSUE OF SATANIC ATTACK

The fifth issue is Satan. Notice what it says, we turn to God and we say:

And don't you allow us to enter into a trial, but rescue us from the evil one. -Matthew 6:13

Now we say this to God and not to Satan, because God controls the universe including Satan's doings. The first issue is God the Father, the second issue is His will. After we sort those two out, we can approach our own needs, which is the third issue. After we sort our own needs out, then we sort our relationships out. We make sure we do not have a chip on our shoulder because of the unmet obligations of other people. Now after we sort all of those four things out, guess who's going to come by and try to goof it all up? Satan's going to come by and say, "God is just like your old man, and you can't trust God's will for you; it'll hurt you. You can't trust this God's motives just because He gave His Son for you." And then he'll say, "And in fact you have some needs, and you know as well as I do the only way you're going to get your needs fulfilled is to worry about them. If you don't worry, you won't do anything." He'll come along and say, "You have no right to forgive that other person. The longer you rub that other person's nose in their wrongdoing, the more they'll learn their lesson. Rub their nose in it some more, so they'll grow up spiritually, confront them, insult them, provoke them to a fight." That's what Satan does. So the fifth thing that we have to avoid is getting sucked into something spiritually stupid because of a thought that Satan has put in our head that will negate the other four issues. If we are careful about doing this, we will be empowered by the Spirit of God to live in a world of relationships.

> "What rips a church apart are people who are preoccupied with what other people should have done."

The last issue is to ask God not to be led into temptation. Literally we ask to be rescued from the evil one. This means that God is sovereign over the plots of Satan. We can quite legitimately talk through any problems that we are having with Satan with the Lord, and we can be rescued. Now there are four areas in which Satan will attack.

He will try to convince us that God's ways are similar to our family of origin. He will try to convince us, as he tried to convince Eve, that God's will is not good.

He'll try and convince us that God has no interest in our needs whatsoever. And He'll try to convince us not to be forgiving. So we need to be careful to keep from being talked into or out of something by the evil one.

Becoming What God Intended

Why do you think that Jesus makes Satan the fifth issue of daily prayer?

How do we know when Satan is trying to convince us that God is not going to take care of us or meet our needs? What is Satan's primary goal for us?

How can we negate Satan's lies?

SUMMARY OF CHAPTER 10
With the Father, we sort out these five issues, based on the acceptance we have in Jesus Christ. As we sort out these five issues, the fruit of the Spirit will powerfully work in our life. We will be led along by a disposition that is characteristic of the person of Christ, we will be able to minister to our own deficits and we will be able to take individual steps into the spiritual life.

TO REVIEW:

What are one or two key insights you've been challenged with this week?

Take a moment to pray and thank the Lord for what He has taught you this week.
Lord, I am thankful for:

11 | ACCEPTANCE & SIN

CHAPTER SUMMARY: We will explore how we are to deal with the effects of sin, and the acts of sin in our lives. Sin effects us internally and it effects the Trinity. When we sin, the Father, Son, and Holy Spirit each respond differently to us. This makes confession of wrongdoing critically important in our lives. When we confess our wrongdoing, God the Father restores His hand of blessing, the Son ceases the judgment of child training or discipline, and the Spirit begins anew the process of character formation.

READING 1 - TRANSPARENCY WITH THE FATHER

Throughout the previous week, have you used the Lord's Prayer as a pattern to work through the five issues that were introduced? Great, you really should do that. Make it a daily exercise to enter into the presence of the Father and walk through the five issues. The concern is not about time, but about the issues of the heart. If we face these issues honestly, and if we look to God as a kind Father who wants the best for us, the first issue will lead us to aggressively address the others. What should happen over a period of days and weeks as the pattern is followed is a shift in the emotions. We'll grow from viewing God either negatively or neutrally, to viewing God positively as our Father.

As we continue to develop our friendship with the Father, we must come to a clear understanding of the effects of sin and the need for transparent honesty before God. In the Christian life, we must be honest with Him concerning sin within.

Probably the most concise and compact section in Scripture on how God relates to sin in the Christian's life is 1 John 1-2. Turn to 1 John, chapter 1. This chapter deals with the relationship between God and sin in the Christian's life. The chapter needs to be carefully understood. The text assumes that with sin comes weakness. Sin is not simply a choice between right and wrong; sin is far more similar to an illness, a disease, a weakness. Sinners are incorrigibly weak. That's exactly what Romans 5:6 says:

For while we were morally weak, at the strategic season Christ died for the ungodly.

Becoming What God Intended

As a result of that weakness, we find ourselves continually sinning. Solving the moral challenge involves more than the simple approach of black and white morality and right and wrong choices.

> The only way out of that weakness is to get to know a Father who helps. Part of the Father's way to help, is for us to be honest concerning sin.

And this is the message which you have heard from him, and we are continually announcing to you: that God the Father is like light, and not a bit of moral darkness is in Him. -1 John 1:5:

The verse is not saying that God is a light bulb. God is qualitatively like light. Everything about Him is open and seen. Nothing is hidden, shameful, or defective. His person is glorious, and open to sight. Everything about Him is glaringly clear; He is the quality of light. Darkness is not in Him at all. Building on the image of light, John says that part of God's will for us is a radical openness about who we are and what's going on inside of us, and in our relationships. Since God is totally open, so should His children be.

In the ancient world and for John and Paul, anything that makes visible and manifest is "light." Do not think of a photon flying through space, but instead light is anything manifest. God is absolutely out in the open (Eph. 5:13-14). We are called to be open about ourselves.

There are three false beliefs that often keep a Christian from being transparent. In 1 John 1, the three false beliefs or sayings (1:6, 8, 10) begin with the phrase, "If we say." We don't say these things out loud to other believers, but we do say them to ourselves. In the Bible the phrase "I or we think" does not appear. Instead, the phrases 'saying' or 'speaking' are used when the Bible refers to what drives our thought life. In one sense, what we think is reflected in our life.

Notice the first thing we say to ourselves when we begin the spiral of sinning:

*If we should be saying that we are having **koinonia** (to have things in common) with Him, and in the darkness we are conducting ourselves in the world (not being open and honest), we are lying and we are not doing the truth. -1 John 1:6*

Truth in scripture is not some abstraction of biblical doctrines. Truth is life as God sees it. Truth is life as it is. If we are saying to ourselves that we have things in common with God, and we're walking around with splotches of darkness all over us, we are not living the truth. Truth is looking at life as God sees it. Let's continue reading:

But if we should be walking in the light as He is in the light, we have things in common with one another. -1 John 1:7

Notice verse 7 carefully: if we are being honest with God, we are trusting Him, and being open with Him, then we are walking in the light as He is in the light and we are having fellowship with each other. We have things in common, and the blood of Jesus His Son is continually cleansing us from every variety of sin. If we live in the light with God, we're not going to be sinless and perfect. The text presumes we are going to have sin. God is perfect in the light, but we're not. As we're being open and honest with Him about who we are, the blood of Jesus the Son will cleanse us from every variety of sin.

> *"Scripture assumes that at our most spiritual, best moments, we are semi-failures. Isn't that wonderfully realistic?"*

The Structure of the Three False Sayings

The three false beliefs and the one true confession are placed in a pattern in 1 John. These false beliefs that occupy a person when he or she is in a spiral of sinning are spread throughout the first chapter of 1 John in the following way:

I. We can fellowship with God and darkness (verse 6).

II. We don't have the weakening principle of sin within (verse 8).

  Confession: But the true Confession brings cleansing (verse 9).

III. An act of sin does not cause present effects.

Note how the three false beliefs we repeat to ourselves are all nullified by one true confession.

We can have the most honest conversation with God we've ever had in our life, and we will still be influenced by sin, we will still have deficiencies in knowledge, and we will still have weakness in relationships.

If we're honest and open with Him, the blood of Jesus Christ will continue to cleanse us, so we can remain in the presence of God, the true place of healing.

Scripture assumes that at our most spiritual, best moments, we are semi-failures. Isn't that wonderfully realistic? If we don't think that's wonderful, we're obviously under the age of 18, or under the age of 25 maybe, and at best naive. Wonderfully enough, the God of Heaven and earth turns to us and says, "Just be open with me, be honest with me, view the world as I view it, and view yourself as I view you." Be open and honest and live in the light, and as we make our life manifest to God, all our weaknesses will continually be cleansed away. Every variety of sin will be cleansed away.

This is wonderful, because it doesn't allow us to delude ourselves into thinking we are religiously perfect. Instead, all we have to do is be scripturally honest and share ourselves with Him.

God is completely open with us; everything about Him is seen. Does He call us to be like this just with Him or with others too?

What are some areas of weakness in your life, both personally, and in your relationships with others?

Share the weaknesses with God the Father, and thank Him that He is willing to work with you as you are, not as you would like to be.

READING 2 - THE THREE FALSE BELIEFS

Let's continue reading (1 John 1:7),

So if in the light we are walking, as He Himself is in the light, we are having things in common with each other when we're open and honest, and the blood of Jesus His Son continually cleanses us.

Now John is the one New Testament writer who consistently draws upon images from the Old Testament. A word like 'cleanse' means to be "religiously acceptable." If a person were cleansed in the Old Testament, it simply meant that he or she could go into the Temple. They were acceptable in the presence of God. John is using the same kind of language. If we're open with God, we'll be acceptable in a relationship with Him.

As we said previously, there are three false beliefs or sayings that set individuals up to be captured by sin. The first false belief is that we can walk in darkness and still have fellowship with God. God calls us to be open and transparent, not to hide or ignore our sin. The second false belief that captures people's minds is that we do not have the weakening sin principle within. Many people latch onto this false belief in order to maintain wrongdoing in their lives. Verse 8 addresses this false belief:

Becoming What God Intended

If we should say that we don't have sin, it's not an influence in us, we are deceiving ourselves, and the truth is not among us. -1 John 1:8

Now remember, don't use the definition of sin as simply a choice between right and wrong. Sin is not that simple. Sin is an emotional climate of moods that produces desires for a quick fix of wrongdoing. Wrongdoing is very similar to an illness incapacitating our will.

This is where many pastors make a profound mistake. When someone walks into the office to admit he or she has a problem, many pastors will say that it's a simple choice between right and wrong. The confessor may nod the head agreeably but within are the questions, "Why am I so weak? Why am I such a failure? Why do I want to run and hide? Why is this thing driving me nuts, if it's just a simple choice between right and wrong?" It is not. Sin is not simply right and wrong.

Paul, in Romans chapter 7, says sin is wholly deceptive. It is captivating, it is confusing, it leads to addictive relationships, and it's far more complex than simple right or wrong decisions. If sin is just a choice, then why do we get so confused?

Verse 1:8 ends with the phrase, " . . . and the truth is not among us." In the text the truth relates to the Bible's insights concerning sin. According to John the apostle, truth does not refer to endless mounds of biblical content regarding sin; rather the truth is the reality of sin within. Within us is the principle of independence generating moods and strong desires to do wrong things, which leads to the death of relationships.

The first two sayings or false beliefs dealt with God and with sin. The first false belief maintained that a believer could dwell in the darkness and fellowship with God, and the second said that we can live without the presence of sin in our lives. Both are equally false. In reality, we are left in tension. We are imperfect as we live our lives out in the presence of a perfect God.

The third false belief alleges that a believer can sin and no effect will occur in the life. When we examine verse 10 we have to be aware of a difference between the language of the Bible, Greek, and the language of today. Verse 10 introduces something that in Greek works differently than in English. Greek has several different ways of expressing time relationships, or tenses, from English. The biblical language has what is called a perfect tense. If we wanted to say that the Titanic sunk and it's still sunk, a perfect tense would be used. Having been sunk in the past, the ship remains today still covered by water. The action in the past has an effect in the present. Perfects can be created in English, but often we do not notice them. The third false belief or saying in 1 John 1:10 is a Greek perfect. The translation should read:

If we should say that we have sinned in the past without any present effect, we are making God a liar and His word concerning this is not among us.

All around us we can find thousands of examples of this mentality. For example, what often happens when an adulterer is confronted within a couple of weeks or months of an affair, is that he says, "What I did really doesn't matter. It doesn't matter to my wife or to me. The kids aren't affected all that much. Yeah, you could call it sin, but it doesn't have any present damage. Everyone will get over it. My wife's better off without me." I can remember walking through a park with a fellow who was involved in adultery. Frankly I said to him, "Do you think this will cause any long-term damage to you or your kids or your wife?" The man simply said, "No." This is similar to a person at ground zero after a nuclear bomb blast saying, "What damage ?"

> "Sin is not simply right and wrong. Paul, in Romans chapter 7, says sin is wholly deceptive. It is captivating, it is confusing, it leads to addictive relationships, and it's far more complex than simple right or wrong decisions."

When we adopt this third false belief, we deny God's view of the damaging effects of wrongdoing. Sin causes self-damage, relational damage, and long-term damage if it's not acknowledged and dealt with. All kinds of things occur when we sin. Things happen in our relationships on earth, and with each member of the Trinity. Sin will affect our relationship to the Father, to the Son, and to the Holy Spirit, and bring about effects in our earthly relationships with one another, and with ourselves.

What happens in a relationship when sin is either ignored or denied?

From your own experience, list three examples in your life where the damage caused by sin was ignored and denied.

1.

2.

3.

How is my relationship with God affected when I choose to ignore or deny the sin in my life?

READING 3 - THE HONEST CONFESSION

What delivers us from the confusion of these three false beliefs and cleanses us so we can live in a healthy way in God's presence, is an honest confession. I rearranged 1 John slightly so that the three false beliefs would stand out, and the antidote-confession would be even clearer. The second false belief concerns the presence of sin within, and the third refers to acts of sin in verse 10. The antidote to all is the confession that we must make:

If we should confess our sins, He is faithful and righteous in order that He should send away (to send away as an issue with the Father and the Son) *our sins, and to cleanse us from every aspect of unrighteousness. -John 1:9*

He is faithful and righteous because Christ has already died for those sins. God is absolutely right in forgiving sin because Christ's life was spilled out for them. He's consistent and faithful, because He will always take very seriously what Christ has already done. He's righteous because if He did not accept the fact that Christ has already died for that sin, He would cheat His Son.

The word for confess simply means "acknowledge." The word, "Confess" is used by John the Baptist in the Gospel of John in this way. John the Baptist saw Jesus coming towards him. As Jesus came into sight, he said to the Pharisees (John 1:20),

"I confess, I deny not, I confess that I am not the Christ."

What does the word confession mean? It means simple acknowledgment.

Confession doesn't mean to have an uncontrollable fear of God. Nor does it mean crying a lot. Confession simply means to say the hardest thing an adult can utter, "I did this."

These are the hardest words to say in the human language—to acknowledge that we have damaged somebody. Is it an easy thing to admit that we've lied? That we've misrepresented, that we have used people and hurt people? Is turning to God and saying, "I did it," an easy thing to do? No. I think "I did it," are the hardest words in life to say to one another and to God. The person who believes that a simple confession of sin to remove guilt is getting off cheaply, greatly misunderstands the concept of confession. The hardest words in life are to say, "Yes, I lied. Yes, I committed adultery. Yes, I committed fornication. Yes, I stole. Yes, I gossiped. Yes, I lost my temper and said bitter things."

Being honest with ourselves and with God is one of the hardest things to do in life.

Acknowledgment is not feeling bad, it isn't crying. It is simply saying, "Yes, I am weak and wretched and I produced that act of wrongdoing." It is simple admission. If I acknowledge my very specific acts of wrongdoing and my actions that have damaged other people, God is completely faithful, consistent, and just to forgive, because Christ has already died for these sins.

Scripture is very sophisticated because the Bible recognizes that breaking out of denial or facing reality is one of the most difficult duties. Counselors know that a major victory has been obtained when a counselee honestly faces his or her wrongdoing. Our responsibility is to get up the nerve to say, "Yes, I did it." Then God's responsibility is to say, "You've been honest with me. I'll send away that sin as an issue between you and myself in our personal relationship. Secondly, I'll clean you up from every aspect of your wrongdoing so that we can freely fellowship and you can be free to do what is right." He makes us acceptable in the face of all kinds of evil. Verse 8 first stated the principle of sin within. Verse 9 says we're supposed to openly acknowledge our wrongdoing, our sins.

> "Now remember, don't use the definition of sin as simply a choice between right and wrong. Sin is not that simple. Sin is an emotional climate of moods that produces desires for a quick fix of wrongdoing."

In 1 John 1:1-10, John has given a clear view of sin. He has told us this: sin is a principle within that produces acts without. Coming with every variety of unrighteousness, an act of sin, if it's not confessed, will always leave a present effect upon us, upon others, and upon God.

We're supposed to be living out in the light, so when we do something wrong, we turn to God and we say, "I've done it." We must get into the habit of doing it quickly. Instead of being a chain smoker, so to speak, where we light one sin off of another, we must deal with each individual sin as it occurs. The goal is to quickly turn to God and acknowledge it to Him.

When we look at 1 John 1:5-10, a question may arise. The question in our minds may be, "Well if sin is such an issue, will it affect my salvation?" This is where 1 John 2:1-2 is extremely helpful. **God looks at sin in a profoundly different way than we look at it.** We can all do ourselves a great favor to view every sin as being joined to the blood of Jesus Christ. God does not view any sin as naked, bare, and separate from the blood of Jesus Christ. Any sin that He deals with, any sin that is an issue, has already been joined to the blood of Christ and He is already satisfied concerning that sin. 1 John 2:1-2 makes that truth clear. These verses contain a parenthetical comment that enables us to understand why God is faithful and just to forgive us, or send away, these acts of sin as issues between us and a loving Father. 1 John 2:1-2 shows us God's attitude and perspective.

Unfortunately, a chapter division occurs here, giving the impression that verse 2:1 introduces a new subject. These verses are not introducing a new subject, but they are explaining God's incredibly generous forgiveness in 1 John 1:1-10. Remember the verses that follow 1:5-10:

> *My children, these things I am writing to you in order that you should not sin, and if anyone might sin, we have a helper personally facing the Father. -1 John 2:1*

Remember something about sin: sin is a weak, vicious, nasty choice. So when we have made a weak, vicious, nasty choice, we have a helper with the Father. If we pretend that our sins are not weak, vicious and nasty, we won't qualify for help because we're minimizing what we have done. "Harmless little sins," don't need any help. If we have weak, vicious, and nasty sins that harm other people and ourselves, then we have a helper, Jesus Christ the righteous, our *paraclete*, or helper who faces the Father.

> "Acknowledgment is not feeling bad, it isn't crying. It is simply saying, "Yes, I am weak and wretched and I produced that act of wrongdoing." It is simple admission."

Notice what we're told about Christ:

And He Himself is the propitiation or satisfaction concerning our sins, and not for ours only, but also for the entire world. -1 John 2:2

Propitiation is the Old Testament word for satisfaction or pleasure. The term is used for the place of propitiation on the Ark of the Covenant, the lid of the Ark that was made of gold. That lid where the blood was sprinkled represented the Lord Jesus Christ. The blood-covered slab of gold was the place of satisfaction. The whole purpose of that place was to make God the Father satisfied concerning sin.

If we say the word "sin" to God, He'll say, "satisfaction." We say, "How can you be satisfied?" He will say, "My Son died for that particular sin. I'm satisfied, are you?" His Son is the satisfaction.

One of the horrible realities within our churches is that a lot of preachers act as if Christ hasn't even died yet. Their proclamation is something like this: "Sin is terrible, no good, and nasty; it sends people to hell. People better not sin." Well, that's not the Gospel! The Gospel is that the God-Man Jesus, God Himself, died for sins. God saw His Son die for those sins and He said, "The issue of sin is settled, I'm satisfied." Now people have to decide what to do with the Son and what to do with God as a Father. Those are the only issues to be settled. The issue of sin has been settled.

What we should be proclaiming to the non-Christian is the Son— what are you going to do with the Son who has already died for your sins?

Such a statement radically changes the message. No longer is it a question of guilt; it's a question of ingratitude.

If God should choose to pay the bills and die for us, what are we going to do with Him? The issue for the non-believer is, "What are you going to do with the Son who already died for your guilt, and has opened the way to Heaven?" The issue for the believer is, "Are we going to continue living in the shadows, separating ourselves from a good Father and not acknowledging our problems to Him?" That's the issue for all of us as His children.

For the nonbeliever and for the believer, Christ is the satisfaction. John 1:29 illustrates this:

The next day, he (John the Baptist) *sees Jesus coming to him. He says repeatedly, "Behold the Lamb of God, the One carrying away the sin of the world."*

This occurred in the wilderness. The language John used is very similar to what's in the Old Testament. Leviticus 16:20-22 describes Yom Kippur - the Day of Atonement. Once a year on that day, all of the iniquity or guilt of Israel was atoned for, or covered. A goat was killed in Jerusalem, and another goat had all of the guilt of Israel pronounced over its head while the High Priest held it. Then, the goat was handed over to a man who led the living animal out into the wilderness where it was set free. The sacrificed goat was supposed to represent Christ's death on the cross, and the other living goat represented His carrying away the sins of the entire world. Like our sins, that living goat just went off into the wilderness and disappeared.

> "We can all do ourselves a great favor to view every sin as being joined to the blood of Jesus Christ. God does not view any sin as naked, bare, and separate from the blood of Jesus Christ. Any sin that He deals with, any sin that is an issue, has already been joined to the blood of Christ and He is already satisfied concerning that sin."

Jesus Christ is God's answer for sin. For the non-Christian, the issue no longer is sin. The issue is what we are going to do with the Savior.

The issue for the believer is what we are going to do with God as a Father. Are we going to live in the shadows or be open with Him about our problems?

Becoming What God Intended

Jesus Christ is God's satisfaction. He bore sin away. That is why, going back to 1 John, God is faithful and just to send away our sins. We will have a healthy relationship if we live in the light and simply acknowledge what we've done wrong.

Now why do we confess our sins; in order to sustain our salvation? No, our helper Jesus Christ the righteous, is very good at saving us until the uttermost. He does a far better job than we could ever do, and we can have confidence in Him. He's the High Priest forever. That being the case, why do we confess sins? This is what happens when we sin—we step out of a relationship with God and over the line into darkness.

Confession of sins is a restoration of sanity. Have you ever heard the line that we confess our sins in order to restore fellowship? Actually, that's putting us on a much higher plateau than where we belong. When we sin and we're not open with God about it, we go into spiritual insanity, and He wants to restore our sanity.

What do you think spiritual insanity is? Why did the author choose this word to explain what happens when we don't confess our sins?

Why does sin affect our relationship with God and how does confession of sin restore that relationship?

Picture your sins-past, present, and future-as already being covered by the blood of Christ. How does that make you feel?

READING 4 - THE INSANITY OF SIN

When we sin as a Christian, here's what an act of sin does to us. Sin causes inward deception and madness. Look at Romans 7:11:

For sin, taking the opportunity through the commandment, totally deceived me, and through it, killed me.

These things are inward problems. When Paul the apostle wrote these words, he was very much alive. The death he spoke of was not physical, but spiritual. He ceased having a positive friendship with God. When we commit an act of sin, it kills our relationship with God, while totally deceiving us. Sin is inherently deceptive and very confusing. When people are caught up in a sinful lifestyle, usually they're horribly confused. The way out is to acknowledge that we've done wrong. Sin causes deception, madness, bondage, and lies (Romans 7:19-23). The worst bondage in the world is to be caught up in slavery to wrongdoing and to sin. Notice Romans 7:19:

> *"God teaches His children to restore their sanity by admitting the lies to Him. He keeps those issues of wrongdoing in front of our face. He is saying, All I want is honesty, not perfection."*

For the good which I am desiring, I am not doing, and the evil which I am not desiring, that I am practicing.

140

The previous contradictions are part of the enslavement. Paul argues that we need to be careful about wrongdoing because it spirals into slavery, or in modern terms, addictions. "One sin won't hurt," is a naive and risky attitude. Such naivete causes a death of relationship and ultimately physical death. So an act of wrongdoing brings internal consequences. We buy into the three false beliefs that are in I John 1 when we commit a sin. When we choose to do wrong, we have run to the shadows, hidden in the darkness, embraced our sin and damaged somebody else.

Confession restores sanity. It doesn't restore salvation, because we're in Christ, and the blood of Christ has already paid for us. In addition, God teaches His children to restore their sanity by admitting the lies to Him. He keeps those issues of wrongdoing in front of our face. He is saying, "All I want is honesty, not perfection. Come into the light and tell me the truth, and the blood of Jesus will cleanse us from every aspect of sin."

In reality, we embrace all three false beliefs in one act of sin. We say that it **doesn't affect God at all**. We can live this way and have things in common with Him. It **doesn't affect others at all**. We can live with one another and have things in common. And it **doesn't affect me at all**.

Why is honesty more important to God than perfection?

How does it make you feel about yourself?

READING 5 - THE TRINITY'S RESPONSE

Sin leads to specific responses from the three members of the Trinity. Romans 6:11 teaches that spiritual life and strength flow from the assumption that we are alive to God in Christ. Before I can choose to do something wrong, the first thing I have to do is act dead to God and alive to the moods and desires within. I have to break fellowship with God as a Father. I have to exclude Him from the situation, so I must render myself dead to Him by ignoring Him. Then, I can walk over to a land of shame and guilt and worthlessness. After ignoring Him, I won't have to do anything else but just stand around in a mood. In a minute or two, I'll end up doing the nasty wrong that I desire to do. Acting like a robot, I don't have to have a conscious thought. I just have to make sure I don't include God in my feeling and thinking.

The Son as our High Priest makes the sin an issue He deals with, and applies child training. Christ protects His own, and even if you don't confess your sins, you're protected, because you have a helper with the Father, Jesus Christ the Righteous. Though He makes the sin an issue, He is the High Priest who saves us to the uttermost.

Child training, God's discipline of His children, is developed in Scripture by both the apostles John and Paul. John develops the admission of sin in 1 John 1. The apostle Paul develops the same teaching, but he uses a different vocabulary. In John the term confession is used, while Paul uses the phrase, "examining ourselves so that we are not judged." 1 Corinthians 11 is where he wrote about confession. Verses 31-32 describe how it works:

> "The one person in the universe who will actually restore our spiritual sanity is God the Father. His presence is wonderfully restorative."

And if we should examine ourselves, we are not being judged. And when we are being judged by the Lord, we are being trained as children in order that we should not be condemned with the world.

Becoming What God Intended

Paul does not call the Lord's response condemnation. Instead, he calls the process child training. Only the children of God can be child trained. The purpose of our child training is to make sure that we're not condemned with the world. Verse 11:30 describes the progressive application of this process:

There have been in the church, on account of this, many among you sick and weak and a number have died. And if we should examine ourselves, . . .

How are we child trained? There are three steps to child training: weakness, sickness, and death. Christ would actually allow us to die? YES. Death is a most effective way to stop a person from sinning. Immediately following our death, whom do we face? The one person in the universe who will actually restore our spiritual sanity: God the Father. His presence is wonderfully restorative. On His right hand is God the Son who is our helper. He saves us to the uttermost. If we don't confess our sins, and they pile up as high as a mountain, God will let them bury us. For some, the burial might bring a sense of relief. Earlier I described walking through the park and talking to an adulterer. He also told me that he had picked out a spot to kill himself. Feeling tremendous pressure, he told me very honestly that it would be better to be dead. This is the same fellow who thought his sin did not affect anybody. He described how he was going to kill himself. He thought it would be better to be dead. Such is the level of pressure God will bring into our lives.

Christ judges us, and we're made weak, sick or taken home. Being taken home is the ultimate restoration. The biblical term to describe this is called the judgment of child training.

One can view this child training as a negative, but the Bible presents it in a most positive light. Hebrews 12:4-8 says the child of God has the privilege of having God the Father as a disciplinarian. The world does not experience the application of God's confronting judgments on His children. But the writer to the Hebrews says (12:9):

. . . how much better to be under subjection to the Father of Spirits and live.

The person who is without spanking is illegitimate (12:6), because any son the Father receives is spanked. This is done because He has *agape* love for us (Hebrews 12:6):

For those whom the Lord has agape love for He child trains or disciplines.

The third person of the Trinity has His own unique response. The Holy Spirit withholds spiritual fruit (Galatians 5:22-23), and He leaves the believer open to the devastating power of the works or habits of the flesh (Galatians 5:19-21). Each member of the Trinity applies pressure in a unique way. The Father withholds His blessings; the Son applies child training; the Holy Spirit does not allow the fruit of the Spirit to develop.

So why do we confess sin? Three reasons exist. Sin affects our relationship with the Father. Secondly, God the Son has to begin to work in our lives to shake us free of our insanity. Third, the Spirit of God quits producing love, joy, and peace, the freeing qualities of the Spirit. We're frozen in our problems, and it's our responsibility to turn to Him and say very simply, "I've done it." As soon as we've said that, He cleanses us, because we've come out into the light and made ourselves vulnerable. We've told Him the truth. We haven't straightened our thinking out; we've just admitted that we've done wrong. Then over the process of time, God as a good Father straightens our thoughts out. Our responsibility is essentially very simple: to acknowledge wrongdoing.

Part of God's desire for us is that we should be open and honest with Him. We should live in the light. In Paul's writing he described light this way: "Whatever makes manifest is light." In other words, light allows us to see and be seen. So walking in the light means we have an open heart and open relationship so that our strengths, characters, weaknesses and sin are all in the open with God the Father. In that way He can help us and we can grow in our walk with Him. God has called us to a rugged honesty about our weaknesses. He assures us that next to His right hand is Jesus Christ the Righteous, our helper. Jesus has already satisfied God concerning any sin we admit or confess. Confession of sin is the beginning step in a restoration of sanity and a restoration of relationship. It has dramatic effects.

Why does God only child-train children of God? How is child training different from condemnation?

Is death, as a result of sin, an act of judgment or mercy on God's part?

Confession

If you're not in a habit of confessing sins, just pull out a sheet of paper and write down the things that you know you've done wrong and you haven't yet admitted to God. Just admit them and get it over with. You'll feel a lot better, and you will have an honest conversation with God. Go through the list and tell Him. Then whenever you commit a sin, right after you commit it, tell Him, because Christ already died for it. It's not going to shock Him. It may embarrass you, but it's not going to shock God.

TO REVIEW:

What are one or two key insights you've been challenged with this week?

Take a moment to pray and thank the Lord for what He has taught you this week.
Lord, I am thankful for:

12 | ACCEPTANCE & SERVICE

CHAPTER SUMMARY: God the Father could not think of a greater or nobler role for His Son than to send Him on a mission of rescue. The Son was sent to serve, to suffer, to ascend to Heaven, and to be rewarded with His reign over the universe and the church. We too are called to participate in the family business of rescue, and to consciously choose to replicate Christ's ministry in our lives. As daughters and sons of God, we have been sent. We are to choose to serve and to suffer. We will ascend in the rapture, and be rewarded by participating in Christ's reign. God could not think of a greater or nobler role for us than to participate in Christ's life pattern. This life pattern gives overall meaning to our lives.

READING 1 - THE SON WAS SENT

Christian service is a great gift God gives His children. On the one hand, that He uses us, illustrates His acceptance, even though we are imperfect people. On the other hand, that He uses us deeply underscores our unity with His Son: we are invited to replicate His ministry. The invitation also reflects the unity of relationship at the heart of everything. We who have been invited into the circle of love predating time, now are asked to join in the great enterprise. Because the Father loves us deeply, He allows us to participate in the goal of Jesus' ministry, the redemption of mankind. He wills to give us the same great goal as He gave to His Son.

In the preceding chapters we have seen different ways God has joined us to the person and work of Christ. He has been identified with us, and we with Him. The key events of His life, the suffering on the cross, His death, the resurrection, and His departure to be with God in Heaven have been counted to be our experience from God the Father's perspective. One final area of identification exists, and this is the only one in which we can choose to participate or not.

> "Because the Father loves us deeply, He allows us to participate in the goal of Jesus' ministry, the redemption of mankind."

When we believed the Gospel, that Jesus died for us and rose again, God identified us with Christ regardless of our feelings or knowledge of such a reality. These things are true from God's side of it, no matter what we feel or think. But one area of identification remains where we have to consciously choose to participate.

A pattern exists in the ministry of Christ, and it starts with being a Son sent by God the Father. He did not send an angel, nor volunteer an Israelite king, but He sent His own Son on a mission from Heaven. Notice what Hebrews 1:1-3 says.

> *In many portions and in many manners, God had previously spoken of old to the Fathers by the prophets. In the last of these days, He spoke to us by a Son. Whom He has placed as the heir of all. Through whom also He made the ages. Who being the outshining of His glory, and the exact representation of His nature, is bearing everything along by a few words based on His inherent power . . . -Hebrews 1:1-3*

This passage argues powerfully for the deity of Jesus Christ. Look at it again carefully. Jesus, the passage states, is the outshining of God's glory, and the detailed, exact representation of God's nature. When the sun shines, does any difference exist between the outshining of the sun and the sun itself? Jesus could not be called the exact representation of God's nature without being able to match Him attribute for attribute. If one is not deity, matching deity is very hard.

Omniscience, knowing everything, omnipresence, being present everywhere, and omnipotence, being infinitely powerful, is either practiced with the ease of the divine or it is impossible in the attempt. *Hupastasios*, the Greek word for nature, is the sustaining structure or nature of a being. This verse says Christ is the exact representation of what sustains God.

My son is unpredictably different than I am, but he has a human nature, a human will, and a human intellect. The fact that he is my son establishes his nature as human. Since Christ is the exact representation of that which sustains God himself, His nature as deity is established. As a Son He shares a common nature with His Father.

This passage also says that Jesus carries everything along by a short utterance. God the Son walked into the emptiness of space and said, "Be and go." Suddenly a universe appeared. Since the beginning of time, His few words have sustained all. How many individuals can create and sustain a universe with three words? The thought implies unusual, if not divine, ability.

> *"We have a God who died for His creation. We do not have an archangel who was volunteered to be a "patsy" for Heaven's sake."*

The passage in Hebrews 1:1-4 continues:

> *Also while bearing everything along by a short utterance from His power, after having made a cleansing concerning sins, He sat down by the right hand of the greatness in the heavens.*

What a combination - the One who bears the entire universe along by a short utterance of power, died for that universe. What a God! He could create everything, and then look at what He created and say, "What I have created is worth dying for." What a compliment to you! All of that creative energy proclaims, "What I made wasn't meaningless. My image marks humanity. I am the only One who knows its value." Because He knows your value, He was willing to die for you and establish your worth forever.

The Son Was Sent to Serve

We have seen who and what the Son is. God invested a Son in this mission of salvation. Now the next step in the pattern of His life was being sent.

Philippians 2:5-8 tells us Christ's perspective regarding His mission, and the perspective that we should have as well.

> *Have this common understanding going on among yourselves which was also in Christ Jesus, though He was in the external display of God continually, He did not assume equality with God something to be firmly held onto. But He emptied Himself of that external display [Just pouring it out on the ground of Golgotha], while taking the external display of a slave. -Philippians 2:5-8*

Becoming What God Intended

Morphae, the Greek term for external display, refers to what is visible and seen. Jesus was visible in heaven as deity. His was the external display of deity. He displayed Himself as divine. Anything God the Father could do, He could imitate. Being the exact representation of the nature of deity, He did not desperately hold on to His equality with God. He willingly exchanged the external display of deity for the service of a slave!

What a contrast! The message should fill the Church. Should not that message penetrate our hearts? The glory of Christianity is that God the Son, who was displaying himself openly as deity in Heaven, looked at that display and thought, "Sinful human beings are worth much more than this display. I'll take their place and become a slave." We have a God who died for His creation. We do not have an archangel who was volunteered to be a "patsy" for Heaven's plan. Jesus didn't hesitate. We were more important to Him than the glory of deity. That is what we are worth to Him. He did not do this to prove a point; He did this to ransom persons. He set aside His glory as casually as we turn off a light as we leave one room to enter another.

Other religions may claim to have wise teachers; they may posture with pride over the greatness of their deities. Christianity rises above them all. Christianity is the only movement and religion that has a noble God. Other so called gods invest nothing in their creation. The Bible claims that at the heart of everything is God's good heart; at the center of all is a God who died for us. The question for the non-Christian is: does he or she want to exist in a Universe with a God who already has suffered in their place?

Think of your daily life for a moment as being on God's servant team. What kind of role have you been playing on Jesus' behalf?

How does what we think or feel affect the different ways in which we are identified with Christ?

READING 2 - THE SON WAS SENT TO SUFFER

Jesus was a Son who was sent on a mission. This mission was one of suffering service. Mark 10:45 says:

For the Son of Man did not come to be served, but to serve, and to give his soul (His life) *a ransom in place of the many.*

Christ invited suffering into His own soul, so that He could present that suffering as a satisfaction to God. In the context of Isaiah 53 and Romans 5, the suffering was for those who would be rescued by His blood, and who would accept His friendship. His service led directly to the cross. As the baby Jesus laid in the manger, the shadow of the cross was already falling across the infant.

Let's continue with Philippians 2:7:

But He emptied Himself, while taking the external display of a slave, being in the likeness of men, and as far as external characteristics are concerned being found as a man, He humbled Himself, becoming obedient unto death, the death of the cross.

Remember the image. Here is the external display of deity. He looks at YOU and says, "This glory is not as important to me as you." Then He steps out of heaven onto the earth to take on the form of a slave. He lives out the life of a man. Then he becomes obedient to death on a cross. You were more important to him than the pain.

The Son Was Rewarded

Notice the result of Jesus' sacrifice in verse 9:

Wherefore also God highly exalted and freely gave to Him the Name or reputation which is above every reputation.

Since Jesus freely set aside His majesty to die on the cross, God the Father gave Him the greatest reputation in the universe. No one has ever done or will ever do the same.

Since the Son has acted so nobly, the Father wants the teeming life of the Universe to acknowledge who the Son is and what He has done. Philippians 2:10 reveals to us the Father's intention:

In relationship to the Name of Jesus, every knee shall bow in the upper heavens, upon earth and under the earth.

Sooner or later, those in Hell, those on the earth, and those who fill the heavens will have to kneel before Christ, acknowledging who He is and the beauty of what He has done. Every non-Christian will have to acknowledge what he or she was worth to God before being sent into outer darkness.

"No greater destiny is possible for a mature daughter or son than to participate in the life and ministry of the first-born Son."

God's Pattern For His Son

Notice the pattern. God sent His Son, His Son served, God's Son suffered, and then after His resurrection, the Son ascended. After His ascension, He was rewarded. God established the pattern for His Son. For you and me He has chosen the same. He could not think of a greater destiny for us than to participate in the life and ministry of Jesus Christ today. No greater destiny is possible for a mature daughter or son than to participate in the life and ministry of the first-born Son.

Have you ever wondered why you have been left on earth? For the same reason God sent Jesus to the earth; to serve, to suffer, and to ascend. Through our adoption as the people of God, we have received a noble charter.

Jesus Shared the Pattern

Note what Jesus Christ did after His resurrection and before His ascension as recorded in John 20:21. He passed on to His disciples the same privilege that He was given, to fulfill the grand purposes of God:

Jesus said to them again, 'Peace to all of you. Even as the Father has commissioned me, also I myself am commissioning you.' -John 20:21

In this same context He breathed on them and told them to receive the Holy Spirit. Also He shared with them the message of forgiveness of sins for others. His life pattern now belonged to them.

What are your feelings about following Christ's life pattern? Excited, apprehensive, motivated, scared? Explain your response.

READING 3 - OUR CHOICE

Our Decision: To Maturely Participate

To participate in Jesus' life and ministry is a great and unique responsibility. Just as the sending of Christ was a non-repeatable event, so this sending of those who trusted in Christ is something that never occurred before.

God did something unique for believers, a privilege Israel did not experience. Paul tells us that God treated the nation of Israel like a young child, who was placed under a guardian or administrator until he reached adulthood. In Galatians 3:23, Paul, referring to the Jews, says:

Before the coming of the faith, we were being kept under guard by the Law.

This is a very interesting image. The Greek verb "guard" means to guard like a garrison. A Greek guardian had two purposes: to keep danger away, and to keep his ward safe. The ward was not in prison but in protective custody, so to speak. The young person was protected, but with no freedom.

Paul says that under the Law a person is in protective custody under an administrator and guardian, or child guide. One responsibility of this guide was to safely take the child to his teacher. Galatians 3:24 explains to us who the law is supposed to lead the child to:

So the Law is a child guide until Christ should come, in order that out of faith we should be made right.

Notice this beautiful image. The Law is taking the nation of Israel by the hand. Every time the nation of Israel slows down, the Law pulls them along, and when they finally get to the teacher, Jesus, the Law breathes a sigh of relief and says, "Here he is, you can teach him now."

Paul's image of the believer is not the ***napios***, the protected child between the ages of one and ten. Paul's image of the believer is the mature son who doesn't need the child guide, who is going to have a relationship of affection and principle with His Father. He is going to participate in the family business. What is the family business? It is all about participating in the life of Jesus Christ and replicating His ministry. Let's look at Galatians 3:25-26.

Faith having come, no longer are we under a child guide, for everyone of you are mature sons through faith in Christ Jesus, (describing the quality of relationship we have) *for whosoever among you were baptized into Christ, have been clothed with Christ. There is neither Jew nor Greek. There is neither slave nor free. There is neither male nor female. For you are all one person in Christ Jesus -Galatians 3:25-26*

We are placed into Christ so that God could relate to us as mature sons. We are not little kids to be patronized and protected. But God says, "I am going to place them in my Son. We will have a relationship of principle and affection. I will ask them to participate in the life of the Son."

No greater privilege could God give a creature in the universe than to participate in the life of the Son. No greater privilege can He give than to identify us with and immerse us completely into Jesus Christ. He did not do this for Israel. Why? Israel had a rulebook; we have the Son of God. Anyone who trusts in Christ is allowed to participate in His life, is placed in Him as a mature daughter or son, and is allowed to participate as an adult.

Why do we have this privilege? God counts us as mature sons because we have believed in His Son. We have looked beyond His humanity, we have looked beyond His enslavement, and we have seen the Son. Because we have seen the Son clothed in human flesh and crucified on the cross, God has turned to us and said, "The rest of the world is blind to Him. Because you have seen Him, I will allow you to participate in His life."

Explain the difference between a protected child who needs a guide, and the mature son, who doesn't. How does their relationship with God differ?

Do you think of yourself as a mature daughter or son of God? Why or why not?

READING 4 - OUR MATURE MISSION

The ability to see the Son as He really is, is the greatest compliment you can pay to God. Correctly perceiving Jesus brings the greatest joy to the Father imaginable. Christ was sent to a world that recognized Him not. His own received him not. As John 1:12 states:

But to those who received Him, He gave the authority to become the offspring of God.

By simple recognition of who He is, we are allowed to participate in His mission. Notice how Galatians 4:4 affirms our adult son placement.

So when the fullness of time came, God sent His mature Son, being begotten out of a woman, having come under the Law, in order that He might buy out those who are under the Law, in order that we should receive adult son placement. -Galatians 4:4

Adult son placement defines the quality of relationship that God wants from us. We may act like kids, but He wants us to respond like adult sons and daughters. We are told not to respond like smothered kids who are over-protected, who are scared of the dark. Nor are we to respond like slaves, who need to be beaten to move, but we are to respond like mature adult daughters and sons. We may act like kids, but He defines the kind of relationship He wants to have with us. He says, "I want a principled, affectionate relationship." We reply, "I can't believe that. Give me a rulebook, beat me and let me act like a kid, but don't expect me to respond with affection and principle." He will not manipulate us, or beat us, or patronize us. He waits for us. We may spend decades foolishly running around, driven by guilt, acting childishly, but He will wait. He has all eternity.

Our Decision: To Maturely Serve

On the one hand, we like Christ have been sent to serve, but on the other hand, our responsibility is not only to make the decision to do so, but also to bring a servant's heart to the mission. The difference between a slave and a person in a principled relationship surfaces right at this point. The slave need only bring his body, but the person who has entered a principled and affectionate relationship has to bring a grateful and appreciative spirit. Gratitude is present because we appreciate that the Son of God became a slave for our benefit.

Becoming What God Intended

We need to have a healthy attitude because we have been the recipients of so much kindness. Go back to Philippians 2:1.

If, and it is true, there is any encouragement in Christ, if there is any tender speaking (tender encouragement) *which comes from agape love, if there is any partnership with the Spirit, if there is any deep emotional responses and tender mercies . . . -Philippians 2:1*

Paul is defining what is involved in *agape* love. The symptoms of *agape* love are emotional involvement and delight in other people. Tender encouragement in Christ and fellowship of the Spirit flows out of love. This is how God has loved us. He is tender, merciful and emotionally involved. He speaks to us in a most intimate and encouraging way. Notice verse 2:

Fulfill my joy in order that you have the same perspective. Have the same love continually. Be one souled - the same perspective have. -Philippians 2:2

Paul is not telling believers to think the same thing, for that is mentally impossible. No two believers on the face of the earth will ever completely agree, unless their brains are deceased. But every believer can have the same perspective. Jesus Christ did not hold on to the external manifestation of His glory, but He simply let go of it and like a slave, seized the cross as a man and died. The apostle says to us three times, "Have the same perspective. Have the same perspective. Have the same perspective." Letting go of our rights, we accept service so we can participate in the perspective and mission of Jesus Christ.

> "The greatest obstruction to service is asserting our own rights. Our rights will always interfere with our sympathy."

We are to have this selfless attitude that Jesus Christ had. When we approach each other, we must not firmly hold our rights, but let go of them instead, in order to meet human need. The greatest obstruction to service is asserting our own rights. Our rights will always interfere with our sympathy.

No greater privilege exists than participating in the mission of Jesus Christ. That is the best thing that God could think of for His own Son. Now He is sharing it with His adopted sons and daughters.

Concern with rank, either in the family or in the church, is a sign of sickness. Being a leader means practicing Christ's kind of leadership: a leader exists for the benefit of others. A wife in the home is to emulate the greatness of Jesus Christ by being a significant helper to the husband. If God the Son did not stubbornly hold onto His glory, but let go of it, every Christian wife can be an imitator of Jesus Christ. The privilege is to choose to serve and be a significant helper. Every leader must recognize that he is not to lead as the Gentiles lead, but to lead as Christ led, by being willing to die for those he is leading. Our understanding of both leadership and service has been revolutionized by Christ.

Our Choice: To Embrace Suffering

> "Every leader must recognize that he is not to lead as the Gentiles lead, but to lead as Christ led, by being willing to die for those he is leading."

Because of Christ's life, even the nature of suffering is changed. Biblical Christianity is not afraid of suffering. The Son of God suffered. Nothing is intrinsically wrong with suffering, if responded to properly. Philippians 3:8 is uniquely stated in Greek. It starts out with four transitional words: "But therefore then indeed." It sounds odd in English and reads odd in Greek. Why does Paul do this? Based on what Christ has done, he has a big point to make. He piles up the transitional words because they act as a great bridge to the grand conclusion. He says:

But therefore then indeed also I count everything to be loss on account of the excellence of the personal knowledge of Christ Jesus my Lord, through whom I have suffered the loss of everything. And I count it but skubala (Greek) *so that I may gain Christ. -Philippians 3:8*

<u>*Skubala*</u> is what is left at the bottom of the garbage can after it is emptied, or what is picked up in the backyard after the dog has done his business, or what is left after the plates are cleaned off.

CHAPTER 12 | **Acceptance** & Service

How could Paul say this? Because it is true. If God Himself chose to die for us, everything selfish or considered significant by this culture is as important as trash. If He sent someone inferior, then its significance is lessened greatly. Since His equal, His Son, embraced the cross for us, then everything we call important is reduced to little. GOD died for us! He became human, a slave, for us. Paul said:

> *I count it to be skubala in order that I might gain Christ, the experience of being conformed to Christ, and be found in relationship to Him, not having my own righteousness, the one out of the Law, but the one through the faith of Christ, the out-of-God righteousness based upon faith. And to know Him, to personally know Him and the power of His resurrection and the fellowship of His sufferings, continually being conformed to His death... (Philippians 3:8b-10)*

Is there any greater privilege in life than to suffer for a loyal friend? Consciously choosing suffering is the right response, because what is involved is deeper than the issue of suffering.

Have you ever chosen to suffer for another's best interest? How did you feel about it afterwards?

What are some rights you may need to relinquish in order to have the same perspective as Christ?

READING 5 - OUR CHOICE: SUFFERING & REWARD

We have the privilege of being loved by a wondrous God. Scripture assumes that His love is deeper than pain. Our world doesn't understand this, but love goes deeper than pain. Take unhappy, unfulfilled, guilt-ridden people, put them in pain, and it will kill them.

> Take a happy person who is delighting in people and who consciously chooses suffering for somebody else's good, and it will ennoble her or him. The same amount of pain will finish some, and be a deepening experience for the other.

What makes the difference? Picture Jesus Christ in the Upper Room. His disciples did not have their feet washed. Jesus, ever conscious of who he was and where He was going, got up, took off his outer garment, tied a large towel about his waist, and washed their feet. We, as believers, knowing who we are and where we are going, can do the same. We have the privilege of participating in the sufferings of life in the same way Jesus Christ suffered. Scripture does not have a problem with pain if it is embraced in a healthy way for the benefit of others. Paul says that one of the most profound experiences in life is to participate in the life experience and the sufferings of Jesus Christ.

At one point in my ministry, some of my very close friends disappointed me deeply. I was confused and crushed for months. A year passed before the experience was sorted out. I could not understand what they were doing. From my own perspective I thought, "My friends are betraying me." During those days, pain racked through me.

"No greater privilege occurs in this life than to experience, even on a small scale, the nobility of the life of Christ."

Becoming What God Intended

I was seated in church on Easter Sunday, flipping through the Gospels, when I read a passage describing Christ telling his disciples that He was about to die. Ignoring their friend's approaching death, immediately the disciples were concerned about who was going to get His job. When I read that, I realized, that was exactly what happened to me. But my response was completely opposite of Christ's. I was hurt and confused and stymied, but His response to disappointment was to continue loving His disciples.

Before that time, I hadn't realized that experience was an opportunity to participate in the life of Christ. Previously I had failed because I became preoccupied with my own pain. After that recognition, I reoriented myself to respond with love, as Jesus did, to the privilege of participating in Christ's life.

No greater privilege occurs in this life than to experience, even on a small scale, the nobility of the life of Christ.

Why are we here? We are called to be a participant, to minister in Jesus' stead. God sent His only Son to earth as the most loving and best thing He could do for us and for Him. Now He allows us to have the privilege of entering His ministry: we are sent to serve, and to suffer.

Our Future: To Reign With Him

Christ's mission came to its completion by His resurrection and ascension into Heaven. In Heaven He was rewarded by being made the Head of the Church and head of the Universe. God the Father gave Him the Name or reputation above all else.

"In the Bible, spiritual responsibility is not given to the clever and well informed. Responsibility is given to those who love Christ and choose to serve, and who love others enough to suffer for them."

Even as God rewarded Christ in Heaven, He opens the same opportunity to us. We are challenged to replicate Christ's ministry. If we do, the significance of that decision will carry on into Heaven itself. For those who have chosen to suffer with Him, will reign with Him. Paul reminded his associate Timothy of this.

If we endure, we shall also reign with Him. -2 Timothy 2:12

When we trust in Christ, God makes our future secure (2 Tim. 2:13). Our part in the future reign is optional. Our place in reigning is dependent upon our choice of serving and suffering for Jesus. Paul took for granted the possibility of reigning with Christ, and He wanted Christians to assume the coming reality of this kingdom. To the Corinthian Christians he wrote:

I want you to reign as kings so that we might reign with you. -1 Corinthians 4:8

Jesus very straightforwardly gave the same as a promise in Revelation 3:21:

He who is overcoming, I will grant to her or him to sit with me on my throne to share my authority, as I also overcame and sat down with my Father to share His authority.

In the Bible, spiritual responsibility is not given to the clever and well informed. Responsibility is given to those who love Christ and choose to serve, and who love others enough to suffer for them. Humanly speaking, we have learned in this world not to trust the promises of the politician, nor to trust the descriptions of their credentials. Who can we trust? We can trust those who have served faithfully and suffered nobly. We can trust Christ with our interests because He died for us.

So how can we look at this life as Christians? In a true sense we are tying up our running shoes for eternity. The real race begins with being ushered into Christ's presence. The reward is to share in His reign.

Our Christian life is a preparation. Now we are making the decisions, accepting the roles, and sharing the suffering that will determine what we will be doing for endless years of time.

What we do does matter not only in this life but in the one to come. In writing to the Corinthians, Paul explained to them that what they built on the spiritual foundation of Jesus Christ does have importance. Christians can either invest significant efforts or little energy at all. Illustrating the point, Paul used the building materials of the ancient world. The cheapest building materials were wood, hay, and straw. The most valuable were gold, silver, and precious stone:

> *For no person can lay a foundation other than the one which is laid, which is Jesus Christ. Now if any person builds upon the foundation with gold, silver, precious stones, wood, hay, straw, each person's work will become evident for the day will show it . . . -1 Corinthians 3:11-13a*

Work done with diligence and care, as represented in the gold, silver, and precious stone, will receive a wage (1 Cor. 3:14). The one who has his or her efforts rejected, as represented in wood, hay, and stubble, will still be saved, but without a reward (1 Cor. 3:15).

The wage is glorious and will be borne throughout eternity. When the Bible describes something as glorious, not only is the miraculous involved, but an element of appropriateness and thoughtfulness exists also. For example, during the ministry of Christ, the disciples noticed a man who was born blind. They wanted to know why. The answer Christ gave them was that the blindness would work out for the glory of God. Then, the man's blindness was healed (John 9). The glorious miracle was appropriate and thoughtful. Blindness was overwhelmed by sight.

W hatever is sacrificed for Jesus, if God approves, will be forever transmuted or strikingly changed into something thoughtfully and appropriately glorious.

If you forgo advancement in your secular job in order to minister in your church, God may advance you over many in His kingdom. If we choose to suffer physically in His cause, the Lord may give special abilities in harmony with the sacrifice. The recipient will have the joyous privilege of using those abilities throughout eternity.

The God of infinite imagination spectacularly filled the earth and the Heavens with wondrous forms of life and beauty. Certainly He will express more power and thought when He rewards those who have been faithful to His Son.

We should never look at death as the end of our lives. In our thinking and planning, we should extend our lives into the thousands of years of the future. This will give great importance to the time we have on earth. Every second, every effort, every sacrifice carries with it eternal implications.

In your thinking and planning, have you extended your life thousands of years into the future? Have you invested significant efforts or little energy into your future?

Is there some way that God has been asking you to suffer? Does this reading today change your perspective?

What excites you most when thinking about your future in heaven?

SUMMARY OF CHAPTER 12

Out of the heart of the Trinity, the Son was sent on an awesome mission. On behalf of the world of people that He created, He came to serve and die. Out of deep appreciation for what He did, the Father raised Him from the dead and rewarded Him. His life created a noble pattern of suffering and reward.

The children of God, the sisters and brothers of Jesus, are called to copy His life pattern. We are called to a mature and affectionate response of gratitude. Christ's reward, reigning over all, carries into eternity, so we are invited into the same prospect. In this way we are challenged to a worthy response. What will our response be?

TO REVIEW:

What are one or two key insights you've been challenged with this week?

What was most helpful and meaningful to you in your study of the *Becoming What God Intended* workbook?

Take a moment to pray and thank the Lord for what He has taught you during this study.
Lord, I am thankful for:

CONCLUSION:
FOR PERSONAL RENEWAL

Without the Trinity, the Christian life does not exist. With the Trinity we discover a breathtaking love streaming out of eternity, engulfing the sins of this world, and inviting those who will to enter a circle of love predating time. To live a vibrant life for Christ, the Christian needs to become a thoughtful and grateful participant in a grand history and wondrous plan.

The Son of God came as a voluntary servant to die for us. In His death, He satisfied the Father's sense of justice and provoked an overwhelming flood of love from the Father's heart. This love was channeled to us through His noble Son. Out of affection for His Son, He will make right anyone who believes in Jesus. Out of a desire, furthermore, to have many other daughters and sons like Christ, God becomes the Father of each believer.

As we relate to this Father with all of our life and heart, the Spirit of God will work to make us like Christ. The fruit of the Spirit, the deep emotional life and character of Jesus will reappear in us. Our challenge will be to make every aspect of our life a place where the life of Christ can be manifested. We are to arrange our life by Spiritual character and insight.

The suffering, death, resurrection, ascension, and present relationship of Christ to the Father are counted to be our own. Throughout eternity we will carry this glorious history with us. God the Father sees us eternally joined to Him. Since the Father perceives us that way, we are exhorted to make these realities the basis of our relationship with God. Our past, with its shame and guilt, and our present negative moods and wrong desires are to be set aside in the pursuit of a principled and affectionate relationship with God. Our family background, good, bad, or mediocre, is lost in the beauty of what Christ has done.

As we pursue our relationships above, certain issues have to be repeatedly sorted out. The Father's person and will, our needs, both small and great, relationships with others, and protection from Satan are all things that we must attend to. We are called to walk realistically with God. When we sin, He cleanses us from its effects as we are open and honest with Him.

One aspect of our identity with Christ we have to consciously choose; the other aspects are given as a gift. We must choose to pattern our life after His. When such a life is freely and lovingly chosen, only then does the pattern have meaning for today. He came to serve, suffer, and ascend to be rewarded. **We are invited to do the same.** We are called into this circle of love.

> Our role in the future is dependent upon many of the choices and efforts
> we make in time. Christ always guarantees our security and acceptance.

So therefore our lives can be an exploration of God's grace, and our efforts can be an expression of gratitude!

SMALL GROUP GUIDE

We welcome you to the use of this Small Group Guide. This is your opportunity to deepen your sense of having an Abba Father in Heaven, and to develop a greater sense of affection and delight from this Father. This is your opportunity to see yourself differently than you normally see yourself (but to see yourself in Christ), and finally to realize on the instinctive level that who you are matters more to God than what you do. Many tens of thousands have profoundly benefited from presentations of this material but more importantly they have been thrilled with how positively their relationship to the Trinity has been affected. The purpose of this guide is to supplement the Becoming What God Intended Workbook. The Becoming What God Intended Workbook is a discipleship study, a journal of your thoughts, and the foundation for the small group meetings.

Here are some questions that will help you to coordinate your group.

1. How is the workbook designed?

The workbook has twelve chapters with five readings each. The Group can structure their group in two ways:

5. **12-week format:** The group can review one chapter per week for each of the 12 chapters.

2. **60-week format:** The group can review one reading per week for each of the 60 readings.

2. Other than the workbook, do I need any other resources for the group?

We strongly encourage you to purchase the 13-videos series to be played at the beginning of your group. Much of the content in the video is not found within the workbook. Group participants have found the videos to further deepen their understanding and experience.

The Group Leader can purchase the video subscription and then play the video at the beginning of the meeting for the entire group. The group members can also purchase it on their own in order to watch the video again at their leisure. Visit **www.WhatGodIntended.org** for more information.

3. Should we read the workbook together?

No. Each person should read the workbook on their own and answer the questions throughout the chapter. Everyone is encouraged to spend time reading the material slowly and carefully and reflect on their responses to the questions.

The group will be discussing the answers to various questions, so be sure to remind group members to come prepared. The quality of your time together will be dependent on everyone's preparedness and participation.

4. Should the group only include Christians?

No. Each chapter begins with the word 'acceptance' and as it's premise, while we were yet sinners, God the Father is continuously recommending His love for us (Rom. 8:28). The workbook creates a solid foundation for which a new believer can grow into *What God Intended*.

5. How long are the group meetings?

We recommend that the groups meet between 1 to 1-1/2 hours

6. How many should be in a group?

Group size can vary and we recommend that the group be no more than seven in order to give everyone ample time to share. Group size will also have an impact on how long your group meets. We don't recommend going beyond 2 hours.

7. What if we have questions?

You may email DrEckman@bwgi.org or Webmail@bwgi.org or call us at 925-846-6264.

RESPONSIBILITIES FOR PROSPECTIVE FACILITATORS

Having a successful experience in the small group depends in large part on the facilitator's desire to love and minister to those in the group and willingness to follow through on all the responsibilities listed below.

ATTEND A TRAINING SESSION
- Develop your skills and understanding of what it will take to succeed
- Meet your on site ministry leader and BWGI contact person for help on difficult questions and issues

PRAY BEFORE EACH MEETING
- For each person in the group
- For the group's effective process and progress each time it meets
- For yourself – for wisdom and guidance of the Holy Spirit
- For your time to prepare and minister

DURING THE MEETING
- Be sensitive to group dynamics and the leading of the Holy Spirit

AFTER THE MEETING
- To follow up on issues that came up needing your care and support

PREPARE
- Do the lesson thoroughly; understand it completely
- Review the facilitator tips before the meeting

CONDUCT THE MEETING
- Arrive early to set up, pray and greet
- Start and end on time
- Reiterate Small Group Agreement
    - Confidentiality – help assure that this is a safe place
    - Completion of the lesson before the meeting
    - Encourage appropriate participation
- Keep each segment to the time allotted
    - But be sensitive to the needs of the group and the leading of the Holy Spirit
    - Stay on topic and minimize rabbit trails or tangents
    - Draw out the shy and curtail the one who tends to monopolize
- Participate as one of the members
    - Model transparency and sensitivity
    - Allow others to respond to questions

SMALL GROUP AGREEMENT
Ask everyone to read and sign.

In order to contribute to an atmosphere of acceptance and trust, I covenant with my group to do the following:
- I will keep all information shared within the group confidential.
- I will make an honest attempt to do the regular readings in Becoming What God Intended.
- I will make every effort to be at the meetings on time.
- I will work at being open about my thoughts and feelings.
- I will be encouraging.
- I will share any significant emotional or physical difficulties with the facilitator.
- I will be patient with group members and not press my opinions upon them.
- I will be willing to believe the best about God the Father.
- I will pray for the Spirit to open my eyes and the eyes of others to Christ's love for each of us.

Signed _____ Date_____

SMALL GROUP LEADER TIPS

1. Always participate in the discussion and activities. You are a part of the group and a fellow learner.

2. Have fun and relax. The Holy Spirit is guiding and convicting. Just enjoy the process of maturing in Christ.

3. It is a risk to share from the heart. Make the group a safe place by praising the efforts of group members.

4. Do not be afraid of silence. Group members may need time to think.

5. Encourage your group to be specific and personal by asking questions like: "Will you give us a specific example?" or "Tell us more."

6. To promote interactive discussion among members, after one person shares an insight, turn to another person and ask if he or she has anything to add to what was just said.

7. You are the model for appropriate sharing and transparency.

8. Not every person has to talk during a session. But if the same person is always silent, you may want to ask him/her something like: "I'm curious, Sue, what are you thinking?"

9. Keep the group safe by not allowing one person to monopolize all the discussion time on personal issues. If someone does talk too much, you can say something like: "Thanks for sharing, but I'm wondering what others might have to say."

10. It is possible that someone may share a traumatic experience from the past (sexual abuse, physical abuse, etc...). It is important that you do not ask any detailed questions about the incident. Simply, be present with the person and thank him/her for sharing so vulnerably. Call this person during the week, and pray for them at the close of the session.

11. If you do not get through all discussion questions, that is okay!! Keep the discussion on task, but allow the Holy Spirit to lead. Sometimes, one question may stimulate an in depth 45 minute discussion that is necessary for your particular group.

12. Show appreciation for the openness and vulnerability of group members by saying something like: "Thank you, for sharing your thoughts."

13. You are not the Bible answer man or the resident expert on every subject. If someone asks a question, and you have no idea how to respond, you can: throw it out to the group, or tell the group you will find the answer during the week.

14. Your job is not to convince anyone of anything. The Holy Spirit changes and convicts the hearts of people.

15. Remember to give advice only if asked - and even then - do so wisely and carefully. Allow people to have their opinions and struggle through their issues.

16. Most often than not people will be gracious and kind. However, if there is a disagreement during a session, do not allow the disagreement to last more than one or two minutes. Say something like: "I'd like to give everyone an opportunity to share, so let's move on to another question. Typically, if someone is going to change their opinion, they will do so one or two days after the initial disagreement. So, do not be concerned with everyone being in agreement, "on the spot."

STRUCTURE OF THE MEETINGS:

Every meeting should follow this agenda. In the "Facilitator Guides" section, you will have an agenda specific to each chapter.

1. (First meeting only) Read the Small Group Agreement on page 157 and ask everyone to agree and sign.

2. (Subsequent meetings) Remind the members of the Small Group Agreement

3. Open with a short prayer

4. Read or ask for a volunteer to read the Chapter Summary

5. Ask the questions listed on the Small Group Chapter Guide

6. End with prayer

SMALL GROUP GUIDES

Chapter 1: Acceptance & Gratitude

1. (First meeting only) Read the Small Group Agreement on page 157 and ask everyone to agree and sign.

2. Open with a short prayer

3. Read or ask for a volunteer to read the Chapter Summary:

"Families of origin are powerful forces that shape our lives. God wants to take us out of our family of origin and place us into His Family because He is the ultimate and intended Father of every person. But growth in the Christian life is directly related to how well we respond to God, the first member of the Trinity, as a Father. Obstacles to growth often arise from one's family background. The solution is to learn how to correctly participate in God's family as to experience an emotionally rich sense of being loved and to have a deep response of gratitude."

4. Have the group share their answers to the following questions which are found within the readings:

   a. (Page 12) "God as a Father is the pivotal person for our inner change and growth, and His family is the context for that change and growth." How did you answer the following question? Explain your answer.

   How does the idea that God wants to become your new father sound to you?
   ☐ **Very exciting. I would love it!**
   ☐ **Neutral, unsure at this time.**
   ☐ **Very intimidating.**
   ☐ **Very presumptuous. I already have a father, thank you.**

   b. (Page 15) What are some unhealthy rules from your family of origin that you try to apply to God's family?

   c. (Page 17) Can you think of someone who has great relational skills and really puts you at ease when you are around them? Share why this person stands out to you.

   d. (Page 19) Describe an example in your life when you were motivated to do something positive for someone in response to their love or concern for you.

5. End with prayer

Chapter 2: Acceptance & Worth

1. Remind the members of the Small Group Agreement (Page 157)

2. Open with a short prayer

3. Read or ask for a volunteer to read the Chapter Summary:
   "God is deeply and eternally affectionate; He wants us to grasp how much He values us. True self-worth comes from knowing how much God loves us. A Christian is worth a Son to God. The cross illustrates that at humanity's worst season and at the time of our moral weakness, Christ died for us. This shows that God values us for who we are to Him and not what we've done or can do for Him, either bad or good. Feeling worthwhile, feeling worth a Son to God, is an essential part of feeling loved."

4. Have the group share their answers to the following questions which are found within the readings:

   a. (Page 23) Who have you depended upon for your feelings of worth? Your parents' view, your spouse's view?

   b. (Page 23) What are some problems that arise from depending on these sources?

   c. (Page 26) Can you think of a time when you bought into "Batting Average Christianity"? How did you feel about yourself and why?

   d. (Page 30) In the "walk with God," God's expression is one of "total understanding marked by real compassion." How is this image of God different or similar to the previous picture of God in your mind?

5. End with prayer

Chapter 3: Acceptance & God the Father

1. Remind the members of the Small Group Agreement (Page 157)

2. Open with a short prayer

3. Read or ask for a volunteer to read the Chapter Summary:
   "The first member of the Trinity is our ultimate and intended Father. He is distinct from the Son and the Holy Spirit. Many times, we fuse our experiences with our earthly fathers, no matter how good or bad, with God the Father. It is important to separate the two and understand who our intended Father is. God has a deeply emotional attachment to us called "*agape* love," and we are to respond to such love with gratitude."

4. Have the group share their answers to the following questions which are found within the readings:

   a. (Page 35) Share your answer to this question and explain your answer. Reflecting on your own earthly father, select the box that would best describe him.

   ☐ My father was basically warm and loving ☐ My father was emotionally distant ☐ My father was a good dad but didn't know how to express himself ☐ My father was never around ☐ Other, describe your father:

   b. (Page 38) Why do you feel Jesus put such a high value on the role of the father?

   c. (Page 39) How does understanding His intention help us put our earthly father into a healthy perspective?

   d. (Page 41) What aspects of God's name, character, works, and reputation help you define a picture of Him? In picturing Him, what first comes to mind?

5. End with prayer

Chapter 4: Acceptance & The Son

1. Remind the members of the Small Group Agreement (Page 157)

2. Open with a short prayer

3. Read or ask for a volunteer to read the Chapter Summary:
   "Salvation is a Person and not a religious system. That person, Jesus, is dedicated to delivering us from our past failures and sin, giving us peace in the present and securing our future with Him. Our Father initiated a relationship with us by sending us Jesus; now it is up to us to respond. If we add our "religious works" on top of Christ's sacrificial death, it feeds our evil conscience. Christ and Christ alone must be allowed to save us and cleanse our evil conscience."

4. Have the group share their answers to the following questions which are found within the readings:

   a. (Page 50) What would it feel like to be totally forgiven of every past sin and failure?

   b. (Page 54) Share your response to this question and explain your answer. Do you ever feel that you need to do certain "Christian things" to feel acceptable to God? If so, check the following boxes that apply:

      ☐ I read my Bible on a regular basis ☐ I have daily prayer time ☐ I share my faith with others ☐ I tithe at church ☐ I (fill in the blank)

   c. (Page 55) How can you combat the "Christ Plus" mentality when your evil conscience is attacking you?

   d. (Page 57) We experience freedom and pleasure when we realize that Christ alone is our acceptance. Conversely, what emotions are prevalent in our lives when we operate off of a performance-based mentality?

5. End with prayer

Chapter 5: Acceptance & The Holy Spirit

1. Remind the members of the Small Group Agreement (Page 157)

2. Open with a short prayer

3. Read or ask for a volunteer to read the Chapter Summary:
   "The Holy Spirit is a permanent down-payment to us signifying God's intention to finish our salvation. Once we accept Christ, the Holy Spirit comes to live within us. The Holy Spirit also has a primary ministry of reminding us that God is our Heavenly Dad, and He wants to have a mature and affectionate relationship with us. We have the status of adult-sons and adult-daughters of God. Our relationship to Him is neither child-like nor slave-like. Instead, God has given us a principled relationship with Him based upon a bond of deep affection and ever-growing character on our part."

4. Have the group share their answers to the following questions which are found within the readings:

   a. (Page 61) Have you ever had someone promise you something and fail to follow through? A broken engagement? A business deal with a friend? A promised vacation with a loved one? How did you feel at the time and what effect did it have on your relationship with that person

   b. (Page 61) Share your response to this question and explain your answer. How did you respond when you read Ephesians 1:13-14, that says God has given you the person of the Holy Spirit as an irrevocable down payment guaranteeing you are His child for all eternity?

      ☐ Skeptical ☐ Thankful ☐ Blown away ☐ Indifferent ☐ Overwhelmed with gratitude

    c. (Page 68) Were fear and suspicion elements that were present in your family of origin? If so, how have they affected your relationships in the present?

    d. (Page 71) How can we respond to God as a mature son or daughter?

5. End with prayer

Chapter 6: Acceptance & Trust

1. Remind the members of the Small Group Agreement (Page 157)

2. Open with a short prayer

3. Read or ask for a volunteer to read the Chapter Summary:

    "Family background affects our understanding and application of concepts like TRUST. God's family runs on trust; trust is at the center of biblical Christianity. Trust is what makes us right with God, and faith brings the emotional power of the fruit of the Spirit into our lives. Each member of the Trinity has entrusted something to us: the Father has entrusted a principled-affectionate relationship to us, the Son has entrusted His work of taking the gospel to the world, and the Spirit has entrusted Himself to us. Now, we must respond with trust in order to actualize these relationships."

4. Have the group share their answers to the following questions which are found within the readings:

    a. (Page 73) Share your response to this question and explain your answer. How was trust exhibited (or not) in your family of origin?

    ❑ There was a high level of trust and respect.

    ❑ There was an occasional level of trust.

    ❑ Trust in our family meant "a lower level of suspicion."

    ❑ Other, explain briefly.

    b. (Page 74) What part does trust play in our relationship with God?

    c. (Page 78) What role does trust play in our righteousness?

    d. (Page 83) How does Biblical faith open up the unseen world?

5. End with prayer

Chapter 7: Acceptance & Our Identity

1. Remind the members of the Small Group Agreement (Page 157)

2. Open with a short prayer

3. Read or ask for a volunteer to read the Chapter Summary:

"A Christian shares the same quality of relationship that Jesus has with the Father. This is because we are identified with Christ by being placed in union with Him. Acceptance of this truth gives us the freedom to have an open and heart-warming relationship with the Father. Our relationship does not depend upon what we have done or how we view our past, but our personal friendship is based upon what Christ has done for us and our being viewed as joined to Him. Our new identity in Christ gives us the courage to deal with our past, allows us to experience a full range of rich emotions and gives us the power to overcome addictive habits and behavior."

4. Have the group share their answers to the following questions which are found within the readings

    a. (Page 87) Christ has come to cut us free from our families of origin, whether they were good or bad. What is your reaction to this statement?

b. (Page 87) How is life in the family of God different from your family of origin?

c. (Page 88) Since learning about your new identity in Christ, are there any self perceptions that have proven to be false? If so, what are they?

d. (Page 91) How could God's view of you with His warm feelings toward you change you when you are down, depressed, or struggling with a particular sin?

5. End with prayer

Chapter 8: Acceptance & Moods: Walking By the Spirit

1. Remind the members of the Small Group Agreement (Page 157)

2. Open with a short prayer

3. Read or ask for a volunteer to read the Chapter Summary:

"Walking by means of the Spirit of God addresses the moods and appetites of the flesh. We can bring our struggles to God immediately, and He will help us sort them out. A healthy relationship to the Trinity delivers us from the power of lusts and moods and brings us spiritual resources."

4. Have the group share their answers to the following questions which are found within the readings

a. (Page 100) According to the metaphor in John 15:1-5, how does the fact that God "lifts up" the branches encourage us to produce spiritual fruit in our lives?

b. (Page 102) Can you identify which moods and negative feelings have caused you to sin the most? Do you have any idea where the underlying pain is coming from to drive those moods? Take a moment and ask the Lord for clarity, wisdom and power to sift through these thoughts. Share about your experience.

c. (Page 106) As you have considered your own personal struggle with sin in the past or present, has anything kept you from coming to God?

d. (Page 109) Why is it important to have feelings in response to truth? Isn't it enough simply to know the truth?

5. End with prayer

Chapter 9: Acceptance & Fruit: Walking By the Spirit

1. Remind the members of the Small Group Agreement (Page 157)

2. Open with a short prayer

3. Read or ask for a volunteer to read the Chapter Summary:

"The Spirit of God has several different ministries in our lives. The Spirit has a radically different ministry to the flesh. We are commanded to walk by the Spirit, to be led by the Spirit, to have the fruit of the Spirit in our lives and to take steps into life by the Spirit. The biblical view says we are put into the God-man. We count ourselves alive to God in the same living relationship that Christ has to the Father now, and we work out of that relationship, so the Spirit of God will empower us to walk with character."

4. Have the group share their answers to the following questions which are found within the readings

a. (Page 112) Why does God feel delight when He looks at you? What do you think is going through His mind?

b. (Page 112) Isolate a mood or a strong desire to do wrong with which you struggle. Take your attention off the feelings and talk about them to God the Father. Notice that the longer you share with the Father, the more the moods and desires dissipate. Do this several times today! Share about your experience.

c. (Page 113) What is the Spirit of God's place in Christian living?

d. (Page 116) Look at the list of the works of the flesh, and for each work write down two emotions that may be working in the person who is captured by the habit.

1. Sexual immorality
2. Sexual impurity
3. Idolatry
4. Strife
5. Envying
6. Drunkenness

How can the Spirit of God address these powerful emotions?

7. End with prayer

Chapter 10: Acceptance & Prayer

1. Remind the members of the Small Group Agreement (Page 157)

2. Open with a short prayer

3. Read or ask for a volunteer to read the Chapter Summary:

"Prayer is not based on the investment of time nor the amount of words. Instead, our prayer life is based on a set of issues we must face daily. We sort those five issues out with the Father, based on the acceptance we have in Jesus Christ. As we sort out those issues, the fruit of the Spirit will powerfully work in our lives. Those issues are: God as a good Father, God's desire/choices for my life, daily needs, forgiveness in relationships and Satanic attack and temptation."

4. Have the group share their answers to the following questions which are found within the readings

a. (Page 124) How is this explanation of prayer different than your own understanding?

b. (Page 129) Are there issues in your life that overwhelm you? Take a few moments now to list your anxieties. Share them with God, and trust Him with them. Thank Him that He is greater than these threats. Ask Him specifically what you want Him to do with those threats. Pray until you are peaceful. Share about your experience.

c. (Page 131) List as many unresolved and hurtful relationships as you can think of, particularly those in which individuals have disappointed you. Be honest!

Now in prayer accept the pain they have caused you, and send away the obligations and resentment you have towards them. Do that because of the cross. Share about your experience.

d. (Page 132) How do we know when Satan is trying to convince us that God is not going to take care of us or meet our needs? What is Satan's primary goal for us?

5. End with prayer

Chapter 11: Acceptance & Sin

1. Remind the members of the Small Group Agreement (Page 157)

2. Open with a short prayer

3. Read or ask for a volunteer to read the Chapter Summary:
    "Sin affects us internally and affects the Trinity. When we sin, the Father, Son, and Holy Spirit each respond differently to us. This makes confession of wrong-doing important in our lives. When we confess our wrong-doing, God the Father restores His hand of blessing; the Son ceases the judgment of child-training or discipline; and the Spirit begins a new the process of character formation."

4. Have the group share their answers to the following questions which are found within the readings

    a. (Page 124) How is this explanation of prayer different than your own understanding?

    b. (Page 129) Are there issues in your life that overwhelm you? Take a few moments now to list your anxieties:

    Share them with God, and trust Him with them. Thank Him that He is greater than these threats. Ask Him specifically what you want Him to do with those threats. Pray until you are peaceful. Share about your experience.

    c. (Page 131) List as many unresolved and hurtful relationships as you can think of, particularly those in which individuals have disappointed you. Be honest!

    Now in prayer accept the pain they have caused you, and send away the obligations and resentment you have towards them. Do that because of the cross. Share about your experience.

    d. (Page 132) How do we know when Satan is trying to convince us that God is not going to take care of us or meet our needs? What is Satan's primary goal for us?

5. End with prayer

Chapter 12: Acceptance & Service

1. Remind the members of the Small Group Agreement (Page 157)

2. Open with a short prayer

3. Read or ask for a volunteer to read the Chapter Summary:
    "God the Father could not think of a greater or nobler role for His Son than to send Him on a mission of Rescue. We too are called to participate in the family business of rescue, and to consciously choose to replicate Christ's ministry in our lives. As daughters and sons of God, we have been sent. We are to choose to serve and to suffer. God could not think of a greater or more nobler role for us than to participate in Christ's life pattern. This life pattern gives overall meaning to our lives."

4. Have the group share their answers to the following questions which are found within the readings

    a. (Page 147) What are your feelings about following Christ's life pattern? Excited, apprehensive, motivated, scared? Explain your response.

    b. (Page 149) Do you think of yourself as a mature daughter or son of God? Why or why not?

    c. (Page 151) What are some rights you may need to relinquish in order to have the same perspective as Christ?

    d. (Page 154) What was most helpful and meaningful to you in your study of the *Becoming What God Intended* workbook?

5. End with prayer

WHAT'S NEXT?

We hope that you have enjoyed the Becoming What God Intended study. Many people have developed friendships in their small group that they have come to enjoy. People have shared how their small groups have continued to meet long after their Head to Heart journey together. The question naturally arises, "What's next?"

Read through one of Dr. Eckman's other books on a variety of topics.

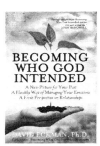

BECOMING WHO GOD INTENDED

"I strongly urge you to get Becoming Who God Intended *and put it to work in your life."*
—Josh McDowell

How Do You See Yourself? How Do You See God?

Whether you realize it or not, your imagination is filled with *pictures* of reality. The Bible indicates these pictures reveal your true "heart beliefs"—the beliefs that actually shape your everyday feelings and reactions to family, friends, and others, to life's circumstances, and to God.

Maybe You're Getting the Wrong Picture. Perhaps you're. . .

- struggling with anxiety, guilt, or habitual sins
- frustrated because your experience doesn't seem to match what the Bible talks about
- wondering if your emotions and feelings fit into the Christian life at all

If so, you may be working from the wrong set of pictures. *Becoming Who God Intended* shows you how you can allow God's Spirit to build new, *biblical* pictures in your heart and imagination.

God Has a Great New Picture for You! Getting the true pictures in your mind—grasping reality from God's perspective—will help bring your thoughts and emotions under control. It will lead you to a life filled with the positive emotions of love, joy, and peace. And you will finally be able to live out the richness of true Christianity . . . the life God the Father has always intended for you.

-≪◆≫-

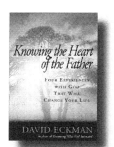

KNOWING THE HEART OF THE FATHER
You 're stuffed full of Christian information. But where is God in all of it?

Maybe You're Thirsting for a felt experience of the Bible's truth.
Perhaps Christianity seems irrelevant to where your heart is really at.

What if you could . . .

1. have an all-encompassing sense that you have a loving heavenly Dad
2. have a sense of being enjoyed and delighted in by Him?
3. recognize that He sees you differently than you see yourself?
4. realize that who you are is more important to Him than what you do?

These four experiences are integral to Biblical Christianity. Discover what often stands in the way of them, and how you can begin to know the heart of the Father in a deeper way as He works these realities into your life.

Take a closer look at the 5-course curriculum:

 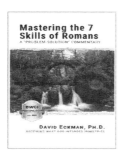  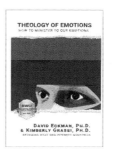 

- **BC101- Foundations of the Spiritual Life** is a discipleship process that leads the student to live within the life of the Trinity so as to experience God as an Abba Father, Jesus as our Identity, and the Holy Spirit as our Helper. The expected outcomes are deeply experiential and relational. These outcomes are such to mark the participant the rest of her or his life.

- **BC102- Theology of Romans** course was designed to give Christians confidence to live their lives out of Trinitarian Theology. Romans is the theological backbone of *Head to Heart*.

- **BC103- Head-to-Heart: Experiencing the Father's Affection.** The Head-to-Heart: Experiencing the Father's Affectionate Acceptance Small Group experience may well be the most effective and most thoughtful group experience presently being practiced in the United States. It is truly transformational with long term positive results in the lives of the participants. The expected outcomes are various, but the most common one is a deepening experience of God the Father's love.

- **BC104- Theology of Emotions** surveys the Old and New Testament's description of the source, function and management of emotions. The purpose is to create a true biblical psychology for the benefit of pastoral counselors, Christian counselors, disciplers, and Bible teachers. As part of this we will examine the place of suffering and how Scripture powerfully addresses the pain of life.

- **BC105- Skills for Living** is a secular version of a Christian mental health program that follows the pattern of *Head to Heart*. It was designed to train counselors in the 60 mental health centers of the universities of Beijing. Skills For Living serves as an introduction to mental health principles, and second, to create a bridge for sharing the Gospel. In this course, parallel Christian books will be used to present the Christian context of the contents.

Other Books by Dr. David Eckman:

Visit www.WhatGodIntended.org
for more information & resources

HEAD TO HEART SMALL GROUP DISCIPLESHIP PROCESS

Head to Heart is unlike any other small group material or discipleship program in a number of special ways. This life-changing journey is not simply about learning the truth of the Bible but integrating the truth into the heart. You will discover a new way of seeing that will change everything because, "how you see, is how you live."™

The Head to Heart process has three key elements:

1. focused Biblical teaching

2. identifying your False Pictures & Beliefs

3. a design of teaching and small groups that help you to integrate God's truth.

Experience the life of the Trinity:

- Discover the Father heart of God.
- Experience the empowerment of the Holy Spirit.
- Live out your Union with Christ.

Many have gone through the exciting transition of knowing something of God to experiencing what God intended. We are delighted to welcome and invite you to the Head to Heart journey!

If you have any questions or would like to talk to someone about next steps, email us at Head2Heart@bwgi.org or contact us at 925.846.6264.

WWW.HEAD2HEART.ORG